Sor Juana

Beauty and Justice in the Americas

Michelle A. Gonzalez

ORBIS BOOKS

Maryknoll, New York 10545

RODMAN PUBLIC LIBRARY

38212003870406
Main Adult
271.9 G643
Gonzalez, Michelle A
Sor Juana : beauty and
justice in the Americas

NOV 2004

Founded in 1970, Orbis Books endeavors to publish works that enlighten the mind, nourish the spirit, and challenge the conscience. The publishing arm of the Maryknoll Fathers and Brothers, Orbis seeks to explore the global dimensions of the Christian faith and mission, to invite dialogue with diverse cultures and religious traditions, and to serve the cause of reconciliation and peace. The books published reflect the views of their authors and do not represent the official position of the Maryknoll Society. To learn more about Maryknoll and Orbis Books, please visit our website at www.maryknoll.org.

Copyright © 2003 by Michelle A. Gonzalez

Published by Orbis Books, Maryknoll, NY 10545-0308.

All rights reserved.

No part of this publication may be reproduced or transmitted in any form or by any means, electronic or mechanical, including photocopying, recording, or any information storage or retrieval system, without prior permission in writing from the publisher.

Queries regarding rights and permissions should be addressed to: Orbis Books, P.O. Box 308, Maryknoll, NY 10545-0308.

Manufactured in the United States of America
ISBN 1-57075-494-2

Library of Congress Cataloging-in-Publication Data

Gonzalez, Michelle A.
    Sor Juana : beauty and justice in the Americas / Michelle A. Gonzalez.
        p. cm.
    Includes bibliographical references and index
    ISBN 1-57075-494-2 (pbk.)
        1. Juana Inés de la Cruz, Sister, 1651-1695. 2. Theology—
Mexico—History—17th century.   I. Title.
BX4705.J728 G66 2003
271'.9002—dc21
                                                    2003009867

"Poetry is not a luxury."
—Audre Lorde

Contents

Preface

The first semester of my doctorate at the Graduate Theological Union, as I struggled with the multiple pressures of studies, work, and adjusting to a new part of the country, I was also introduced to the figure that is the focus of this study, Sor Juana Inés de la Cruz. I learned of Sor Juana from a (seemingly) casual suggestion from my advisor at the time, Alejandro García-Rivera. As a Cuban-American who had often been given the impression that the intellectual history of Latin America was at best inconsequential and at worst nonexistent, I found the discovery of Sor Juana a moving event. Through her work I discovered a rarely mentioned piece of theological history. As a Roman Catholic, I was intrigued by the fact that she was a woman religious. Not only did I find a Latin American who was writing theology and philosophy in the seventeenth century, but this person was a woman. Sor Juana was a woman who struggled against the preconceived notions of gender that constrained her intellectual pursuits, aware that her sex severely limited her life, her options, and her work.

Unlike Sor Juana in her cloister, who complained of the isolation and loneliness she felt without an active community of scholars to discuss and share her work, I have been blessed with a network of colleagues, mentors, and friends who have encouraged and nurtured my scholarship. I am eternally indebted to those people and institutions without whom this study would not have been possible. This book began as my dissertation on the theological contribution of Sor Juana in light of the methodology of Hans Urs von Balthasar.[1] My dissertation coordinator, Alejandro García-Rivera, has been an extremely supportive mentor to me. I am indebted to the other members of my committee, Margaret R. Miles, Peter J. Casarella, and Emilie L. Bergmann for their time, suggestions, and insights. The staff and faculty at the Graduate Theological Union provided a stimulating and encouraging environment for my academic pursuits. I would also like to thank the Hispanic Theological Initiative (HTI) and the Fund for Theological Education (FTE) for their funding throughout my doctoral studies. In addition to monetary support, the HTI opened up a community of scholars and colleagues that has been invaluable. I would also like to thank Robert Ellsberg at Orbis Books for his support of this project.

The friendships I have made throughout the years have also been sources of inspiration and support. The Academy of Catholic Hispanic Theologians in the United States (ACHTUS) has been an extremely fruitful and challenging venue for addressing the questions and concerns of Latino/a theologians. I would like to thank in particular Ada María Isasi-Díaz, Ana María Pineda, María Pilar Aquino, Roberto S. Goizueta, Orlando O. Espín, Francisco Lozada, and Eduardo Fernández for their friendship and encouragement throughout the years. My new colleagues at Loyola Marymount University have been a model of collegiality and support. I would also like to thank LMU for awarding me a New Faculty Summer Research grant in the summer of 2002, allowing me the time to finish this project. My research assistant at LMU, Rebekah Walter, deserves a special note of thanks for her work on my bibliography. My family has always been a source of comfort and *apoyo* throughout the years. Most importantly, however, I would like to thank my husband, Scott Barklow. I am grateful for his love, his support, and his patience.

Notes

[1] *A Latin American* Ressourcement: *The Theological Contribution of Sor Juana Inés de la Cruz in Light of the Methodology of Hans Urs von Balthasar* (Ph.D. Diss., Graduate Theological Union, Berkeley, CA, 2001).

Introduction

"What sort of beauty will save the world? "[1]
—Fyodor Dostoyevsky

Very few women's voices emerge in the history books and theological texts of the late seventeenth century in Latin America. In fact, many would argue that there are few substantial figures in this region, male or female, whose impact is significant beyond their local context. Latin America has historically been set apart from the rest of the New World. Octavio Paz writes in his monumental study of the life and era of Sor Juana Inés de la Cruz, "I will reiterate a point I have often made: our history, from the perspective of modern Western history, has been ex-centric. We have no age of critical philosophy, no bourgeois revolution, no political democracy: no Kant, no Robespierre, no Hume, no Jefferson."[2] The difference of Latin America's history has been historically judged as "other" or inferior. Since Latin America *seemingly* has no Kant or Jefferson, it is seen as having nothing to contribute to other cultures and nations intellectually. Paz does not find the equivalent of the traditional philosophical greats in the Spanish New World. I disagree.

I maintain that one can find Kants and Jeffersons in Latin America,[3] voices that have been ignored due to the marginalization of Latin American culture, history, and scholarship. Granted, these thinkers are different from their European and North American counterparts. Since they do not carry the prestige and weight of Western European history behind them, they appear insignificant, or significant solely on a highly contextualized level. However, their impact resonates in less obvious ways. If these figures do not have a historical trajectory of scholarship that has seriously engaged and been influenced by their thought, this is due to their marginal status. Their weight has yet to be assessed, for their voices have yet to be the object of careful study and consideration. In addition, the very nature of their writing differs from contemporary interpretations of authentic theological and philosophical discourse.

The poetry, dramas, and prose of seventeenth-century Mexican writer Sor Juana Inés de la Cruz provide an especially eloquent challenge to Paz's assumption that Latin America failed to experience an era of critical philosophical thinking. Her theological and philosophical texts contest the assumption that the history of philosophy and theology can be written omitting colonial Mexico. For contemporary theology, her ideas on theological aesthetics constitute an important historical resource for this blossoming area of study. Sor Juana scholarship is of special interest for liberation theologies that strive to recover marginalized historical voices within the Christian theological tradition. For these theologies in particular, the relationship between Beauty, Justice, and Truth found in Sor Juana's theology resonates strongly with current scholarship on aesthetics, social justice, and epistemology.

The retrieval of Sor Juana's theology as a resource for contemporary theology, especially for liberation theologies, is a timely study that engages various pressing questions that are currently at the forefront of theological reflection. Since their inception in the 1960s, liberation theologies have contained a substantial amount of emphasis on praxis (the Good) in response to the overwhelmingly predominant focus of modern theologies on truth claims and the authenticity of theological reflection (the True). In the past decade, after a substantial exile, Beauty has returned to consideration as a serious subject for theology in the work of various theologians. For liberation theologies, therefore, the question becomes not "How does one relate orthodoxy to ortho-praxis?" but rather "What is the relationship between the True, the Good, and the Beautiful?" Part of that answer, I contend, can be found in Sor Juana's theology.

Contemporary theology, and liberation theologies in particular, can be enriched by the theological aesthetics of Sor Juana Inés de la Cruz. This study of Sor Juana arrives at an important moment, for the relationship between theological aesthetics and the ethical imperatives of liberation theologies is currently a lively subject of theological speculation. Does the current interest in aesthetics diminish the role of ethics in liberation and contextual theologies? Or do they in fact, as some have argued, *ground* the importance of social justice? Sor Juana's theology, which incorporates aesthetics, ethics, and epistemology, presents an alternative where all three are present. The aesthetic is never explored at the expense of justice. Sor Juana joins the increasing chorus of voices that have been painstakingly recovered by theologians working to bring the marginalized to the center of theological reflection.

This retrieval of Sor Juana, therefore, occurs within the framework of historical research in liberation theologies. The present study begins in chapter 1 with an exploration of the theological landscape in which this text is situated. After a brief introduction of Sor Juana, I turn to some of the concerns surrounding a theological assessment of her work and her various contributions. The remainder of the chapter demonstrates both the importance of historical retrieval and the relevance of theological aesthetics to the theological project of contemporary liberation theologies, including North American feminist, Black, womanist, Latino/a, and Latin American theologies. Since much of Sor Juana's writing is in literary form, I give special attention to the relationship between literature and theology. Chapter 2 is a substantial introduction to Sor Juana's life, writing and historical context, drawing from a selection of her corpus and from secondary scholarship in literary theory, philosophy, and theology. After an overview of Sor Juana's life and writing, I depict the colonial era in Mexico (then known as New Spain), emphasizing the significance of the baroque worldview. I then consider the colonial Mexican philosophical and theological context. Sor Juana, after all, did not write in a vacuum; she was actively involved in the theological and philosophical debates of her contemporaries. Finally, I locate Sor Juana in light of the milieu of the cloistered woman religious in seventeenth-century New Spain.

The heart of my study of Sor Juana's theology is found in chapters 3 through 5. The organization of these chapters is centered on the role of the three transcendentals: Beauty, the Good, and the True.[4] The importance of aesthetics, ethics, and epistemology is pivotal to understanding Sor Juana's theology. Chapter 3 begins by exploring Beauty. Drawing substantially from Sor Juana's allegorical drama *El Divino Narciso*, as well as from numerous poems, this chapter highlights the importance of Beauty in both the form and the content of Sor Juana's theology. Chapter 4 moves to an exploration of the theme of justice. Through her dramas, poetry, and prose, Sor Juana explores the marginalization of women, Latin American Indigenous, and African peoples. Chapter 5 concludes this section with a discussion of epistemology in Sor Juana's corpus.

Chapter 6 returns the reader to the modern era, where the connection between the Good and Beauty is explored in contemporary theology, with special attention to the role of aesthetics in liberation theologies. Chapter 7 concludes this study with an examination of insights gleaned from Sor Juana's theology and their implications for the broader theological arena, highlighting directions suggested for future work in theological aesthetics and liberation theologies. Through my study of Sor Juana's theology, I hope not only to alter understandings of the history of Christian thought by expanding its sources and voices, but also to transform the manner in which contemporary theologians approach and express the theological task.

Notes

[1] Fyodor Dostoyevsky, *The Idiot*, Penguin Classics, trans. David Magarshack (London: Penguin, 1986), 394.

[2] Octavio Paz, *Sor Juana: Or, the Traps of Faith*, trans. Margaret Sayers Peden (Cambridge, MA: Harvard University Press, 1988), 16.

[3] For my purposes I am using the examples of philosophers as cited in the Paz quote. In an ideal setting, Latin America would not in any way have to measure and justify itself against Europe and North America.

[4] This format is not atypical for theological aesthetics. Hans Urs von Balthasar's trilogy begins with Beauty (*Herrlichkeit*) moves to the Good (*Theodramatik*), and ends with Truth (*Theologik*). Also see Alejandro García-Rivera, *The Community of the Beautiful: A Theological Aesthetics* (Collegeville, MN: The Liturgical Press, 1999).

Chapter 1

Setting the Stage

"We are a bit uneasy about beauty."[1]
—Rubem A. Alves

Ignored or forgotten by present-day Latin American liberation theology, Sor Juana Inés de la Cruz is a compelling seventeenth-century Mexican figure whose work offers a significant voice both to the history of Christian thought and to contemporary theology. Still, though the name Sor Juana may ring foreign to the ears of theologians, throughout the halls of Spanish and Latin American Studies departments around the world this "tenth muse" of the Americas is recognized as one of the greatest figures in Spanish literature. Long considered solely as a literary figure, Sor Juana is increasingly being studied for the philosophical and theological nature of her writing, and this interest in her work is accompanied by a renewal in the study of colonial Mexican philosophy and theology. Scholars who study her religious writing consider her to be the first female theologian of the Americas. Through her poetry and plays Sor Juana offers a theological voice that expands contemporary understandings of the very form and method of theological elaboration. Her theological aesthetics is not only a historical resource for contemporary theology, but also offers a Latin American voice to this increasingly emergent field which places Beauty at the center of the theological task.

In order to develop Sor Juana's historical and contemporary contributions to theology, her work must be explored in light of

1

this field. While an isolated study examining the theological themes found in Sor Juana's writing might be one way to examine her theological voice, I have opted for a more intentional engagement of Sor Juana's thought with contemporary theology. My reasons are twofold. First, the claim that Sor Juana's work is theological cannot be isolated from the discipline of theology itself. Instead, it must be viewed in light of theological elaborations, with the aim of demonstrating how her work affirms, challenges, and expands theological understandings. Second, and more strategically, in order to recover a marginalized voice so that its full impact can be assessed in light of dominant discourse, one must explicitly engage that discourse. Far from holding this to be an isolated study that explores a slight and easily forgotten theologian, I intend to pursue the broader implications of Sor Juana's corpus for contemporary theology.

Sor Juana offers a different way of viewing things. She did not write treatises and essays, but plays and poetry. Her writing may not have aided in the founding of a nation, but her voice speaks of the birth of a people. As noted by Gustavo Gutiérrez in his comprehensive study of the ethics and theology of Bartolomé de Las Casas, "There are figures in history—few, to be sure—who will leap the barriers of time to become the contemporaries of all ages. These are people who immerse themselves so deeply in their own age that they remain relevant long after historical anecdotes and others of their own time are simple memories of the past."[2] Sor Juana Inés de la Cruz is such a figure. A study of her writing reveals a substantial resource of creative thought and also provides a window into a better understanding of an era that merits rigorous historical and theological studies. Her voice emerges today as a much needed font of knowledge and creativity. The fact that she is a woman is extremely significant. Sor Juana offers a Latina American's voice in an era and culture where women were discouraged from public, intellectual scholarship. Her writing constitutes not only a historical theology, but also a critical interlocutor for contemporary theology. While this contribution is not limited to the areas of Latin American, Latino/a, and feminist theologies, her work is of special interest to these theologies as a contextualized historical resource of a marginalized woman's voice. As a theological aesthetics, her writing is a Third World resource to this increasingly studied topic in contemporary theology. This study explores Sor Juana's theological contribution to theology through her theological aesthetics, an area that has been integral to the task of various liberation theologians for some time now. In their quest for alternative resources that express the faith and lives of marginalized peoples, liberation theologians have often turned to the aesthetic as a vital resource for theological expression.

Sor Juana Inés de la Cruz

Who was Sor Juana Inés de la Cruz? While the following chapter will treat her life and context in more detail, a few introductory comments are in order. Somewhere between the years 1648-1651 a young girl named Juana Ramírez de Asbaje y Santillana was born in the town of Nepantla, Mexico. Nepantla, an Aztec word, means "land in the middle."[3] It is ironic and telling that Juana entered this world in such a place, for it is in Nepantla that she spent most of her life, struggling within the tensions, contradictions, and paradoxes of her culture, her Church, and her vocation. The daughter of unwed parents, her mother was a *criolla* and her father a Spanish military officer.[4] Around the age of thirteen Sor Juana went to live in the court of the viceroy of New Spain (colonial Mexico) as the lady-in-waiting of the marcioness of Mancera. She stayed there for three years. In 1667 she entered into the ascetic, cloistered Order of Discalced Carmelites, which she left after a short time. She later joined the order of the Hieronymites. The significance of her decision to join a religious order is a point of tension in contemporary Sor Juana scholarship, for interpretations abound.

At a young age Sor Juana was extremely interested in intellectual studies. She was an avid reader, and by her mid-teens was recognized as the most erudite woman in Mexico. Her reputation as a scholar was a crucial factor in her gaining a position in the viceregal court.[5] Learning was her first love. In her autobiographical narrative, *La respuesta a Sor Filotea* (*The Answer*), Sor Juana describes begging her mother to allow her to dress like a man so that she might attend the university. At the age of six or seven, having learned to read and write, "I heard that in Mexico City there was a University and Schools where they studied the sciences. As soon as I heard this I began to slay my poor mother with insistent and annoying pleas, begging her to dress me in men's clothes and send me to the capital, to the home of some relatives she had there, so that I could enter the University and study."[6] Sor Juana's desire for a life of scholarship and study was perhaps a significant factor in her decision to enter cloistered life.

The biography written by her confessor states that Sor Juana hesitated to enter the convent, fearing that life there would impede her studies. However, there were few other choices for women in her era short of marriage, and this was not an option for Juana.[7] As she herself writes, "I took the veil because although I knew I would find in religious life many things that would be quite opposed to my character (I speak of accessory, rather than essential matters), it would, given my absolute unwillingness to enter into marriage, be the least unfitting and the most decent state I could choose."[8] Due to her aversion to marriage, Sor Juana's only other alternative, as a woman in her social class, was cloistered life.

Sor Juana's time in the convent was focused primarily on fierce intellectual study and scholarship. She read in the fields of literature, philosophy, theology, and science. The estimates of the amount of books in her library range from the hundreds to the thousands. She also amassed scientific and musical instruments. Her poetry and plays were in high demand for both Church festivities and court occasions, and it is in these milieus that her writing was read, sung, and dramatized. She states that she never wrote for own personal pleasure, but only in response to requests and for commission. "What is more, I have never written a single thing of my own volition, but rather only in response to the pleadings and commands of others; so much so that I recall having written nothing at my own pleasure save a trifling thing they call the *Dream*."[9] This seemingly exaggerated remark, where she names *Primero sueño* (*First Dream*), one of the most complex poems in the Spanish language, a mere trifling, demonstrates the weight of requests Sor Juana received for her work.

Though part of a cloistered order, through the popularity of her works and her friendships Sor Juana was able to live a very public life. In fact, to ecclesial authorities Sor Juana's life was too

public. "Her worldly life brought down upon her the criticism of
the more sinister, more fanatical element in the church."[10] While
I will treat the controversial later years of Sor Juana's work in the
following chapter of this study, it is worth noting that the final
years of her life remain clouded in intrigue and uncertainty. After
a public chastising by a neighboring archbishop, Sor Juana responded to him in writing and shortly afterwards renounced her
public life as an author. Did this result from ecclesial pressure?
Or was it a conversion of sorts on her part? Modern scholars will
never know. However, contemporary scholarship has made one
thing clear: this was a time of emotional turmoil in her life. Two
years after her renunciation, Sor Juana died from an illness she
contracted while caring for the sick in her convent.

Sor Juana Inés de la Cruz has long been heralded throughout
the Spanish-speaking world for her literary talent. She remains,
however, relatively undiscovered in the mainstream theological
academy of the United States, despite the fact (or due to the fact)
that she lived and wrote in Mexico. George Tavard attributes
this "disregard" for Sor Juana's works to a general "indifference"
Anglo North Americans have toward the scholarship of Spanish-
speaking peoples.[11] Secondary scholarship categorizes Sor Juana's
writing for the most part as literature.[12] Recently, scholarship
surrounding Sor Juana has flourished, especially in the fields of
women's studies, Chicana/o studies, and philosophy.[13] Meanwhile,
her theological contributions have been essentially ignored.[14] This
reduction of her work is pervasive, due to the above-mentioned
bias raised by Tavard (to which I would add the general bias
against women's scholarship), and to the very limited definition
of theology operative today.

Any attempt to recover a female voice within the current patriarchal paradigms must simultaneously reinterpret the very disciplines in which it seeks to insert such voices. As Roberto S.
Goizueta observes, "If the achievements of women do not appear in our history books, it is not only because the contributions
of women to human history have been ignored but, even more
so, because our very conception of what counts for human history is itself skewed, or distorted."[15] Scholars must therefore be
aware of the pervasive sexism contained in the definitions of philosophy and theology. The style of writing deemed "appropri-

ate" for women limited their modes of expression, and this limitation is simultaneously their greatest constraint and the wellspring of their creativity. I raise this point in order to recognize that the "form" of women's philosophies and theologies does not necessarily mirror what is stereotypically considered academic discourse. This does not, however, diminish the value and intellectual import of these texts. One must recognize the error that occurs when scholarship is reduced to traditional male discourse, and must also remember that the absence of women from philosophy is not only based on their explicit exclusion, but also "a failure to read some thinkers in the right way, a failure of recognition, a hermeneutic blindness."[16]

Scholars are increasingly recognizing Sor Juana's significance as a theologian. She has been labeled the first woman theologian in the Americas.[17] In her study, *Sor Juana Inés de la Cruz: Religion, Art, and Feminism*, Pamela Kirk provides an examination of a significant portion of Sor Juana's corpus, positing it as theological. Kirk notes that two-thirds of Sor Juana's work is religious and those texts "occupy a middle place between literature and theology."[18] Their ambiguous classification is an indication of the era in which they were produced.

> This remarkable variety of literary expressions offers a challenge to the theologian because of contemporary expectations of the genre of theological discourse as prose reflection and critical argumentation. Sor Juana's age was accustomed to receiving religious content not only through sermons, works of theology, and books of devotion, but also through sacramental dramas. . . . Because she was adept at using these popular forms, consideration of her theology from this angle can also be instructive for the theology of our time in its search for alternative expressions of theological content.[19]

A study of Sor Juana's work provides an alternative theological vision. This is offered both in its aesthetic content and aesthetic form. Sor Juana's work differs from mainstream contemporary theological expression in two ways. Her writing will not necessarily resemble that of traditional male discourse. The one time

Sor Juana assumed a male theological form of writing, she was severely reprimanded for her actions. One must keep in mind that the forms of theological expressions in Sor Juana's day and age differed radically from what is categorized as academic theology today.

Sor Juana's contribution to theology occurs on various levels. First of all, viewing her as a theologian challenges the very nature of theological discourse. This occurs in questioning the method and structure of contemporary theology, as well as its androcentric presuppositions. In turn, historical recovery and research is pursued through Sor Juana studies, where a woman's lost voice is retrieved in light of the contemporary situation. Sor Juana also offers an alternative that challenges Eurocentric understandings of the history of Christian thought. Contrary to the notion that seventeenth-century Mexico was an intellectual wasteland, Sor Juana scholarship demonstrates the opposite. Contemporary theology is increasingly engaging literature, the arts, and theological aesthetics. Sor Juana's work contributes to this interdisciplinary exchange in a distinct Latin American manner. The methodological implications of Sor Juana's theology, accompanied by the revision of Christian history through the inclusion of a Latin American woman's voice and the incorporation of literature as theological expression, resonates with the theological projects of contemporary liberation theologians. Therefore, this study is of special, though not exclusive, concern for these theologies that strive to incorporate voices from the underside of history as central to contemporary theology.

Liberation Theologies: *Ressourcement* and Theological Aesthetics

The twentieth-century birth and growth of liberation and contextual theologies, especially in the Third World and among U.S. minorities, is the greatest theological development of the twentieth century. These theologies, which have exploded onto the theological arena, challenge Eurocentric, patriarchal, de-historicized assumptions about theological construction. They highlight the importance of social location and a preferential option for the oppressed and marginalized. While not wishing to collapse the distinctiveness of the variety of both liberation and contextual theologies, generally speaking these voices emerge from the underside of history, critically engaging the historical Christian tradition and contemporary understandings of theological sources, norms, and loci.[20]

A central feature of liberation theologies has been their emphasis on the contemporary context and struggles of oppressed peoples. However, equally important is the predominance of historical *ressourcement* within liberation theologies. The term *ressourcement*, though not traditionally associated with liberation theologies, is being increasingly embraced by U.S. minority theologians.[21] The *ressourcement* movement in twentieth-century Roman Catholic theology was an appeal for theologians to return to historical sources to inform contemporary understandings. This movement must be understood in light of Vatican II and the theology preceding the Council. As noted by Dominican theologian Yves Congar, who is perhaps one of its most significant figures, "The movement of thought that prepared the way for the Council can be described as a 're-sourcement' in the sense meant by Péguy, who coined the word—a rising up of vitality from the source into the present, rather than a simple return to the sources of Christian faith, although this also certainly took place."[22] As highlighted by Congar, *ressourcement* does not represent a return to historical sources applied uncritically to the present. Instead, it entails a revival of historical sources.

In light of the retrieval of Sor Juana's theology, liberation and contextual theologies add a critical edge to *ressourcement*. Unlike my Western European counterparts, through my background in Third World, U.S. minority, and feminist theologies, I turn to the Christian historical tradition with a hermeneutics of suspicion that questions the power dynamics and historicity of theological discourse. This critical edge allows for the inclusion of a theological voice such as Sor Juana's, which has historically been marginalized and forgotten. Liberation and contextual theologies benefit from the project of *ressourcement* because historical studies, especially in Latin American liberation theology, remain scarce.[23] A retrieval of Sor Juana's work is to Latin American theology what *ressourcement* was to the early European proponents of this movement. A Latin American *ressourcement*, through a study of Sor Juana, emerges in the spirit of both the *ressourcement* movement and theologies from marginalized contexts. This is a distinct Latin American contribution, grounded and informed by a larger theological tradition.

In North America, paralleling the irruptions from the underside in Latin America, were the voices of women and U.S. minorities.[24] In contrast to other U.S. liberation theologies (i.e. Black, Hispanic), feminist theology developed as the struggle of an oppressed majority. The invisibility of women within religious institutions fueled the outrage and fervor behind this movement. As noted by Elisabeth Schüssler Fiorenza, "Women are not only the 'silent majority' but we are also the 'silenced majority' in the Roman Catholic Church. . . . This deliberate or unconscious silencing of women in the Church engenders our ecclesial and theological invisibility."[25] The 1968 publication of Mary Daly's *Church and the Second Sex* marks the birth of this movement in the United States.[26] Many consider Schüssler Fiorenza, along with Daly and Rosemary Radford Ruether, the "foremothers" of feminist theology. In their work, one finds a hesitancy to give Christian tradition, Scripture, and theology any sort of normative status due to its androcentric foundation. Therefore, women's experiences and struggles for liberation often become the central commitment and norm in their work. Fundamental to these theologians' work is recovering women's intellectual histories, as well as the implications of this task. Through privileging gender as a primary analytic category, feminist theologians seek to highlight the ideologies operating in historical and current understandings of Christian tradition.

One cannot downplay the significance of historical theology for all liberationist projects. Feminist theologians hold historical retrieval as the second step in the tripartite method of their theologies. The initial hermeneutics of suspicion that deconstructs the Christian tradition with an awareness of the self-serving partiality that accompanies it is followed by a hermeneutics of retrieval (or historical research) in order to recover marginalized women's voices. These two steps inform the third, a feminist reconstruction of Christian sources, symbols, and practices.[27] As noted by Elizabeth A. Johnson, "Negatives alone do not nourish.

Feminist religious scholarship also searches for ignored, suppressed, or alternative wisdom both inside and outside of that mainstream, for bits and pieces that hint at the untold stories of the contributions of women and the possibility of different construals of reality."[28] The historical retrieval of marginalized women's voices must always proceed with caution. Too often, as Rosemary Radford Ruether warns, if we skim the surface in a quest for women in Christian history, we only uncover those women whose lives and stories have been canonized by patriarchal ideologies in order to serve as models of submission for women. The feminist scholar must move beyond this to uncover a more substantial treatment of these women's lives and discover those women who have been silenced, yet not lost, within Christian tradition. These "lost" women, who are either not found in the history books of Christianity or depicted as heretics, are the true font for contemporary feminist theologians. They present an alternative to patriarchal Christianity. "Occasionally a woman in the tradition stands out as so powerful and so central that she can neither be silenced nor sanitized."[29] Not only is it impossible to "sanitize" Sor Juana's life and work, but she also stands as a forgotten woman within the history of Christianity. Contributing to her absence within the history books about Christian thinkers is her context as a Latin American woman. As a Third World woman, she suffers the double marginalization of being a woman and Latin American.[30]

Feminist theologians are not alone in their efforts to uncover an alternative understanding of Christian history and theology. Black liberation and womanist theologians have made historical recovery central to their theological task and a key resource for constructing contemporary theologies. As Dwight Hopkins elaborates, this is central to the theological method of Black theology: "For a contemporary and constructive Black theology of liberation, we must engage a faith in freedom that anchors the seemingly infinite variety of Black folk's striving to name themselves with their own language, bodies, and spirits; hence a cultural foundation for Black theology."[31] Black liberation theology emerged in the mid 1960s as an explosive theological movement in the United States. Nurtured by Church leaders and academic theologians, Black liberation theology claims that the Christian

God is a God of liberation and love. Black theologians promoted a message of self-love for African-Americans, as children of God born in the image of God. Included in this message is the denouncement of racism, which defies God's will for humanity and stands in contrast to the kingdom of God. The 1969 publication of James H. Cone's *Black Theology and Black Power* marked the birth of the academic branch of this movement.[32] Womanist theology emerged in the mid-1980s as a Black feminist theological movement that both draws from and critiques Black and North American feminist theologies. Womanists highlight the shortcomings of early Black theologians regarding the category of gender in their work and also critique feminists for the racism prevalent throughout White feminist scholarship and social justice movements. Womanist theologians use a multidimensional analysis of race, class, and gender as their hermeneutical lens for the theological task.

Black and womanist theologies must be rooted in Black sources, both historical and contemporary. Whether it is the spirituals, the speeches of Malcolm X, the writing of Zora Neale Hurston, or the contemporary fiction of Alice Walker, an interdisciplinary retrieval of the cultural expressions of Black peoples is fundamental to the methodology of Black theologians.[33] Delores Williams, for example, highlights the significance of literature for womanist theology. Williams "affirms the value of imaginative literature as a source for theology and for shedding light on the nature of women's experience."[34] Williams uses the work of Margaret Walker, Zora Neale Hurston, and Alice Walker as sources for Black women's experience. "The literature used in this study illustrates the symbiotic relationship between the imagination and the theological task. Women's imagination and women's reason must not be separated. The imagination must have equal status with reason in theological construction, so that the voices of many diverse women can speak of the God they know."[35] In this statement, Williams suggests that the use of literature as a theological resource leads to a reconceptualization of rationality and knowledge. Rationality includes the symbolic, the poetic, and the imagination.

Central to Black theology's task is bringing forth those voices that have been written out of the history of Christian theology.

However, this concern does not exhaust the impulse behind Black theologians' historical research. Also fueling this *ressourcement* is an awareness that as peoples from the underside of history, African-Americans carry with them a set of assumptions and presuppositions different from that of the dominant White intellectual milieu. Latin American liberation theologian Gustavo Gutiérrez speaks very clearly of this concern for all liberation theologies when he stresses that the questions of the nonperson, who is the subject of liberation theology, create a radically different starting point for theological reflection.[36] Nonpersons, as "those human beings who are considered less than human by society, because that society is based on privileges arrogated by a minority," are the forgotten masses.[37] To make an uncritical correlation between the theological concerns and styles of those nonpersons with those of dominant theology is to be methodologically naïve, as James H. Cone emphasizes:

> The situation of being an American slave created certain kinds of theological problems, but they were not the same theological problems of White slave masters or others who did not live out their lives as slaves. Therefore, to use European or Western theological and philosophical methodologies as a means of evaluating the significance of Black reflections on the slave condition is not only theoretically inappropriate but very naïve. To evaluate correctly the slaves' theological reflection on their servitude in relation to divine justice, it is necessary to suspend the methodology of the enslavers and to enter the cultural and religious milieu of the victims.[38]

The contemporary theologian seeking to retrieve a marginalized voice must therefore proceed cautiously, careful not to impose the hermeneutic of the oppressor upon that of the oppressed. This is fundamental to the conversion of the theological task as a whole. If liberation theologies are to be effective in their revision of theology, they must transform it both in content and form. Marginalized sources must not be inserted uncritically into existing, oppressive paradigms. Instead, liberation theologians call for a methodological revolution in theology. Theologians must acknowledge the narrow manner in which their rhetoric and sources have been historically constructed.

The implications of liberationist historical research are especially strong in the area of theological method. An alternative vision of theology includes a reconsideration and expansion of the very form of theological elaboration. This is of special concern in this study of Sor Juana. A striking feature of the historical research done by liberation theologians, especially Black theologians, is the inclusion of aesthetic resources to the theological "canon." When they examine spirituals, rap, prayers, literature, and/or the blues in their efforts to find an authentic expression of African-American faith, Black theologians have entered the realm of theological aesthetics, deliberately or not.

Theological aesthetics is a growing area in contemporary theology. Though not necessarily a theological "school" or "field" per se, those authors working on theological aesthetics constitute a conversation or particular theological style grounded in their concern for Beauty. Theological aesthetics holds that in the encounter with Beauty there is an experience of the Divine. An emphasis on the aesthetics is based on the belief that within the realm of symbol, imagination, emotion, and art one finds a privileged expression of the encounter with the Divine and its articulation. The emphasis on the metaphorical and the poetic, however, does not come at the expense of the metaphysical.

In its response to the demands of the scientific and rationalist worldview produced by the Enlightenment, theology has suffered a great loss. Roberto S. Goizueta situates this loss as a consequence of Western rationalism, which led to the divorce of form from content and the marginalization of aesthetic form as unacademic.[39] Goizueta emphasizes a deep-seated loss in modern theology. In its struggle to become an "academic" discipline, theology has lost its form, its beauty and, consequently, its ability to reflect the glory of the God whom it claims as its focus. As a result of this, Goizueta continues, theology has lost the ability to speak as a significant voice. "[W]e have become irrelevant to the faith communities that we claim to represent, and, therefore, increasingly desperate in our attempts to say *something* that actually *matters* to people—not least of all to ourselves. Theology has indeed become academic."[40] In highlighting the traditional forms

in which theology was once communicated, especially in noting
narrative, metaphor and poetry, Goizueta builds on the work of
Swiss-born theologian Hans Urs von Balthasar, whose articulation of a theological aesthetics includes poetry, drama, and literature as resources.

Often considered the younger sibling of Latin American liberation theology, Latino/a theology has reached a historical moment where its identity and direction are at a crossroads.[41] As a
theology that remains critically engaged with and informed by
the struggles, commitments, and concerns of the Latino/a population, Hispanic theology offers an essential contribution to the
contemporary theological academy and worldwide Christian
churches. This contribution is rooted in the methodological starting point and commitment of Hispanic theologians. From its inception, Latino/a theology has sought to speak both for and from
the history, spirituality, and contemporary situation of U.S. Latino/a
communities. In the past decade there has been a surge of scholarship by Hispanics, offering various distinct contributions to
Latino/a theology. The more recent work in the areas of aesthetics, epistemology and metaphysics, rooted in the liberation paradigm, challenges and expands the scope and method of Latino/a
theology. Today, U.S. Latino/as struggle to articulate a theology
that incorporates the insights of its socio-cultural location, as it
confronts and connects with the larger theological conversation.

There are four concerns which characterize U.S. Latino/a theology: the faith of the people as a source and norm for theology,
the emphasis on the particular as a way of discovering the universal, the need to include the silenced and marginalized voices
of Latino/a peoples in theological discourse, and a contestation
of dualistic epistemological and ontological constructions.[42] The
significance and privilege given to popular faith and devotions in
Latino/a theology is found in the emphasis on popular religion
and daily life (*lo cotidiano*). Theology must take into account the
manifestation of God's revelation and love in the lives and practices of marginalized peoples. Linked to this conviction is Latino/a
theology's consistent use of the particular story as an entry point
in order to reveal a larger universal truth. It is in the "little stories"
of Guadalupe's apparition and the Good Friday devotion at San
Fernando Cathedral in San Antonio, Texas, where the "big story"

of God's love and accompaniment of marginalized peoples is told.[43] By lifting up these particular narratives, the third concern found in Latino/a theology is demonstrated, a consistent effort to recover the faith, struggles, and histories of marginalized and oppressed peoples. Through their preferential option for the poor, where poverty is understood not only as economic, but cultural and anthropological, Latino/a theologians struggle to include marginalized voices within the larger theological discourse. This commitment to inclusion is based on the belief that here one finds God's privileged locus of revelation.

The last shared concern is the explicit rejection of dualisms in Latino/a theology. In the privileging of the mixture, diversity, and in-betweenness of Latino/a peoples, there is a rejection of dualistic understandings of the human. *Mestizaje/mulatez* are ontological and epistemological categories.[44] Through the emphases on *mestizaje/mulatez*, community, daily life, and popular religion, Latino/a theologians are not merely attempting to bring forth the particular religious reality and practices of Hispanics, they are also seeking to transform the very discourse of theology. Theology cannot continue to label and limit itself through neat, dualistic oppositions. Instead, Latino/a theology offers a way to speak of the diversity, messiness, and beauty of reality.

Emerging from these concerns is the historical recovery of marginalized voices and traditions of Latino/a peoples. This can be seen in the work of Virgilio Elizondo on Our Lady of Guadalupe, Alejandro García-Rivera on San Martín de Porres, and Orlando Espín on popular religion.[45] María Pilar Aquino offers a succinct definition of the role and significance of this historical research when she redefines the Conquest paradigm of discovery as an actual "covering" of rich cultures, traditions, and religious practice. She writes, "This is so because the Iberian powers in Latin America – as well as the powers that succeeded them – really *covered*, concealed, and hid dramatically two realities, falsifying their truth in the process."[46] Aquino raises the need for Latino/a peoples to "un-cover" the historical marginalization and suppression of their cultures and traditions in order to discover the rich history of Latino/a peoples and cultures.

A last area of scholarship within Latino/a theology I wish to highlight is aesthetics. Mirroring its rising presence in contemporary theology, theological aesthetics is a growing field in Latino/a theology that broadens the scope and nature of Latino/as' theological method.[47] Those scholars working on aesthetics, both Latino/a and non-Latino/a, approach the field via two avenues: methodological and ontological. The theologian who emphasizes the ontological dimensions of aesthetics examines the metaphysics of Beauty as a transcendental. Scholars in this area, who include Alejandro García-Rivera and Edward Farley, note the demise of Beauty as central to theology and seek its recovery.[48] On the methodological end of the spectrum we find theologians that incorporate aesthetic resources within their theologies. The above-mentioned efforts in Black theology are examples of this. Then there is a third category within theological aesthetics, the scholarship of those who share ontological and methodological concerns. The writing of Hans Urs von Balthasar may provide the best example of this, since the most well-known dimension of von Balthasar's theology is his theological aesthetics, culminating in the seven-volume *Glory of the Lord*.[49] Theological scholars consider it to be one of the twentieth century's greatest achievements within theology.[50] Situated as the first part of von Balthasar's enormous trilogy, his aesthetics seeks to simultaneously recover Beauty as a transcendental and as the aesthetic form of theology. The trilogy itself is based on the three transcendentals of being: the Beautiful (*Herrlichkeit*), the Good (*Theodramatik*), and the True (*Theologik*). The order of the trilogy is not arbitrary. The manifestation, or theophany, of the aesthetics leads to the encounter of the dramatics. As von Balthasar writes, "God does not want to be just 'contemplated' and 'perceived' by us, like a solitary actor by his public; no, from the beginning he has provided for a play in which we all must share."[51] The theo-drama, in turn, is followed by the theo-logic, which treats the human articulation of the dramatic event. All three components of the trilogy are saturated with literature, poetry, and dramas as theological resources. As a significant amount of Sor Juana's writing falls under the heading of literature, this area of theological aesthetics is of particular interest for this study.

To propose literature as a theological resource is not new to theology. From Dante's works to the poetry of Gerard Manley Hopkins, historically literature has been an aesthetic voice within theology. Theologians have used literature as a resource to tap into and reveal the theological imagination of humanity. Often this is done in an ad hoc manner that does not explicitly challenge the implications of aesthetics for theology. A theological methodology that places literature in *explicit* conversation with theology, however, is often characterized by the ambiguity and tension of its interdisciplinary task. Gregory Salyer, in his introduction to *Literature and Theology at Century's End*, discusses the uncertainty of the field.[52] Noting that often those who pursue this field are challenged to justify the validity of their work, Salyer emphasizes the strain in this field of theological scholarship. Tensions aside, however, one cannot ignore the vitality and growing interest in this area of Christian thought.

Latin American theology is a theology that does not often come to mind when one engages the area of literature and theology. However, literature plays a significant role in informing the theological elaborations of Latin American theologians. Latin American liberation theology speaks of God's manifestation in the victims of history. More specifically, this theology is characterized by reflection on God's grace and action among the poor in history. As defined by Gustavo Gutiérrez in his monumental work *A Theology of Liberation*, for the Latin American liberation theologian, theology is "critical reflection on Christian praxis in the light of the Word."[53] This definition highlights the critical and praxiological emphasis of the theological task. With its emphasis on the poor, Latin American liberation theology offers a revolutionary shift in theological method, for it radically departs from the traditional interlocutor of contemporary theologies. Unlike other "postconciliar" and "progressive" theologies, which are concerned with the question of the skeptic and the nonbeliever, Latin American liberation theology concerns itself with the nonperson.[54] As such, the interests and questions of this theology differ from its counterparts, challenging traditional notions of theological scholarship. Within the institutional Roman Catholic Church, the conferences of Latin American bishops both at Medellín (1968) and at Puebla (1979) are significant moments in the development of Latin American liberation theology, where the Church articulated a commitment to the struggles of the poor.

In a recent article on theology and literature in Latin America,

Luis N. Rivera-Pagán has highlighted the significance of literature as an avenue for tapping into the Latin American consciousness and imagination. "The Latin American existential drama, in all its manifold complexities, has expressed itself fundamentally, and in a magnificent way, in our literature, especially our novels, not in philosophical treatises."[55] Rivera-Pagán argues for the use of literature as a vehicle for unearthing the intellectual heritage of Latin American peoples. This would transform the stereotype that in Latin America there is no critical intellectual history. Rivera-Pagán cites the work of Ernesto Sábato who recounts, "Not long ago, a German critic asked me why we Latin Americans have great novelists but no great philosophers. Because we are barbarians, I told him, because we were saved, fortunately, from the great rationalist schism. . . . If you want our *Weltanschauung*, I told him, look to our novels, not to our pure thought."[56]

While I am in agreement with both Sábato and Rivera-Pagán's assessments of literature as revelatory of the Latin American imagination, I am hesitant to reduce that literary production to the purely imaginative. The philosophical plays and literature of twentieth-century philosophers Jean-Paul Sartre and Albert Camus are clear examples that contest this reduction. In a specifically Latin American context, there are two contemporary examples. The first is seen in the influence of the literature of José María Arguedas on the theology of Gustavo Gutiérrez. As Brett Greider has demonstrated, Gutiérrez holds Arguedas's literature to be a significant resource in elaborating a theology that emerged from the context and culture of the people.[57] A second instance is the anthology entitled *Filosofía, teología, literatura: Aportes cubanos en los últimos 50 años*.[58] Editor Raúl Fornet-Betancourt brought together philosophers, theologians, and literary scholars in order to approach their fields in an interdisciplinary perspective. This book is an illustration of the growing number of collaborations in the fields of literature, theology, and philosophy in the Latin American context.

To conceive of many of the contributions of liberation theologians under the rubric of aesthetics could be seen as problematic for some. After all, Beauty has at times been portrayed as detracting from justice. However, aesthetics, whether named explicitly as theological aesthetics or not, has become a central aspect of liberation theologies. This should not be surprising, for the rewriting of history upon which liberation theologians embark must entail a reimagining of the very discourses that constitute theology. Within this revision of Christianity, the context that shapes these alternative voices is a central feature of the inclusive reconstruction of Christian theology. Thus, to set the stage for my retrieval of Sor Juana's voice, I turn to the life and times of this tenth muse, who constantly struggled against the limitations her culture, society, and church placed upon her intellectual pursuits and her theological voice.

Notes

[1]Rubem A. Alves, "From Liberation Theologian to Poet: A Plea That the Church Move from Ethics to Aesthetics, from Doing to Beauty," *Church and State* 83 (1993): 23.

[2]Gustavo Gutiérrez, *Las Casas: In Search of the Poor of Jesus Christ*, trans. Robert R. Barr (Maryknoll, NY: Orbis, 1993), xv.

[3]In an interesting twist, the theme of Nepantla is becoming increasingly popular for Latino/a theologians as a means of identifying the ambiguity of bicultural peoples. See Daisy Machado, "Kingdom Building in the Borderlands: The Church and Manifest Destiny," in *Hispanic / Latino Theology: Challenge and Promise*, ed. Ada María Isasi-Díaz and Fernando Segovia (Minneapolis: Fortress Press, 1996), 63-72; Rudy Busto, "The Predicament of *Nepantla*: Chicana/o Religions in the 21st Century," *Perspectivas* 1 (Fall 1998): 7-21; Orlando O. Espín, "Immigration, Territory, and Globalization: Theological Reflections," *Journal of Hispanic/Latino Theology* 7:3 (2000): 46-59; Michelle A. Gonzalez, "*Nuestra Humanidad*: Toward a Latina Theological Anthropology," *Journal of Hispanic/Latino Theology* 8:3 (February 2001): 49-72.

[4]A *criollo/a* is a person of Spanish descent born in the New World.

[5]As noted by Sor Juana scholar Dorothy Schons, "She had devoured any and every book that came within her reach. At the age of fifteen she had already established a reputation as the most learned woman in Mexico. . . . It was because of her learning that she gained a position at the viceregal court." Dorothy Schons, "Some Obscure Points in the Life of Sor Juana Inés de la Cruz," in *Feminist Perspectives on Sor Juana Inés de la Cruz*, ed. Stephanie Merrim (Detroit: Wayne State University Press, 1991), 39.

[6]Sor Juana Inés de la Cruz, *The Answer/La Respuesta: Including a Selection of Poems*, critical ed. and trans. Electa Arenal and Amanda Powell (New York: The Feminist Press at the City University of New York, 1994), 49. (OC 4: 446.241-246). In order to provide accessibility to Sor Juana's work for an English-speaking audience, translations of Sor Juana's work will be used

in the body of my text. Whenever possible, I have used published translations of Sor Juana's corpus. Unfortunately, the entirety of her work has not been published in English. In the cases where an English translation is unavailable, translations are my own except those translated by Ellen Calmus, which are indicated by (EC). In addition, I will include references to the most recent edition of Sor Juana's works: Alfonso Méndez Plancarte and Alberto Salceda, eds., *Obras Completas de Sor Juana Inés de la Cruz*, 4 vols. (Mexico: Instituto Mexiquense de Cultura; Fondo de Cultura Económica, 1995). I will note all citations using the abbreviation OC, followed by volume: page number. verse/ poem number. The verse numbers will be cited for the longer works, and poems will be cited by their poem numbers.

[7]Schons, "Some Obscure Points," 40.

[8]Sor Juana, *The Answer/La Respuesta*, 51. (OC 4: 446.268-273).

[9]Ibid., 97. (OC 4: 470-471.1264-1267).

[10]Schons, "Some Obscure Points," 47.

[11]As noted by George Tavard, "Well known in her native Mexico and in the generality of the Spanish-speaking world, Juana Inés de la Cruz has remained largely unknown to the educated public of English-speaking North America, in spite of the fact that good scholarly investigations of her life and works have been done in the United States." George Tavard, *Juana Inés de la Cruz and the Theology of Beauty: The First Mexican Theology* (Notre Dame, IN: University of Notre Dame Press, 1991), 1.

[12]I am in no way disputing the fact that the form of the majority of Sor Juana's work is literary. However, the content cannot be limited to literature.

[13]See bibliography.

[14]The two book-length exceptions to this are the above cited study by Tavard and Pamela Kirk, *Sor Juana Inés de la Cruz: Religion, Art, and Feminism* (New York: Continuum, 1998). Also see Elina Vuola, "Sor Juana Inés de la Cruz: Rationality, Gender, and Power," *Journal of Hispanic/Latino Theology* 9:1 (Aug. 2001): 27-45. Ivone Gebara also uses Sor Juana's writing as one of many resources for a Latin American feminist theology that addresses women's experiences of evil and salvation. See *Out of the Depths: Women's Experience of Evil and Salvation* (Minneapolis: Fortress Press, 2002).

[15]Roberto S. Goizueta, " 'Why are you frightened?' U.S. Hispanic Theology and Late Modernity," in *Cuerpo de Cristo: The Hispanic Presence in the U.S. Catholic Church*, ed. Peter Casarella and Raúl Gómez (New York: Crossroad, 1998), 62.

[16]Donald Beggs, "Sor Juana's Feminism: From Aristotle to Irigaray," in *Hypatia's Daughters: Fifteen Hundred Years of Women Philosophers*, ed. Linda Lopez McAlister (Bloomington, IN: Indiana University Press, 1996), 108.

[17]In a brief article discussing the theological contribution of Sor Juana, Beatriz Melano Couch writes, "Scholars who have studied Sor Juana speak of her greatness as a literary figure, philosopher, and woman of science. My

study of her works has brought me to the conclusion that she was also a theologian: indeed, the first woman theologian in all the Americas." Beatriz Melano Couch, "Sor Juana Inés de la Cruz: The First Woman Theologian in the Americas," in *The Church and Women in the Third World*, ed. John C.B. Webster and Ellen Low Webster (Philadelphia: The Westminster Press, 1985), 54.

[18]Kirk, *Sor Juana*, 10.

[19]Ibid., 12-13.

[20]For an excellent article on the common method of liberation theologies see Peter Phan, "A Common Journey, Different Paths, the Same Direction: Method in Liberation Theologies," in *A Dream Unfinished: Theological Reflections on America from the Margins*, ed. Eleazar S. Fernandez and Fernando F. Segovia (Maryknoll, NY: Orbis Books, 2001), 129-151.

[21]See M. Shawn Copeland, "Tradition and the Traditions of African American Catholicism," *Theological Studies* 61:4 (Dec 2000), 632-655; Roberto S. Goizueta, "A *Ressourcement* from The Margins: U.S. Latino Popular Catholicism as Lived Religion," *Theology and Lived Christianity*, ed. David M. Hammond (Mystic, CT: Twenty-Third Publications/Bayard, 2000), 3-37.

[22]Yves Congar, *I Believe in the Holy Spirit*, vol. 2, trans. David Smith (New York: Seabury Press, 1983), 150.

[23]The two major studies that come to mind are Gutiérrez's above-cited monograph on Las Casas and Alejandro García-Rivera, *St. Martín de Porres: "The Little Stories" and the Semiotics of Culture* (Maryknoll, NY: Orbis, 1995).

[24]While an overview of the global movement of Third World theologies is far too extensive to undertake at this juncture, one should note that in both Asia and Africa, similar developments in liberation theology, though distinct in their focus, are occurring. In 1976, the formation of the Ecumenical Association of Third World Theologians (EATWOT) clearly marks the beginning of diverse theological expressions from the Third World in conversation with each other and recognizing their common struggles.

[25]Elisabeth Schüssler Fiorenza, "Breaking the Silence – Becoming Visible," in *The Power of Naming: A Concilium Reader in Feminist Liberation Theology*, ed. Elisabeth Schüssler Fiorenza (Maryknoll, NY: Orbis, 1996), 161-162.

[26]Some would argue that in fact Valerie Saiving's essay, "The Human Situation: A Feminine View," is actually the first feminist theological text. While not disputing this fact, I find the impact of Mary Daly's book to be the fundamental public moment for feminist theologians. Valerie Saiving, "The Human Situation: A Feminine View," *The Journal of Religion* (April 1960).

[27]Rosemary Radford Ruether describes this methodology: "One can speak of three moments or stages in the development of feminist theology, although these stages do not simply succeed each other in mechanical fashion, but are constantly developing in interaction with each other. . . . The first moment of feminist theology is the critique of the masculine bias of theology. . . . The second moment in feminist theology is one which seeks alternative

traditions which support the autonomous personhood of women. . . . The third moment of feminist theology then takes the form of tentative efforts to restate the norms and methodology of theology itself in the light of this critique and alternative tradition." Rosemary Radford Ruether, "The Future of Feminist Theology in the Academy," *Journal of the American Academy of Religion* 53:4 (Dec. 1985): 706-709.

[28]Elizabeth A. Johnson, *She Who Is: The Mystery of God in Feminist Theological Discourse* (New York: Crossroad, 1992), 29. In the later work of Roman Catholic theologian Elizabeth Johnson there is a fourfold method of ideological suspicion, historical reconstruction, ethical assessment of texts, and hermeneutics of suspicion, applied to remembrance, proclamation, and celebration. Elizabeth A. Johnson, *Friends of God and Prophets: A Feminist Theological Reading of the Communion of Saints* (New York: Continuum, 1998), 160-161.

[29]Ruether, "The Future of Feminist Theology in the Academy," 708.

[30]Ruether's monumental study, *Women and Redemption: A Theological History* (Minneapolis: Fortress Press, 1998), is an excellent overview of European and North American women's theological contributions. While her chapters that examine contemporary theologians include Third World women's voices, the historical chapters do not.

[31]Dwight N. Hopkins, *Shoes That Fit Our Feet: Sources for a Constructive Black Theology* (Maryknoll, NY: Orbis, 1993), 126.

[32]James H. Cone, *Black Theology and Black Power* (New York: Seabury Press, 1969; rev. ed., Maryknoll, NY: Orbis Books, 1998).

[33]On the importance of spirituals for Black theology, see James H. Cone, *The Spirituals and the Blues* (Maryknoll, NY: Orbis, 2000). On the interdisciplinary nature of Black theology see Dwight N. Hopkins, *Introducing Black Theology of Liberation* (Maryknoll, NY: Orbis, 1999); for womanist theology, see Stephanie Y. Mitchem, *Introducing Womanist Theology* (Maryknoll, NY: Orbis, 2002). On the significance of Zora Neale Hurston for womanist theologians, see Katie Geneva Cannon, *Katie's Canon: Womanism and the Soul of the Black Community* (New York: Continuum, 1996).

[34]Delores Williams, "Black Women's Literature and the Task of Feminist Theology," in *Immaculate and Powerful: The Female in Sacred Image and Social Reality*, ed. C.W. Atkinson, C.H. Buchanan, and M.R. Miles (Boston: Beacon Press, 1985), 88.

[35]Ibid., 107.

[36]"The questions asked by the 'nonperson,' the 'nonhuman,' . . . have to do with the economic, the social, and the political, and yet this does not make for a nontheological discussion, as some seem to think. That would indeed be a facile solution. It is a matter of a different theology. The difference is clearly seen in the real world, where persons live and die, believe and hope, and where it is reprehensible to obscure social conflict with generic affirmations and a false universalism." Gustavo Gutiérrez, *The Power of the Poor in History* (Maryknoll, NY: Orbis, 1993), 212.

[37]Ibid., 91-92.

[38]Cone, *The Spirituals and the Blues*, 65.

[39]Roberto S. Goizueta, "U.S. Hispanic Popular Catholicism as Theo-poetics," in *Hispanic/Latino Theology: Challenge and Promise*, ed. Ada María Isasi-Díaz and Fernando F. Segovia (Minneapolis: Fortress, 1996), 261.

[40]Ibid., 262.

[41]As Latino/a theologians use both terms, I will be using Hispanic and Latino/a interchangeably in this study. For a philosophical study of the issue of naming within the Latino/a community see, Jorge J.E. Gracia, *Hispanic/Latino Identity: A Philosophical Perspective* (New York: Blackwell, 2000).

[42]The "people" is a term often used by Latino/a theologians to designate the Latino/a community in the United States. While at times designating the entire Latino/a community, some scholars emphasize a certain group within the community. For those Latino/a theologians who are influenced significantly by Latin American liberation theology, "the people" often designates the poor. Roman Catholic Latino/a theologians often define their work in terms of popular Catholicism. In these cases, "the people" designates Roman Catholic Latino/as. See Orlando O. Espín, *The Faith of the People: Theological Reflections on Popular Catholicism* (Maryknoll, NY: Orbis, 1997); Roberto S. Goizueta, *Caminemos con Jesús: Toward a Hispanic/Latino Theology of Accompaniment* (Maryknoll, NY: Orbis, 1995). For a Protestant discussion of Latino/a theology's method see José David Rodríguez, "On Doing Hispanic Theology," in *Teología de Conjunto: A Collaborative Hispanic Protestant Theology*, ed. José David Rodríguez and Loida I. Martell-Otero (Louisville, KY: Westminster John Knox Press, 1997), 11-21. For a Roman Catholic perspective see María Pilar Aquino, "Theological Method in U.S. Latino/a Theology: Toward an Intercultural Theology for the Third Millennium," in *From the Heart of Our People: Latino/a Explorations in Catholic Systematic Theology*, ed. Orlando O. Espín and Miguel H. Díaz (Maryknoll, NY: Orbis, 1999), 6-48.

[43]On the "little stories" and "big story" see García-Rivera, *St. Martín de Porres*.

[44]*Mestizaje* designates the cultural and biological mixture of Spanish and Indigenous; *mulatez* names the mixture of Spanish and African.

[45]See Virgilio Elizondo, *Guadalupe: Mother of the New Creation* (Maryknoll, NY: Orbis, 1997); García-Rivera, *St. Martín de Porres*; Espín, *The Faith of the People*.

[46]María Pilar Aquino, "The Collective 'Dis-covery' of Our Own Power: Latina American Feminist Theology," in *Hispanic/Latino Theology: Challenge and Promise*, 241-242.

[47]See Peter Casarella, "The Painted Word," *Journal of Hispanic/Latino Theology* 6:2 (Nov. 1998): 18-42; Alejandro García-Rivera, *The Community of the Beautiful: A Theological Aesthetics* (Collegeville, MN: The Liturgical Press, 1999); Roberto S. Goizueta, "Fiesta: Life in the Subjunctive," in *From*

the Heart of Our People, 84-99; Jeanette Rodríguez-Holguín, "La Tierra: Home, Identity, and Destiny," in *From The Heart of Our People*, 189-208.

[48]García-Rivera, *The Community of the Beautiful*; Edward Farley, *Faith and Beauty: A Theological Aesthetic* (Burlington, VT: Ashgate, 2001).

[49]English translation of *Herrlichkeit: Eine theologische Äesthetik.*

[50]As noted in the opening words of Louis Dupré's often-cited overview of von Balthasar's aesthetics, "Hans Urs von Balthasar's seven-volume *Herrlichkeit*, completed by 1969, ranks among the foremost theological achievements of our century." Louis Dupré, "The Glory of the Lord: Hans Urs von Balthasar's Theological Aesthetic," in *Hans Urs von Balthasar: His Life and Work*, ed. David L. Schindler (San Francisco: Ignatius, 1991), 183.

[51]Hans Urs von Balthasar, *My Work: In Retrospect* (San Francisco: Ignatius, 1993).

[52]Gregory Salyer, "Introduction," in *Literature and Theology at Century's End*, ed. Gregory Salyer and Robert Detweiler (Atlanta: Scholars Press, 1995), 1.

[53]Gustavo Gutiérrez, *A Theology of Liberation*, 15th anniversary ed. (Maryknoll, NY: Orbis, 1988), 11.

[54]Gutiérrez, *The Power of the Poor in History*, 91.

[55]Luis N. Rivera-Pagán, "Theology and Literature in Latin America," *Journal of Hispanic/Latino Theology* 7:4 (May 2000): 19.

[56]Ernesto Sábato, *The Angel of Darkness*, trans. Andrew Hurley (New York: Ballantine Books, 1991), 194, cited in Rivera-Pagán, "Theology and Literature," 19.

[57]Brett Greider, *Crossing Deep Rivers: The Liberation Theology of Gustavo Gutiérrez in Light of the Narrative Poetics of José María Arguedas* (Ph.D. Dissertation, Graduate Theological Union, Berkeley, CA, 1988).

[58]Raúl Fornet-Betancourt, ed., *Filosofía, teología, literatura: Aportes cubanos en los últimos 50 años* (Aachen: Concordia Reihe Monographien, Band 25, 1999).

Chapter 2

Sor Juana Inés de la Cruz

Her Life and Context

"Among flights of your pen I go, different from myself."[1]
—Sor Juana Inés de la Cruz

Sor Juana Inés de la Cruz lived in a world very different from modern-day Latin America. The colonial era in Mexico was marked by the influences of the Baroque, court life, and the birth of a Spanish population born in the Americas. It is one of the least-studied eras in Mexican history, and pivotal for understanding the cultural context of her life and writing. Her personal history and intellectual concerns were shaped by the contours and characteristics of her era. In addition to the broader characteristics of her cultural milieu, Sor Juana's context includes the fact that she was a cloistered woman, a significant dimension to consider in exploring her work. An examination of Sor Juana's biography is an especially vital component of any Sor Juana study, since the last years of her life are clouded with mystery and uncertainty. In addition, as Sor Juana is probably an unfamiliar figure to the modern student of theology, a general overview of her life, of the writing she did which is significant to her biography, and of her cultural and intellectual climate is central for a recovery of her theology. In order to understand, for example, her particular theological contribution, we must establish the contours of the theology of her era.

My overview of Sor Juana's life and the writing relevant to this account will be followed by an examination of the culture, society, and intellectual climate of colonial Mexico, with special attention to the philosophy and theology that was characteristic of Sor Juana's era.

Before beginning my attempt to contextualize Sor Juana and her life, I must highlight the ambiguity that clouds this task. While the modern-day scholar can pool resources from the fields of history, literary studies, theology, and philosophy in order to better understand Sor Juana, the results of these efforts are always incomplete. Modern scholars' judgments are understandably colored by their context and hermeneutic. In addition, it is impossible for the present-day reader to have a clear picture of Sor Juana's world, due to the inevitable gaps in information. The ambiguity surrounding the events of Sor Juana's life has led to divergent interpretations by contemporary scholars. I will highlight some of the more pressing debates among *sorjuanistas*, though I will not treat them exhaustively.[2] The reader is encouraged to consult the endnotes of this chapter in order to explore the work of those scholars engaged in contemporary discussions regarding Sor Juana's history and identity. These debates are significant, for they contribute to the mold in which Sor Juana has been cast for the contemporary reader, often ignoring the nuances of her writing and context. In my exploration of her life and work I emphasize the role of her theological vocation. As I will demonstrate, extreme caricatures of her story often lead to a diminishment of the importance of theology and vocation for Sor Juana. This in turn contributes to the marginalization of her theological contribution.

My remarks on Sor Juana's life and culture are not intended to be exhaustive, but simply a means of setting the stage for an understanding of her writing and giving the reader a glimpse of the world in which she wrote. This chapter should be seen as an effort to interpret Sor Juana's life, without claiming to offer a complete picture. The picture is framed, and thus limited, by the concerns of a modern theological audience. I therefore proceed with caution. The goal of this study is not to retrieve a historical theology, but instead to explore a historical contribution to contemporary theology.

Background

The attempt to portray Sor Juana's life accurately is a daunting task. There is a broad spectrum of interpretations of her life, piety, and sexuality, and any effort to claim an accurate depiction risks staunch criticism from opposing camps. Questions abound. Does her love poetry to women imply, as some contemporary scholars hypothesize, that she was a repressed lesbian? Or was she merely emulating the style and the language of her male contemporaries? Did she enter into the convent solely to study and escape the possibility of marriage, or did she have a sense of Christian vocation? Did the Catholic Church silence her for daring, as a woman, to write theology? Is she the first feminist in the Americas?

The answers to these and other questions remain ambiguous, in part, due to Sor Juana's silence on these topics. *Sorjuanista* Asunción Lavrin notes that while Sor Juana has given literary scholars a wealth of material to study, she was a bit stingier with historians.[3] What the modern scholar knows about Sor Juana is very sparse, and this contributes to the plurality of interpretations and hypotheses surrounding her life. A Jesuit named Diego Calleja wrote a biography of Sor Juana shortly after her death, but it is framed as a spiritual biography that seemingly idealizes and mythologizes Sor Juana in a manner similar to hagiography, making some of its claims questionable. In addition to this biography, scholars have the scattered comments Sor Juana herself wrote as another primary resource. These comments are found in various poems, her secular comedy *Los empeños de una casa* (*The Trials of a House*), and the prose piece *La respuesta a Sor Filotea* (*The Answer*).

From the start, Juana Ramírez de Asbaje's history is questionable. Even her date of birth is contested. Her biographer Calleja states that she was born on November 12, 1651. However, a baptismal certificate dated December 1648 for a girl named Inés, whose godparents were the siblings of Juana Inés's mother, is a persuasive document for a 1648 birth year. Unfortunately, as her parents were unmarried, her birth is not recorded in the church registry. Juana Ramírez had four sisters and one brother. Her parents' names were Pedro Manuel de Asbaje and Doña Isabel Ramírez de Santillana. According to Juana her father was Basque. The mystery surrounding her father is one that continues to puzzle *sorjuanistas*.[4] He was at the margins of her life.

Sorjuanistas know a bit more about her mother, Isabel Ramírez. Strong and independent women characterize Sor Juana's family.[5] Isabel Ramírez never married either of the two men that fathered her children: Pedro Manuel and Diego Ruiz Lozano. Sor Juana shares her father with her first three siblings. After her father died, Sor Juana's mother managed his hacienda for over thirty years. Sor Juana emerges from a family where women had strong leadership positions. This is significant, for Sor Juana herself was a fiercely independent woman who struggled against exterior forms of authority and control over her life. Her mother was clearly a model of female autonomy and power for Juana when she was growing up.

In *The Answer* Sor Juana tells us that at the age of three she learned to read, after pleading with one of her older sisters' teachers to instruct her. As mentioned in chapter 1, she begged her mother to dress her as a boy to send her to the university in Mexico City. Since this was clearly not going to happen, Sor Juana instead studied the books found in her grandfather's library. Her grandfather, yet another shadowy man in Sor Juana's past, lived with her family until his death. As Octavio Paz emphasizes, by reading her grandfather's books Juana made her first entry into a world in which she would later struggle in life to remain included, a world with clear gender divisions that Sor Juana sought to blur. "Her grandfather's books opened the doors to a world which neither her mother nor her sisters could enter: a man's world."[6] We learn in *The Answer* that Sor Juana had odd habits that accompanied her studies; they reveal some of the flavor of her personality. "I would abstain from eating cheese, because I heard tell that it made people stupid, and the desire to learn was stronger for me than the desire to eat."[7] In addition, as a child Sor Juana would do such things as cutting her hair to monitor the efficiency and capacities of her intellectual skills. If her hair grew out before she had learned a particular subject Sor Juana would "cut my hair right off to punish my dull-wittedness, for I did not think it reasonable that hair should cover a head that was so bare of facts—the more desirable adornment."[8] These early years as an avid reader in her grandfather's study mark the birth of one of the greatest scholars in Mexican history. Her time with his books, however, was short-lived. For reasons unknown to the modern reader, around the age of eight Juana went to Mexico City to live with relatives.

The years Sor Juana lived with her family in Mexico City are lost to us today. The reasons for her departure are unknown, as is how she occupied herself throughout her stay with her extended family. After several years living with them, at the age of thirteen, Juana's family presented her to the court of Viceroy Don Antonio Sebastián Toledo and Vicereine Doña Leonor Carreto. Juana joined the court as a lady-in-waiting. Doña Leonor will appear in Sor Juana's poems under the name of Laura. Of particular note concerning the viceroy and vicereine is their love of literature.[9] An interesting account, reported by Calleja, is of the viceroy being so impressed by Juana's knowledge that he called forty (male) scholars in Mexico City to the palace in order to have an intellectual debate with Juana. In the end, she outwitted all of these men. Though the historical accuracy of this account may be questionable, what is clear is that even during her time in the court, Juana was known for her vast knowledge and deft intelligence.

The viceroyalty was a temporary governing position in New Spain, with each leader designated to rule for only a short period of time. Sor Juana saw four viceroys in her public lifetime.[10] Of the four, Don Tomás Antonio de la Cerda, the Marquis de la Laguna, and his wife, María Luisa Manrique de Lara y Gonzaga, Countess of Paredes de Nava, would have the greatest impact on Sor Juana's career as an author. They lived in Mexico from 1680 to 1688. Sor Juana had the most fruitful and public period of her writing career during their reign. María Luisa, the Marquise and wife of the viceroy, had a close relationship with Sor Juana. Both she and her husband frequently visited the convent, and they were patrons of her work. *Sorjuanistas* have María Luisa to thank for the publication of Sor Juana's works in Spain. The first volume of Sor Juana's works was published in 1689 in Madrid, sponsored by María Luisa. In 1692 a second volume of her work was published, again with the vicereine's aid. The third volume of her work was published posthumously in 1700. Today her corpus stands with 65 sonnets, 62 romances, a prolific amount of poems in other forms, two comedies, three *autos sacramentales* (allegorical dramas), 16 sets of *villancicos*, one *sarao*, and two farces.[11] María Luisa had a great love for literature and the arts, and she and Sor Juana shared a mutual admiration. Sor Juana's relationship with María Luisa is the source of contemporary speculation surrounding Sor Juana's sexual identity.[12] María Luisa was an authority figure in Sor Juana's life, commissioning much of her writing. Many of Sor Juana's poems use the language of passion and love to describe María Luisa. However, Sor Juana's poetry emulated the male Spanish greats. It is therefore difficult to discern the impulses behind Sor Juana's language. As Jean Franco indicates, "I am not denying that the passion that many have detected in the poems addressed to the Countess is real nor that they are indeed love poems; but it is impossible to separate personal love from love of the body politic, and love of the body politic included the recognition of authority."[13] This more recent discussion surrounding Sor Juana's sexuality is not the first aspect of her life that has led to debate among contemporary scholars.

A person with whom Juana came in contact during her time in the court, one who would become one of the major players throughout the rest of Sor Juana's life, was the Jesuit Antonio Núñez de Miranda. He was a powerful figure in the colonial Church, with extremely odd, almost fearful, attitudes toward women. On his contact with women he writes, "With women, I must have great caution not to make eye contact. I must not allow them to kiss my hand, nor allow myself to look at their face or clothing, nor visit any of them unless I have a qualified and inevitable motive; in short I must be cautious and prudent."[14] During her time in the court Núñez de Miranda encouraged Sor Juana to enter the convent. Aware of her academic gifts as well as her distaste for marriage, he felt the convent was the best venue to monitor Sor Juana's growing public notoriety and intellectual aspirations.[15] This was not an easy task, given Sor Juana's background and financial situation. As Norma Salazar highlights, "Joining a religious community was usually expensive. Elaborate initiation ceremonies were costly and required substantial dowries. Juana had no money of her own and no male family members to provide a dowry. A wealthy sponsor furnished the several thousand pesos needed."[16] Around the age of sixteen Juana entered the Order of the Discalced Carmelites as a novice. However, after three months, she left that order for health reasons. In 1669 she took the veil in the convent of San Jerónimo, to the Order of the Hieronymites, an order known to be a bit more lenient than the Carmelites. Núñez de Miranda would become Sor Juana's confessor for a significant portion of her cloistered life.

Scholars have several theories regarding Sor Juana's entry in the convent. For the most part, contemporary *sorjuanistas* downplay the role of religious faith and vocation in her life. This understanding of Sor Juana is flawed, I contend, for it is based on a very narrow definition of religious vocation. Too often, the diminishment of Sor Juana's vocation leads to downplaying the significance of Sor Juana's theological and philosophical writing. I begin with Octavio Paz, since his study overshadows so many of the others. Paz, while not denying Sor Juana's Catholic faith, does not see her as called to a vocation as a woman religious. "Nothing in Sor Juana's earlier life reveals a particular religious disposition. . . . Nor, it must be admitted, did she demonstrate excessive piety during the twenty-six years she lived in San Jerónimo."[17] For Paz, Sor Juana's lack of religious inclinations in her earlier years and her failure to exhibit an adequate sense of piety inform his claim.[18] In a different vein, Dorothy Schons interprets Sor Juana's entry into the convent as purely conditioned by the societal structures of her era. As a woman of "illegitimate" birth with no desire to marry, the convent was the only safe and viable option for her.[19] These interpretations of Sor Juana's decision to join a religious order hold Sor Juana to feminine standards of piety. In other words, because Sor Juana did not express her faith in the manner typical of the women of her era (through mystical writing and mortification, for example), she is not interpreted as pious. Schons does not even entertain the possibility of a sense of vocation in Sor Juana. Paz holds that she did not fulfill the criteria of a devout sister. If there is anything Sor Juana's life clearly demonstrates, however, is the fact that she was an atypical woman.

Asunción Lavrin explores this vein. "There is no doubt that Sor Juana was a very devout and profoundly Catholic woman. However, unlike other women religious in her era, she never spoke profoundly about her interior life."[20] Although Sor Juana does not express her spiritual life in the manner typical of women of her era, this does not mean that she did not have a spiritual life. While I am not saying that Sor Juana necessarily entered the convent out of a profound sense of vocation or calling as traditionally understood for women religious, there is no clear evidence that she did not have a sense of calling, albeit different from the women with whom she shared a cloistered life.

The words of Sor Juana herself shed light on this. Perhaps the most frequently cited expression of Sor Juana's motivations for taking the veil are found in the lines of La Respuesta when she writes, "I took the veil because, although I knew I would find in religious life many things that would be opposed to my character (I speak of accessory rather that essential matters), it would, given my absolute unwillingness to enter into marriage, be the least unfitting and most decent state I could choose."[21] She continues by listing those aspects of her personality that she sees as unsuitable for cloistered life: her desire to live in solitude, to have the freedom to study, and to have a space to study undisturbed. While this text expresses hesitancy in joining an order, it does not do so based on a lack of faith or vocation. Instead, Sor Juana worries over the way her personality will fit into the structure of the cloister. She is concerned that her overwhelming need to study undisturbed stands against the very nature of communal, convent living.

In the end, sorjuanistas will never know Sor Juana's motivations for entering the convent. Those Sor Juana scholars who downplay any sense of vocation in Sor Juana construct her vocation in the gendered models of her era. In other words, because she did not express a sense of calling in the manner typical of other women, she must not have had one. But we need to consider how such vocations were traditionally expressed by the men of Sor Juana's era. Scholars did not hesitate to measure Sor Juana's writing against her male contemporaries. Perhaps an expanded study of piety and devotion would aid in better understanding her life and calling.

The reasons behind Sor Juana's entry into convent life play a significant role in interpreting of her final years. After enjoying a very public life as a writer and intellectual, protected in part by the viceroy and vicereine, in 1690 Sor Juana's situation took a dramatic turn. In this year Sor Juana's critique of a male theologian's analysis of Christ's greatest demonstration of love (*fineza*) entitled *La carta atenagórica* (*The Letter*) was circulated without her authorization. Accompanying her critique was a letter written under the pseudonym Sor Filotea (which means lover of God), criticizing Sor Juana's intellectual pursuits. Sor Juana scholars today generally acknowledge that the author of this critique was the Bishop of Puebla, Manuel Fernández de Santa Cruz, and that Sor Juana was aware of his role in these events. Fernández names the object of Sor Juana's critique as a fifty-year-old sermon written by the prominent Jesuit theologian Antonio Vieira. Though the actual object of Sor Juana's critique is a matter of debate among *sorjuanistas*, the perceived target of Sor Juana's *Letter* in the eyes of her contemporaries was Vieira.[22] Her response to that publication, *La respuesta* (*The Answer*), an autobiographical defense of women's right to intellectual pursuits, was completed the following year. Within four years of producing *The Answer*, Sor Juana renounced her public life. In 1695 she died during an epidemic in the convent.

Within the murkiness surrounding these last years, two other sets of documents also play a key role. The first is a letter, the *Carta de Monterrey* (*Letter from Monterrey*). This letter, discovered in the late twentieth century and authenticated as Sor Juana's, reveals that in 1682 Sor Juana broke her relationship with her confessor. The break lasted for ten years. Prior to the discovery of this letter, *sorjuanistas* assumed that it was Núñez de Miranda that ended the relationship with her. This letter disputes an oversimplified depiction of Sor Juana's last years where she is a victim, silenced by the Church. For example, attributing the break to Núñez de Miranda is a major tenet in Paz's depiction of the final years of Sor Juana's life; he interpreted this termination as a step in the progressive "cold war" between Sor Juana and the Church. Instead, it was the independent Sor Juana who dismissed her confessor, not vice-versa. She was not entirely stripped of her agency.

The second set of papers consists of the five documents of renunciation that she signed in 1693. Of the five documents, not one mentions her renouncing her pursuit of letters. These documents must be understood in light of their context of her renewal of vows on the twenty-fifth anniversary of her profession. As theologian Pamela Kirk has argued, they may signal a time of spiritual renewal for Sor Juana on that anniversary, versus a total rejection of her intellectual life.[23] Also noted by Kirk is the fact that her death a month before the end of this penitential year leaves unanswered the question of whether she would have resumed writing at its end. Scholars do know, however, that Sor Juana did not in fact renounce her books and writing at the end of this year. At the time of her death Sor Juana had almost two hundred books in her library and fifteen files of writing on secular and sacred themes. This could possibly have been the most liberating time of Sor Juana's life, when she was free to write for herself, rather than on demand for public events.[24]

What else do scholars know that can shed light on these incidents? *Sorjuanistas* have established that Sor Juana was never persecuted by the Inquisition, as many detractors as she had; she also had supporters.[25] However, as Elías Trabulse indicates in his recent interpretation of Sor Juana's last years, her bishop had the authority to sanction her without the tribunal of the Inquisition. These judicial processes were handled secretly. Trabulse speculates that Sor Juana could have been the subject of an episcopal trial at the local level. The same month (April 1693) when Sor Juana turned from her pursuit of letters, Antonio de Aunsibay y Arena, a vicar general for the Episcopate who was also in charge of the bishop's local branch of the Inquisition, visited Sor Juana's convent. The proceedings that followed this visit are unknown today, though shortly afterward Sor Juana took her vow of silence. The contents of her cell at the time of her death reveal that her renunciation was directed at the public dimension of her writing.[26] In other words, while she relinquished her library at the time of her renunciations, she either did not do so completely, or immediately began a new one. She also continued her role of convent accountant, a position she had held prior to these events. She resumed her relationship with her confessor in 1692. In the last years of her life, Sor Juana exercised extreme mortification and penitence, something she had not practiced in prior years. Núñez de Miranda had always been critical of Sor Juana's public life. In Sor Juana's era the sphere that was the most monitored was women's access and participation in the public realm, especially with regard to preaching, publication, and participation in debates. Sor Juana did all these things, in her own way, through her publicly performed pieces and her circulated writing.

At the time of her censure Sor Juana's fame had spread across Spain and its colonies. In what modern scholars interpret as an autobiographical speech by the character Leonor in Sor Juana's comedy *Los empeños de una casa* (*The Trials of a House*), Sor Juana reveals her awareness of her fame:

> Inclined toward my studies
> from earliest childhood
> with such ardent poring
> with such anxious care
> that a short time contained
> the fatigues of long years.
> I turned time, industrious,
> to the most intense labors
> till soon I received
> such extravagant praise,
> that the laurels I earned
> were thought naturally mine.
> In my country I was
> the most esteemed object
> of those adorations'
> collective applause. [27]

Accompanying this fame was a depiction of Sor Juana almost as an oddity, different from all other women. Sor Juana was well aware that to some she was almost a freak of nature. "I have only myself as my whole lineage."[28] In the first volume of the modern edition of her complete works appears a romance by Sor Juana that was written in response to a poem where she is compared to a Phoenix. Known even today as the Phoenix of Mexico, Sor Juana was quite conscious of the implications of this "flattery." The poem describes, for example, the phoenix as a sideshow freak. "What would the mountebanks not give to seize me and display me, taking me round like a Monster, through by-roads and lonely places in Italy and France, which are so fond of novelties, where the people pay to see the Giant's head. . . . Not that! Your fortune you'll not find with that Phoenix, you merchants; for this is why it is confined behind thirty locks, in the convent."[29] In her analysis of this poem, Stephanie Merrim indicates its baroque intricacies: "In this magnificent burlesque of the baroque esthetic of the bizarre and of her role as a prodigious Phoenix of Mexico within it, even as she writes of herself as a literal monster, Sor Juana proves herself eminently aware of the considerable 'monstrous' implications of being considered one."[30] The monstrosity of her fame and the manner in which she was revered contributed to the ecclesial vigilance over her writing.

There are two "camps" which interpret Sor Juana's final years: the Catholic interpretation sees her renunciation as a turn to spirituality and devotion, while the secular camp sees Sor Juana as a woman persecuted by the Church. Both positions are ideological, for they are based on a desire to depict Sor Juana as either converting to or surrendering to the desires of the institutional Church. Both are too simplistic. Sor Juana clearly transgressed the established norms for women religious. She did so in a very public manner. She also entered the realms of philosophical and theological speculation, trespassing on male claims to truth and authority. It is interesting to note, for example, that while the Bishop of Puebla chastises her for her secular pursuits in his *Carta de Sor Filotea*, he does so in response to her most explicitly theological text. *La carta atenagórica* is Sor Juana's writing that most clearly resembles male theological writing.

In the end, scholars may never know the exact reasons for Sor Juana's renunciation. Did the Church persecute her? I do find that she was under pressure from ecclesial authorities to curb her writing. She writes, "In persecuting me, world, what is your point? Where is my offense, when I only wish to put beauties in my intellect, not intellect in my beauties? I do not value treasures or riches; it always gives me more pleasure to put wealth in my thought than thought in my wealth."[31] In a similar vein she laments, "Let us pretend that I am happy, sad Thought, for a while: perhaps you can persuade me, although I know it is the contrary.

. . . Let my intellect serve for once as a relief. . . . If my intellect is my own, why must I always find it so inept in alleviating me, so keen to harm me?"[32] Was she forced to silence herself? This matter is clouded with uncertainty. Did she have a spiritual conversion? I disagree with Constance M. Montross's hypothesis that "In 1693, apparently convinced of the spiritual dangers of her intellectual activity, Sor Juana stopped writing and gave up her library."[33] However, Kirk's theory that her silence was in fact a part of a prescribed period of penitence and spiritual reflection, whether voluntary, encouraged, or coerced, offers an interesting hypothesis. One cannot deny, however, that in the hierarchical and rigidly compartmentalized culture of New Spain Sor Juana defied social norms and gender constraints. She contested her society and Church's rejection of women's abilities to claim an authoritative voice. She was simultaneously a product of and a challenge to her colonial, Baroque milieu.

The Baroque in New Spain

A survey of the Baroque in New Spain is fundamental both to a study of Sor Juana and to any broader treatment of Mexican cultural and intellectual history, for the often ignored Baroque was an era that left a lasting imprint on Mexico. As Mariano Picón-Salas has noted, "This part of our past is the least known and the most misunderstood of our whole historical and cultural evolution. The Baroque, however, was one of the elements that remained rooted in our culture for a very long time. Indeed, in spite of nearly two centuries of rationalism and modern criticism, we Spanish Americans have not yet fully emerged from its labyrinth."[34] I agree with Picón-Salas's thesis of the significance of the Baroque and the unfortunate ignorance surrounding it. First, the colonial era, which frames the Baroque in New Spain, is one of the least-examined eras of Mexican history.[35] The historical imagination surrounding Mexican history and culture often jumps from the Conquest to the modern era. Second, the imprint of the Baroque that Picón-Salas describes is fundamental. The colonial era was a time when the *criollo*, the Mexican-born Spaniard, was developing his or her consciousness and identity.[36]

The seventeenth and eighteenth centuries thus constitute an extremely formative period for Mexican identity in the Americas, as it distinguished itself from identity in the European Spanish culture.

The Baroque era was a time of paradox. This is due, in part, to the attempt in Baroque times to resolve and maintain the medieval world view that was slowly deteriorating in the wake of scientific, political, and economic revolutions throughout Europe and the Americas. It is interesting that within this chaos Louis Dupré, in his work *Passage to Modernity: An Essay in the Hermeneutics of Nature and Culture*, finds "a comprehensive spiritual vision" uniting Baroque times.[37] Describing the Baroque in general, Dupré defines it as an era where "religion and politics were cut from the same cloth, indeed the most intensely political issues were precisely the religious ones."[38] The unity of religion and politics is an especially significant feature to emphasize in studying Sor Juana's life and writing. The interconnectedness of the secular and the sacred that characterizes the Baroque is a prominent dimension of Sor Juana's story.

Moving from Dupré's broad brush-strokes to the specific context of New Spain, one finds a particular manifestation of the Baroque in the Americas. The society of New Spain was constructed in such a way as to mirror Spain. It was influenced by the extremely conservative and orthodox Counter-Reformation. Spain therefore attempted to shut out any Enlightenment ideas, which were seen as tinged with Reformation ideologies. While this proved an extremely complex task in Europe, the isolation of New Spain made it easier to contain cultural and political influences on the public. As Irving A. Leonard notes, "In this situation ideas, whether secular or religious, were carefully screened in Spain and excluded, as far as possible, from the New World so as to protect the incompletely Christianized natives from contamination."[39] Spain's isolationist tactics were motivated by a concern that the inadequately evangelized native peoples would somehow be more susceptible to corruption by Enlightenment or Reformation ideas. However, this isolation was not absolute, for advances in science were slowly shattering New Spain's medieval world view.[40]

It was possible to control the influx of knowledge and ideas in

New Spain, due to the fact that a small elite white minority controlled a large indigenous population. Baroque society was rigidly hierarchical. In New Spain the top of the hierarchy was occupied by the European-born Spaniards. Below them were the *criollos*, people of Spanish descent born in the New World. The *criollos* rarely held positions of power and were resentful of the Spanish elite. The clergy was divided into two groups: diocesan priests and those in religious orders. People of African descent, depending on their skin color, were able to exist on various social levels, though always subordinate to the *criollos* and the Spaniards. The *indios* were at the lowest rung of the social ladder. Colonial scholar Margo Glantz describes Baroque society as highly compartmentalized. The society resembled an armoire, with very defined sections based on race, birthplace, and class.[41] The irony of New Spain's Baroque era is found in its attempts to neatly classify peoples, while simultaneously holding ambiguities in tension.[42] The Baroque offered a distinct manner for dealing with the sharp contrasts and contradictions of life: the rich and the poor, morality and barbarism, idealism and realism. The comprehensive manner in which this occurred, touching practically every aspect of culture, caused an utter transformation of society. The irony of the Baroque is perhaps best seen in the simultaneous evangelization and massacre of the Indigenous. The paradox of this world view was seen in the resolution and justification of these two acts.

Directly preceding the colonial era was the conquest of the Americas. Contributing to the distinctiveness of the Baroque era in New Spain is its proximity to a time before the arrival of the Spanish, when the Aztec empire was the dominant political power. This nearness to the era of Aztec rule marked the colonial era. "The Aztec state was military and theocratic."[43] The Aztecs were a war-like people who terrorized and dominated various ethnic groups in the region. Their conquest of other indigenous groups was characterized by the superficial adoption of the religious beliefs of conquered tribes. They would assume cultural practices and deities of the tribes they assimilated into their empire. Therefore, a transculturation would occur, the conquered ethnic group becoming part of the Aztec people, the conquered group's cultural and religious symbols becoming a part of the Aztec world view.[44] "Just as an Aztec pyramid often covers an older structure, so this theological unification affected only the surface of the Aztec consciousness, leaving the primitive beliefs intact. The situation prefigured the introduction of Catholicism. . . . Everything was prepared for Spanish domination."[45] In other words, the Aztec manner of religious appropriation, directly tied to their military conquests, facilitated the paradox of the *Conquistador's* sword and the missionary's cross. Sor Juana's writing is marked by this presence of Indigenous peoples and cultures, including a poem written in the Nahuatl, and she includes Indigenous characters in her dramas. In addition, she addresses questions concerning Aztec religious practices and their functions as prefigurations of Christianity.

In comparing the histories of Latin America and the United States, one finds the influence of religion behind both examples of the colonization of the "New World." Yet while the English fled Europe in search of religious freedom, the Spanish *Conquista* was rooted in a commitment to spread and maintain orthodox Catholic faith. This distinction, coupled with the distinctively Spanish Counter-Reformation, produced what is called today the Baroque in New Spain. Though it is a lengthy quotation, I think this is best expressed in these words of Irving A. Leonard:

> In contrast to the more northerly parts of Europe the Hispanic people reacted to humanism by trying to reintegrate a medieval religiosity with science, but the end result was largely a blend of the two intellectual movements. A neo-scholasticism became the methodology of a neo-orthodoxy without diminishing the dilemma of Christendom. . . . The effect was a tendency to shift from content to form, from ideas to details, to give new sanctions to dogmas, to avoid issues, and to substitute subtlety of language for subtlety of thought; it served to repress rather than liberate the human spirit, and to divert by spectacles, by overstatement, and by excessive ornamentation. Such, in essence, was the spirit of the so-called "Baroque-Age" as manifested in the Hispanic world.[46]

In his discussion of the longevity and intensity of the Baroque's impact on Latin American cultures, Leonard provides various factors that must be considered. They are as follows: Spain's isolation of the New World in its formative years; the Church's massive influence and control in the New World, even in "secular" society; and the Church as the patron of the arts. In addition, the above-mentioned social immobility, especially for the *criollos* and the *indios,* played a significant role in maintaining colonial structures.

The features I have indicated of the Baroque as a culture are also characteristic of baroque literature. The writing style of the Baroque was dense and opaque, clearly marked by its world view. As Leonard notes, "Excess energy expended itself chiefly in allegory of obscure symbolism and in an exaggerated verbalism, relieved now and then by savage satire."[47] The language of the Baroque was excessive and ornate. The baroque literature of New Spain is characterized by its emulation of the Spanish greats, including Luis de Góngora, Francisco de Quevedo, and Pedro Calderón de la Barca. This world was predominantly male, written by and read by men. Sor Juana, of course, is a notable exception. She is recognized as the most important colonial writer in Mexico, in spite of the fact that she was a woman and was therefore excluded from schools of higher learning. Instead, Sor Juana made use of her time in the court and in the convent locutory, or receiving room, the only two places men and women could meet for intellectual conversation.[48] Sor Juana, however, was not an exception in that she was a woman writing. There were other women writers in colonial Latin America, especially in the context of convent life. What distinguished Sor Juana were her forays into what was understood as "masculine" discourse and the public nature of her writing. Her theological and philosophical writing, as well as her secular poetry and plays, contrast drastically to the mystical writing of other nuns of that culture. In addition, her connections to the court—both before and during her cloistered life—set her apart from other women religious.

New Spain was a courtly culture, and the viceroyalty was the center of society. The viceroy of New Spain was also the governor, captain general, and presiding officer of the *Real Audiencia.* In order to maintain the loyalty of the viceroy to the Spanish court and curb personal ambition, the appointments of viceroys were for very short terms.[49] Many checks and monitors were placed on the office in order to control the local power of the viceroy and ensure his loyalty to Spain. While Spain could attempt to control the local power of the viceroy through governmental constraints, it could not control the influence the viceregal court had upon the broader colonial society, where the court set the moral and aesthetic tone. In addition to offering a connection to European culture, the court also served as the secular alternative to the other dominant institution of Sor Juana's time, the Roman Catholic Church. The viceregal court was one center of power in New Spain; the Church was the other. Colonial Mexico's society was strongly Catholic, both in the institutional presence and power of the Church, as well as in popular culture. The intermeshing of politics and religion that characterized the Conquest continued in Sor Juana's era.

One particular feature of the Roman Catholicism of Sor Juana's context was the predominance of the Jesuit influence. This occurred on two very important fronts. First, Jesuit theology and practice emphasized the establishment of a relationship between indigenous and Christian religions. This relationship was characterized by attempts to discover prefigurations of Christianity in indigenous practices and beliefs. An example of this endeavor is seen in the work of Jesuit Carlos de Sigüenza y Góngora, a close friend of Sor Juana's. Sigüenza y Góngora was a mathematician, astronomer, historian, and cartographer. A second key feature of the markedly Jesuit character of colonial Mexico is found in the predominance of Jesuit intellectual centers, especially universities and seminaries.[50] The Jesuits arrived in New Spain in 1572, and through the establishment of their schools became a great intellectual influence in the New World.[51] The Jesuits were much more open than their predecessors to the beliefs of indigenous peoples. Georgina Sabat de Rivers traces Sor Juana's interest in indigenous populations to the Jesuit influence, seen especially through her relationship with Sigüenza y Góngora.[52] Like the society surrounding her, Sor Juana's world was colored by the preoccupations of the Jesuits. In addition to exerting influence over the Catholic climate, Jesuits were also in key institutional positions. Sor Juana's confessor, Antonio Núñez de Miranda, for example, was in charge of the Inquisition in New Spain. In a society where the Church played such a key role, at the levels of both infrastructure and intellectual influence, theology was fundamental. As this was an oral culture, the reigning theology was a reflection of the salon and the pulpit. Sor Juana participated in both these dimensions of theological elaboration, through the nature of her writing, and its public dissemination.

Philosophy and Theology

A Scholasticism influenced by Renaissance Platonism and hermetic thought characterized the philosophy and theology of seventeenth-century New Spain.[53] Renaissance humanism also played a significant role.[54] Baroque philosophy in colonial Mexico was extremely eclectic, though with a strong Thomist foundation. It was an era, as Mauricio Beuchot notes, on the cusp of modern philosophical reflection. "Although in the seventeenth century the foundation continued being Scholasticism, it was a Scholasticism in contact with hermetic philosophy and a nascent modern philosophy."[55] Much like the philosophical character of her era, Sor Juana is often viewed as a figure on the verge of modernity. Her philosophical and theological interlocutors were those of her contemporaries. The authors she read, cited, and engaged in discourse were representative of those thinkers appearing throughout the intellectual centers of New Spain. Her writing mirrors that of her male contemporaries.

While hermetic, Platonic, and Neoplatonic influences are prevalent in New Spain, Thomism remained the predominant paradigm. As noted by Constance M. Montross, "Scholasticism and Aristotelianism dominated intellectual life in post-Counter Reformation America. At the universities, two of the principal chairs were devoted to Scholasticism and Aristotelian logic."[56] In Sor Juana's era of Mexican culture, Thomism was taught not only at the university, but also in convent schools. The Thomist foundation was the filter through which other philosophical ideas were received. An example of Sor Juana's Thomism is found in her belief that the secular sciences are tools that can be utilized in the articulation of theology.[57] Much like her philosophical contemporaries, Sor Juana drew from a variety of sources that were not contradictory in her intellectual context. Her unsystematic methodology was characteristic of her era.

Contemporary *sorjuanistas* have too often emphasized non-Christian influences on Sor Juana's thought and downplayed the Christian philosophical elements. This trend, coupled with efforts to question a sense of vocation in her life, contributes to a depiction of her life and work that downplays an understanding of her as a Christian thinker. Mexican philosopher Mauricio Beuchot is critical of the lack of secondary scholarship addressing the influence of Thomism on Sor Juana's writing. Instead, he notes, *sorjuanistas* often emphasize the hermetic and Neoplatonic elements of her corpus at the expense of those influenced by Scholastic philosophy.[58] A major emphasis in Beuchot's scholarship on Sor Juana is the Thomism found in her poetry. His work focuses on Aquinas's impact on both Sor Juana's philosophical content and her rhetorical style.[59]

In the colonial era, literature, poetry, and mythology played a significant role in philosophical elaborations. Theologically, they were used as rhetorical devices to express the Christian message, especially in the realm of kerygmatic theology. Kerygmatic theology strives to elaborate Christian teaching, especially in the area of doctrine. Beuchot situates Sor Juana's allegorical dramas as key examples of this form of theology.[60] The nature of this theology was public, seen in the preaching and distribution of sermons, the singing of *villancicos* at liturgical celebrations, and the performance of religious dramas. The task of the public theologian was to bring forth the Christian message in a language that was accessible to a broader public. For members of the clergy, the pulpit was the clearest avenue. For our tenth muse, it was necessary to seek other options. Sor Juana could not stand at the pulpit. However, she still found a means to express herself theologically in the public realm. Her allegorical dramas and sung poetry were public vehicles to transmit Christian doctrine.

Contemporary theologians are not accustomed to think of poetry, literature, and plays as theological discourse. In the contemporary era, where faith is often counter-posed with reason, theological discourse seeks to stand on academic ground. As a result, it has lost much of its original flavor, seeking to prove its validity rather than assume it. In Sor Juana's era, at a time on the brink of modernity (yet not there) such concerns were not operating. Sor Juana is part of a tradition that not only speaks to her context and the theology of her time, but one that continues to exist today, though often marginalized from academic centers of reflection. Like Seneca, Russell, and Sartre, Sor Juana uses drama and poetry as a form of philosophical reflection.[61] She stands among those thinkers who offer alternative constructions of philosophical method.

Though Thomism was the predominant paradigm, hermetic philosophy left a clear impact on Sor Juana's corpus, seen for example in her allegorical drama *El Divino Narciso* and her epistemological poem *Primero sueño*. The Platonic hermeticism of seventeenth-century Mexican philosophy found its roots in the Florentine Renaissance. This Renaissance Platonic hermeticism was the result of a convergence of diverse intellectual currents and ideas, including Platonism, elements of the *Corpus Hermeticum*, and the Cabala. Astronomy, physics, and the occult also play a prominent role.[62] However, hermetic philosophy was not the only avenue through which seventeenth-century philosophers and theologians came into contact with non-Christian philosophers. Patristic authors, such as Clement of Alexandria and Augustine, provided additional avenues through which thinkers such as Sor Juana learned of Plato, Aristotle, and Plotinus.[63]

Hermetic thought attempted to synthesize Plato and Aristotle, and was influenced by Neoplatonism. It was believed that the founder of this philosophy was the mythological Hermes Trismegistus.[64] A large body of literature was developed under his name, touching on the areas of philosophy, the occult, magic, and astrology. During the popularity of hermetic texts and philosophy during the Renaissance, it was believed that the Egyptian priest Hermes wrote the texts in remote antiquity. The *Corpus Hermeticum* was in fact written between 100-300 C.E., by various authors, most likely Greek.[65] As Frances A. Yates has indicated, the texts are an eclectic philosophical mixture: "They contain popular Greek philosophy of the period, a mixture of Platonism and Stoicism, combined with some Jewish and probably some Persian influences."[66] The content of the texts ranges from Egyptian magic rites to a creation account that resonates with the Genesis narrative.

Hermes is a legendary figure who supposedly lived in the time of Moses. According to hermetic mythology, Plato was inspired by hermetic thought. The hermeticism that became popular in New Spain had its roots, as mentioned above, in the Florentine Renaissance. The significance of hermeticism in fifteenth-century Italy cannot be underestimated.[67] As an era that was characterized by a revival of classical texts, the belief that Hermes was in fact Plato's predecessor and inspiration motivated the privileging of hermetic philosophical texts. The discovery that these texts were in fact older than first assumed, and that the Egyptian priest Hermes was in fact imaginary, was devastating to Renaissance hermetic Platonism and Neoplatonism.

Hermeticism, however, did not die with this discovery. One figure who is representative of efforts to maintain a Renaissance attitude towards Hermes Trismegistus is the seventeenth-century German Jesuit hermetic philosopher Athanasius Kircher. Kircher dated the works of Hermes to the time of Abraham and interpreted elements of hermetic texts as prefigurations of Christianity.[68] Building on Latin translations of hermetic texts that originated in Italy, Kircher maintains an analysis of hermeticism steeped in Egyptology. He interpreted the Platonic doctrine of ideas, for example, as originating in Egyptian philosophy.[69] The writing of Kircher was widely available and extremely influential upon the intellectual centers of New Spain. From her citations it is clear that Sor Juana was familiar with Kircher's work.[70] One cannot, however, over-emphasize the influence of hermetic thought on Sor Juana. While Sor Juana drew from hermetic texts, she also had other philosophical and theological resources. Elements of Kircher's hermeticism, however, are found in three of Sor Juana's major works: *La respuesta*, *Primero sueño*, and *Neptuno alegórico*.[71]

Octavio Paz links the prevalence of hermetic thought to the Egyptianism that marked Sor Juana's era. Focusing on the figure of Kircher, Paz notes that

> Kircher believed that in the Egyptian civilization he had found the universal key for deciphering all the enigmas of history. Naturally, that was the Egypt of the hermetic tradition. . . . In Kircher's work Jesuit syncretism reaches a totality that embraces all times and all places. Catholic

Rome is the center upon which all religions converge, and the prefiguration of that center, a true bridge between Christianity and other religions, is ancient Egypt and her prophet Hermes Trismegistus.[72]

Paz also presents Kircher as a vital link between fifteenth-century Neoplatonic Florence and the seventeenth-century Americas. Sor Juana's admiration of Kircher is clear from her writing. As a resource, he provided her with three strands of intellectual thought clothed in the orthodoxy of a German Jesuit: Neoplatonic hermeticism, syncretism, and astrological speculation.[73] Sor Juana, like her era, drew from various philosophical strands and was in no way systematic. While Sor Juana's intellectual climate was very diverse, her daily life was regimented. Convent life in seventeenth-century Mexico was a world that was very controlled and dominated by hierarchy and authority. The fluidity of the different intellectual ideas that flowed through her convent cell and locutory contrasted sharply with the structured life she led as a cloistered nun.

Convent Life

The prevalence and significance of the convent in the culture of New Spain cannot be underestimated. Both in their number and roles, convents were a significant presence. In colonial Mexico the convent played a much more significant role than in other regions of the Spanish empire. One is surprised to hear, for example, of the number of convents in colonial Mexico City: there were sixteen in 1650. This compares with, for example, three convents on the entire island of Cuba.[74] Convents were financially dependent on the philanthropy of the colonial elite. Women of Spanish descent were favored for entry in the convent; "racial purity," without African, Jewish, or Moorish ancestry, was essential for acceptance in a convent. As Asunción Lavrin, one of the leading scholars of convent life in the Americas emphasizes, this led to the creation of an elitist culture within the convent, based on economic and racial stratifications.[75] Lavrin notes that the convent served as a symbol of both Spanish society and the triumph of

Christianity in the New World. The convent was also seen as a space to protect these elite women and their virtue.[76] In a patriarchal culture, the role of the convent, as a feminine space controlled by the masculine clergy, had a significant function in the reinforcement of the subordination of women to male authority.

Why did women enter the convent? For many, especially those of the racial and economic upper classes, it was the only alternative to marriage. Octavio Paz defines taking the veil in terms of a profession, "But in her time the convents were filled with women who donned their habits because of worldly considerations and needs, not as a response to a divine call. Sor Juana's case was no different from the girls of today who seek a career that will offer both economic security and social respectability. The religious life, in the seventeenth century, was a profession."[77] The role a sense of vocation played in women's decisions to enter the convent should not be underestimated; at the same time, one must recognize the societal considerations that entered into the picture when a woman decided to take the veil. The cloistered nuns could not leave the convent, though they could receive company. The locutory was in many ways a salon for the nuns where they could visit with their guests.

For the seventeenth-century cloistered woman, life was characterized by a paradigm of authority and obedience: to her confessor, the larger Church, the superiors of her Order, and civil authorities.[78] The direct control of the clergy was exemplified in the nun's relationship of obedience to her confessor. Lavrin notes, for example, that the vow of obedience was one of four in monastic life. Antonio Núñez de Miranda, S.J., Sor Juana's confessor, defined the vow of obedience as the renunciation of one's own personal volition to that of one's prelates. Sor Juana's public chastisement by her bishop Fernández de Santa Cruz can be interpreted as a site where Sor Juana's intellectual "disobedience" to the norms of her day and her struggles for intellectual freedom were reprimanded. These struggles over obedience and authority are not exclusive to Sor Juana. However, due to the public nature of Sor Juana's writing, her story gives one of the clearest pictures of the tensions between authority and obedience in her era.[79] Denial of the self in service and obedience to the Church is the dominant paradigm.

There were several features found in seventeenth-century convent spirituality: spiritual exercises (which Sor Juana wrote for her convent), devotion to the Sacred Heart, devotion to the crucified Christ, visions and dreams, an understanding of the body in opposition and in conflict with the soul. The body had to be disciplined in order for the soul to flourish. The body had to be silenced and abused in order for the soul to dominate the will of the human. It is interesting to note that in the last two years of her life Sor Juana subjected herself to mortifications and flagellations typical of her era; her confessor could barely control her excessive conduct.[80] Prior to that there is no record of any such behavior on her part.

One cannot stress sufficiently that Sor Juana was not the sole woman religious writing in seventeenth-century New Spain. Writing was, in fact, a common practice in convents. As collections such as *Untold Sisters: Hispanic Nuns in Their Own Words* demonstrate, Sor Juana must be understood within the literary canon of women religious writing in the Americas.[81] She must be placed in the context of her fellow women writers. A simplistic interpretation of the events surrounding the last years of her life, for example, could lead one to interpret the controversy surrounding her writing as merely based on the fact that she is writing. In other words, the act of her writing is interpreted as her wrongdoing. This was not the case. The same year that Sor Juana Inés de la Cruz began writing her autobiographical defense to Bishop Manuel Fernández de Santa Cruz, María de San José, a woman religious also in New Spain, was asked by that same bishop to begin writing her spiritual autobiography. As Kathleen Myers and Amanda Powell emphasize in their introduction to María de San José's writing, "Madre María's visionary journals stand in sharp contrast to Sor Juana's highly reasoned document. . . . Sor Juana describes a calling to the life of letters, while Madre María's is to the life of the *perfecta religiosa*, the ideal nun."[82] The content and form of her writing are what led to Sor Juana's problems with ecclesial authorities.

Unlike the many seventeenth-century Latin American women religious whose writing was often hidden and forgotten, Sor Juana stands as the exception to the rule. Both her brilliance and her subject matter set Sor Juana apart. "Sor Juana did not emerge from a vacuum. Writing was a common enough activity in the cloisters. However, prior to Sor Juana, none of the works of these women seems to have been published or to have received much public attention."[83] The public nature of Sor Juana's works was one feature that distinguishes Sor Juana. Not only was her writing read abroad in Spain and circulated in Mexico, she often wrote for public court and ecclesial events. Yet another feature that sets apart Sor Juana's work is its content. Mysticism was the predominant form of women religious' writing. Unlike her contemporaries, whose writing emphasized their efforts to achieve the perfect state of religious life, Sor Juana rarely discussed such matters in her own work. In fact, when she did write about the duties of religious life, they were often described as obstacles that conflicted with her time for study.[84] Sor Juana never describes mystical experiences or acts of penitence in her writing.

The convent was the locus of feminine culture, especially in the realm of mysticism. Often the writing and devotions of nuns were mystical visions studied and admired by others. Jean Franco has noted that by constructing the nun as the mystic, the institutional Church could control both the production and interpretation of women religious' visions and their documentation. Also, as a form of truth that could not be judged "rationally," mystical truth claims were often problematic. The clergy took on the task of interpreting the mystic nun and her visions. While intending to subordinate women, the clergy instead created a space for female expression. "By subordinating women on the grounds of their lesser rationality and relegating them to the domain of feeling, the clergy unwittingly created a space for female empowerment."[85] While exiled to the mystical, this was, nonetheless, a space for women's writing and devotions.[86] Sor Juana transformed the intellectual arena of the convent, creating a milieu for philosophical and theological reflection.

Notes

[1] "Y diversa de mí misma entre vuestras plumas ando" (OC 1:158.51) (EC).
[2] *Sorjuanista* is the term for a Sor Juana expert.
[3] Asunción Lavrin, "Sor Juana Inés de la Cruz: Obediencia y autoridad en su entorno religioso," *Revista Iberoamericana* 61 (July-Dec. 1995): 606.

[4]For a Freudian analysis of Sor Juana's absentee father and its relationship to her writing, see Ludwig Pfandl, *Sor Juana Inés de la Cruz: La décima musa de México*, ed. Francisco de la Maza (Mexico: UNAM, 1963).

[5]Octavio Paz, *Sor Juana: Or, The Traps of Faith* (Cambridge, MA: Harvard University Press, 1988), 67.

[6]Ibid., 79.

[7]Sor Juana Inés de la Cruz, *The Answer/La Respuesta: Including a Selection of Poems*, critical ed. and trans. Electa Arenal and Amanda Powell (New York: The Feminist Press at the City University of New York, 1994), 49. OC 4:445.235-237.

[8]Ibid., 51. OC 4:254-268.

[9]Paz, *Sor Juana*, 89.

[10]Don Antonio Sebastián Toledo and Vicereine Doña Leonor Carreto would leave a few years after Sor Juana took the veil. In 1673 a new viceroy was named, Don Pedro Nuño Colón de Portugal, who died four days after entering office. Fray Payo Enríquez de Rivera was named viceroy the following year. As a cleric his viceroyalty was characterized by the institutional joining of Church and State. He retired after holding the position for six years. The following viceroy was Don Tomás Antonio de la Cerda, the Marquis de la Laguna, and his wife, María Luisa Manrique de Lara y Gonzaga, Countess of Paredes de Nava (1680-1688). Count de Galve replaced him in 1688.

[11]A *villancico* was a poem set to music that was sung at religious holidays, usually in an ecclesial setting; a *sarao* is a celebratory song accompanied by a dance.

[12]Some scholars have hypothesized, for example, that Sor Juana's poetry to María Luisa, which at times uses the language of lovers, implies that Sor Juana was in fact a lesbian. At the same time, all of Sor Juana's poetry must be understood in light of the body of literature from which it emerges. Sor Juana often assumed a "male" voice in her writing, and one cannot discern whether Sor Juana's use of loving language with regards to María Luisa was the result of rhetorical convention or motivated by erotic love. I mention this debate, for it is a conversation in contemporary Sor Juana scholarship. However, because of the uncertainty surrounding this matter, I leave this question open. Also, I find it problematic to label a seventeenth-century figure with the contemporary label of lesbian. See Alicia Gaspar de Alba, "The Politics of Location of the Tenth Muse of America: An Interview with Sor Juana Inés de la Cruz," in *Living Chicana Theory*, ed. Carla Trujillo (Berkeley, CA: Third World Woman Press, 1998), 136-165; Gaspar de Alba, *Sor Juana's Second Dream* (Albuquerque, NM: The University of New Mexico Press, 1999); Paz, *Sor Juana*; Nina M. Scott, " 'Ser mujer ni estar ausente, / no es de amarte impedimento': las poemas de Sor Juana al la condesa de Paredes," in *Y diversa de mí misma en vuestras plumas ando: Homenaje internacional a Sor Juana Inés de la Cruz*, ed. Sara Poot Herrera (Mexico: El Colegio de México,1993), 159-170.

[13]Jean Franco, *Plotting Women: Gender and Representation in Mexico* (New York: Columbia University Press, 1989), 50.

[14]Antonio Núñez de Miranda quoted in Juan de Oviedo, *Vida exemplar, heróicas virtudes y apostólico ministerio del venerable padre Antonio Núñez de Miranda, de la compañía de Jesús* (México, D.F.: Herederos de la viuda de Francisco Rodrígues Lupercio, 1702), 153. Cited in Norma Salazar, *Foolish Men!: Sor Juana Inés de la Cruz as Spiritual Protagonist, Educational Prism, and Symbol for Women* (DeKalb, IL: LEPS Press, 1994), 63.

[15]Short of marriage or convent life, there were very few options for *criollas* in New Spain. For an excellent overview of the culture and daily life of women in New Spain, see Pilar Gonzalbo Aizpura, *Las mujeres en la nueva España: Educación y vida cotidiana* (Mexico: El Colegio de México, 1987).

[16]Salazar, *Foolish Men*, 30.

[17]Paz, *Sor Juana*, 105.

[18]Marie-Cécile Bénassy-Berling agrees with this, simultaneously affirming Sor Juana's faith. See Marie-Cécile Bénassy-Berling, *Humanisme et religion chez Sor Juana Inés de la Cruz: La femme et la culture au XVIIe siècle* (Paris: Éditions Hispaniques, 1992), 103. Anita Arroyo defines Sor Juana's vocation as philosophical. Her true vocation was intellectual, not religious. For her, knowledge exemplified the path to God. Anita Arroyo, *Razón y pasión de Sor Juana* (Mexico: Editorial Porrúa, 1980), 142.

[19]Dorothy Schons, "Some Obscure Points in the Life of Sor Juana Inés de la Cruz," in *Feminist Perspectives on Sor Juana Inés de la Cruz*, ed. Stephanie Merrim (Detroit: Wayne State University Press, 1991), 46-47.

[20]Asunción Lavrin, "Espiritualidad en el claustro novohispano," *Colonial Latin American Review* 4:2 (1995): 174.

[21]Sor Juana, *The Answer/La Respuesta*, 51. OC 4: 446.268-274.

[22]Until recently, the hypotheses surrounding these events assumed that Sor Juana's critique was in fact directed toward Vieira's sermon. However, today this is being contested. Elías Trabulse has put forth a theory based on the discovery of *La carta de Serafina de Cristo*, dated February 1, 1691, directed at Fernández de Santa Cruz. In this letter, which Trabulse attributes to Sor Juana, the author ironically and defiantly states that the true object of *Atenagórica* was actually Núñez de Miranda. The author was in fact refuting his book entitled *Comulgador penitente de la Purísima* (1690). In this book, Núñez de Miranda argues that Christ's greatest *fineza* (demonstration of love) was the Eucharist. The author of *Serafina de Cristo* contests this. In refuting him, however, the author also rejects a foundational rule of the *Congregación de Purísima*, a powerful group of clergy and political laity. Trabulse interprets this move as political suicide on Sor Juana's part. Sor Juana is not only refuting a powerful Jesuit, she is also contesting this group of elite people, who include the current viceroy. Elías Trabulse, *Los años finales de Sor Juana: Una interpretación (1688-1695)* (Mexico: CONDUMEX, 1995), 18-20. Trabulse's interpretation has been contested recently by other *sorjuanistas*. See Marie-

Cécile Bénassy-Berling, "Actualidad del sorjuanismo (1994-1999)," *Colonial Latin American Review* 9:2 (December 2000): 279.

[23]Pamela Kirk, *Sor Juana Inés de la Cruz: Religion, Art, and Feminism* (New York: Continuum, 1998), 147-148.

[24]Bénassy-Berling, "La modernidad de Sor Juana Inés de la Cruz como católica," in *"Por amor de las letras" Juana Inés de la Cruz: Le donne e il sacro. Atti del convegno di Venezia 26-27 Gennaio 1996*, ed. Susanna Regazzoni (Rome: Bulzoni Editore, 1996), 108.

[25]Trabulse, *Los años finales de Sor Juana*, 28-31.

[26]Trabulse thanks historian Teresa Castelló Yturbide for copying the ledger of the contents of Sor Juana's cell at the time of her death, thus giving today's scholars this information. Ibid., 37.

[27]OC 4:37.307-324 (EC).

[28]OC 1:146.49.

[29]Sor Juana, *The Answer/La respuesta*, 179. OC 1:147.49.

[30]Stephanie Merrim, *Early Modern Women's Writing and Sor Juana Inés de la Cruz* (Nashville: Vanderbilt University Press, 1999), 31.

[31]OC 1:277.146.

[32]OC 1:5-6.2.

[33]Constance M. Montross, *Virtue or Vice? Sor Juana's Use of Thomistic Thought* (Washington, DC: University Press of America, 1991), x.

[34]Mariano Picón-Salas, *A Cultural History of Spanish America: From Conquest to Independence*, trans. Irving A. Leonard (Berkeley, CA: University of California Press, 1966), 87.

[35]See Paz, *Sor Juana*. For a study of colonial Latin America see Francisco Javier Cevallos-Candaui et al., eds., *Coded Encounters: Writing, Gender, and Ethnicity in Colonial Latin America* (Amherst, MA: The University of Massachusetts Press, 1994).

[36]Yolanda Martinez-San Miguel has done a significant amount of research in this arena. See *Saberes Americanos: Subalternidad y epistemología en los escritos de Sor Juana* (Pittsburgh: University of Pittsburgh Press, 1999).

[37]Louis Dupré, *Passage to Modernity: An Essay in the Hermeneutics of Nature and Culture* (New Haven, CT: Yale University Press, 1993), 240.

[38]Ibid., 238.

[39]Irving A. Leonard, *Baroque Times in Old Mexico: Seventeenth-Century Persons, Places, and Practices* (Ann Arbor, MI: University of Michigan Press, 1959), 24.

[40]Ibid., 21-24.

[41]Margo Glantz, *Sor Juana Inés de la Cruz: ¿Hagiografía o autobiografía?* (Mexico: UNAM, 1995), 42.

[42]Arroyo, *Razón y pasión*, 131.

[43]Octavio Paz, *The Labyrinth of Solitude: Life and Thought in Mexico*, trans. Lysander Kemp (New York: Grove Press Inc., 1961), 92.

[44]For an excellent study of the conquests see Robert Ricard, *The Spiritual*

Conquest of Mexico (Berkeley, CA: University of California Press, 1966).

[45]Paz, *The Labyrinth of Solitude*, 92.

[46]Leonard, *Baroque Times in Old Mexico*, 27-28.

[47]Ibid., 31.

[48]Paz, *Sor Juana*, 45.

[49]The viceroy was not permitted to bring his children to New Spain, and he was monitored by a royal inspector who visited the court. Ibid., 21-23.

[50]Leonard, *Baroque Times in Old Mexico*, 25.

[51]Georgina Sabat de Rivers, *En busca de Sor Juana* (Mexico: UNAM, 1998), 277. Bénassy-Berling echoes a similar sentiment. See *Humanisme et religion*, 68.

[52]Sabat de Rivers, ibid., 280.

[53]On the Neoplatonism of Sor Juana's era see Octavio Paz, *Sor Juana*; Robert Ricard, "Refleciones sobre 'El sueño' de Sor Juana Inés de la Cruz," *Revista de la Universidad de Mexico* 30:4, 25-32. On hermeticism see Frances Amelia Yates, *Giordano Bruno and the Hermetic Tradition* (London: Routledge, 1964); Francisco de la Maza, *Sor Juana Inés de la Cruz en su tiempo* (Mexico: SEP, 1967).

[54]Mauricio Beuchot, *The History of Philosophy in Colonial Mexico*, trans. Elizabeth Millán (Washington, DC: The Catholic University of America Press, 1998). Marie-Cécile Bénassy-Berling also emphasizes the humanism of the era; Bénassy-Berling, *Humanisme et religion*, 145.

[55]Beuchot, "Los autos de Sor Juana: Tres lugares teológicos," in *Sor Juana y su mundo: Una mirada actual*, ed. Sara Poot Herrera (Mexico: Universidad del Claustro de Sor Juana, 1995), 355.

[56]Montross, *Virtue or Vice?*, x, citing John Tate Lanning, *Academic Culture in the Spanish Colonies* (New York: Oxford University Press, 1940). Also see Mauricio Beuchot, *Estudios de historia y de filosofía en el México colonial* (Mexico: UNAM, 1991).

[57]See Montross, *Virtue or Vice?*, 45. Bénassy-Berling is another *sorjuanista* who has highlighted the prevalence of Thomism in Sor Juana's milieu. Bénassy-Berling defines Thomism as the operational language imposed on Sor Juana by its sheer dominance. Bénassy-Berling, *Humanisme et religion*, 142.

[58]Beuchot, *Sor Juana: Una filosofía barroca* (Mexico: UNAM, 1999), 61.

[59]See Beuchot, "El universo filosófico de Sor Juana," in *Memoria del Coloquio Internacional Sor Juana Inés de la Cruz y el Pensamiento Novohispano* (Mexico: Instituto Mexiquense de Cultura, 1995), 29-40; Beuchot, *Sor Juana: Una filosofía barroca*, 25-70; Montross, *Virtue or Vice?*

[60]Beuchot, "Los autos de Sor Juana," 357.

[61]Ibid.

[62]Paz, *Sor Juana*, 164-165.

[63]For a detailed study of the role of Platonic, Aristotelian, and Neoplatonic philosophy in *Primero sueño* see Alberto Pérez Amador Adam, *El precipicio de faetón. Nueva edición, estudio filológico y comento de* Primero sueño *de*

Sor Juana Inés de la Cruz (Frankfurt: Vervuert, 1996).

[64]For more information on hermetic philosophy see J. Festugière, *La révélation d'Hermès Trismégiste* (Paris: Belles Lettres, 1989); Yates, *Giordano Bruno and the Hermetic Tradition*.

[65]Yates, *Giordano Bruno*, 3. In 1614, Isaac Casaubon dates the *Corpus Hermeticum* between 100-300 C.E., challenging the authorship of Hermes.

[66]Ibid., 3.

[67]Yates recounts that in 1460, a Greek manuscript was brought to Florence that contained a copy of the *Corpus Hermeticum*. Though the manuscripts of Plato were ready, waiting to be translated, Cosimo dé Medici ordered that the texts of Hermes be translated immediately. Plato was translated after the translation of Hermes was complete. Ibid., 13.

[68]Ibid., 416.

[69]For a more detailed discussion of Kircher's hermeticism see ibid., 416-422.

[70]Beuchot assumes that Sor Juana never directly read the work of Hermes in a systematic fashion. Beuchot, "Sor Juana y el hermetismo de Kircher," 5.

[71]Octavio Paz had highlighted the Neoplatonic elements in *Primero sueño*, especially in Sor Juana's understanding of the soul in relationship to the divine as First Cause. In addition, Paz grounds Sor Juana's depiction of the chain of being, also in *Sueño*, in Plotinus' philosophy. See Paz, *Sor Juana*, 373-375.

[72]Ibid., 166.

[73]Ibid., 176.

[74]Bénassy-Berling, *Humanisme et religion*, 36.

[75]Asunción Lavrin, "Vida conventual: Rasgos históricos," in *Sor Juana y su mundo*, 37.

[76]See María Dolores Bravo Arriaga, "La excepción y la regla: Una monja según el discurso oficial y según Sor Juana," in *Y diversa de mí misma en vuestras plumas ando*, 36.

[77]Paz, *Sor Juana*, 104.

[78]Asunción Lavrin, "Sor Juana Inés de la Cruz," 606.

[79]Bravo Arriaga echoes Lavrin when she emphasizes the various features that characterize the life of the nun: hierarchy and authority, silence, and self-denial, both physical and intellectual. Devotion and spirituality were defined by obedience to the hierarchy. Bravo Arriaga, "La excepción y la regla," 36.

[80]Lavrin, "Espiritualidad en el claustro novohispano," 170-171.

[81]Electa Arenal and Stacey Schlau, *Untold Sisters: Hispanic Nuns in Their Own Words* (Albuquerque: University of New Mexico Press, 1989). For an account of Sor Juana in light of early modern women's writing see Merrim, *Early Modern Women's Writing*.

[82]Kathleen A. Myers and Amanda Powell, "Introduction," in *A Wild Country Out in the Garden: The Spiritual Journals of a Colonial Mexican Nun* (Bloomington, IN: Indiana University Press, 1999), xviii.

[83]Asunción Lavrin, "Unlike Sor Juana? The Model Nun in the Religious

Literature of Colonial Mexico," in *Feminist Perspectives on Sor Juana Inés de la Cruz*, 76.

[84]Ibid., 68.

[85]Franco, *Plotting Women*, xiv.

[86]Arenal and Schlau also present the convent as a space for female subculture. The Church thus represses women and simultaneously provides a space for their expression. Arenal and Schlau, *Untold Sisters*, 6.

Chapter 3

Beauty

*"Let us rejoice, Beloved, and let us go see ourselves
in your Beauty."*[1]
—San Juan de la Cruz

The contention that a significant portion of Sor Juana's corpus is theological is not original to this study. In a brief article discussing the theological contribution of Sor Juana, Beatriz Melano Couch writes, "Scholars who have studied Sor Juana speak of her greatness as a literary figure, philosopher, and woman of science. My study of her works has brought me to the conclusion that she was also a theologian: indeed, the first woman theologian in all the Americas."[2] Sor Juana is a forgotten theological voice whose work is increasingly the object of study. Perhaps her greatest contribution to contemporary theology is found in the aesthetic form of her theology. Beauty is not merely a theme in her corpus. Through the privileging of myth, metaphor, and symbol as the most authentic and valued forms of theological expression, Sor Juana transforms the very nature of theological writing. The fact that Beauty is central to Sor Juana's theology is of key importance, but equally significant is the aesthetic form of her writing as poetry and drama.

In this chapter I begin my assessment of Sor Juana's theology by examining the role of Beauty in her corpus. My decision to begin with Beauty is intentional. While I do not intend to imply that Sor Juana has in any way a systematic exposition of her theology (nothing comparable to Hans Urs von Balthasar's trilogy, for example), her writing can be gathered under the themes of Beauty, the Good, and the True.[3] My decision to begin with Beauty is motivated, in part, by my desire to explore the methodological implications of Sor Juana's writing. My study of the role of Beauty in Sor Juana's theology is twofold, engaging excerpts of her poetry and *El Divino Narciso*. An examination of aesthetic themes in Sor Juana's poetry as a major portion of her corpus is an essential aspect of any study exploring her theological import. The allegorical drama (*auto sacramental*) *El Divino Narciso* (*The Divine Narcissus*) is Sor Juana's most theological text.[4] This drama is the clearest expression of Sor Juana's theological aesthetics. In the *loa* preceding this drama one finds Sor Juana's defense of indigenous peoples and their religious practices. For these reasons, the *loa* will be treated in chapter 4 of this study, under the section examining the role of the Indigenous in Sor Juana's theology. *El Divino Narciso* is an especially important piece, for it argues for the significance of aesthetics with regard to the content and form of theology. Because of the theological weight of this play, the majority of this chapter will examine *El Divino Narciso*.

Poetry

The first two volumes of Sor Juana's four-volume *Obras completas* (in its most recent edition), which total over one thousand pages (including notes), contain her poetry. Of course, to limit the consideration of her "poetic" writing literally to poems is to degrade the lyricism of many other genres of her writing, especially her allegorical dramas. With perhaps a bit of exaggeration, Sor Juana wrote in her *Respuesta* that to write in verse is "so natural to me that indeed I must force myself not to write this very letter in rhyme."[5] To attempt to summarize the role of Beauty in Sor Juana's poetry is a daunting task, due to the sheer number of poems that discuss beauty theologically and to the unsystematic nature of Sor Juana's writing.[6] Therefore, I have chosen to focus on two significant dimensions of the role of Beauty in Sor Juana's poetry. The first is the role of order and proportion in Sor Juana's definitions of Beauty. The second is the role of Beauty as it relates to Sor Juana's Marian poetry. The Marian dimension of Sor Juana's poetry illuminates certain aspects of Sor Juana's concept of God and Christology.

Like Augustine of Hippo, Sor Juana had a passionate and dedicated interest in music. Apparently, her convent cell was littered with various musical instruments along with her hundreds of books and scientific devices. A treatise she wrote on music has, unfortunately, been lost. Also like Augustine, she found beauty in harmony and proportion. In a poem written for the Condesa de Galve she writes, "in the proportions of its parts alone does beauty consist."[7] Beauty is found in the proportion of the parts and is thus associated with order and harmony. Later in the poem, she has the voice of Music saying: "Loveliness is nothing more than a proportion which orders some parts well with others: for it does not suffice that they be lovely absolutely, if relatively lovely they are not. . . . Thus, Beauty is not only in that the parts be excessively lovely, but that each with the others have relative proportion. So nothing represents Beauty better than Music."[8] Music represents the highest abstraction of beauty, for it contains the ultimate harmony. Sor Juana also holds beauty as relational, for it only exists in relationship. Beauty is not found in individuality, but rather in the harmonious relationship of the parts to the whole. Beauty cannot stand alone, but almost always exists in community. Only in the beauty and harmony of its parts can the whole be beautiful.

Order and harmony not only apply to the beauty that is created by the human imagination. Instead, Sor Juana situates the beauty of nature in its order. In a *loa* written in honor of Fray Diego Velázquez de la Cadena, the reader finds the allegorical character of Nature surveying the ordered process of the cosmos.[9] In this survey, Nature observes the precise order of humanity. "All being so measured, all having such order, the Sea swells not a drop, nor Earth wane by a point, . . . making their qualities, now twinned, now opposed, a circle so perfect, a mysterious chain."[10] Demonstrating the deftness of her writing, Sor Juana repeatedly uses the word chain (*cadena* in Spanish) to honor the very person for whom the *loa* is intended (Fray Diego Velázquez de la *Cadena*). Nature is in charge of regulating the order of the natural world. Sor Juana finds the harmony of nature in its order *in relationship*. Noting the complexity, diversity, and beauty of the natural world, Nature observes the interrelatedness of the parts that constitute the whole. In this order one finds the "circular beauty" of the world. The significance of relationships is fundamental to Sor Juana's understanding of natural, created beauty. Still, as her Marian texts demonstrate, when Sor Juana speaks of divine Beauty, the category of glory reigns stronger in her descriptions of Mary, God, and Jesus Christ.

In his *Confessions*, Augustine distinguishes two types of beauty. The first is beauty that is pleasing in and of itself. Augustine makes a distinction between this and beauty that is "fitting because it is well adapted to some other thing."[11] George Tavard finds a similar distinction operating in Sor Juana's theology, due to the Platonic and Augustinian influences found therein.[12] I concur. Like Augustine, who saw measure, number and weight as the Trinitarian imprint on creation and its beauty, Sor Juana privileged order when speaking of the natural world.[13] Contrary to the emphasis on order and harmony found in certain of Sor Juana's description of beauty, when one turns to her Marian texts, one finds a definition of beauty based on glory. The glory of Mary is grounded in the glory of God.

Mary has a very prominent role in Sor Juana's corpus. Most of Sor Juana's religious poetry contains Marian themes.[14] Whether this is due to Sor Juana's own personal devotion or to the demands placed upon her is unknown to us today. Pamela Kirk argues that Sor Juana has an enthusiastic rendering of Mary that is atypical of the writing of other women religious, creating "a religious symbolic system that has at its center a female figure of power and radiance, nearly a goddess."[15] Contesting this view, *sorjuanista* Margo Glantz reminds us that while Mary is an essential figure in Sor Juana's corpus, this is a product of circumstance, for the poetry in Sor Juana's era was most often written based on requests and demands, not the personal fancy of the poet. Glantz raises an important point. However, while Mary as the subject of her poetry was perhaps not Sor Juana's choice, the way in which she depicted Mary was entirely her creation. The theological significance of Sor Juana's writing lies in the manner in which Mary is theologically constructed.

Sor Juana's *villancicos*, a significant number of which were written for Marian feasts, are a central resource for understanding the role of beauty in Sor Juana's poetry. A *villancico* is a poem with short lines, frequently put to music and sung in churches on religious holidays in Sor Juana's era. As a performed theological genre, these poems constituted a poetic and musical form of public theology. In Sor Juana's *villancicos*, Mary is constantly described in terms of her beauty as a reflection of God's glory. The celebration of Mary's conception resulted in two series of Marian *villancicos* (1676 and 1689). Mary's immaculate conception is a strong theological theme in Sor Juana's corpus. This doctrine is one of the places where one finds a clear theological development in Sor Juana's writing. In the 1676 series, Sor Juana held that Mary was born with original sin, yet was immediately liberated from it. In the third *villancico* of this series the refrain begins by asking, "Who is that Queen of the earth and heaven?" The refrain continues,

> She is the bird of grace, by God eternal
> conceived without stain,
> for she is for glories, for she is for graces,
> in an instant God freed her from blame
> to be his Mother.[16]

Shortly after her birth Mary is freed from the mark of sin that tarnishes all of humanity. A second aspect of Marian theology that shifts in these texts is the relationship between sin and beauty. While Mary is described in this earlier series as free from sin and beautiful, the two attributes are not explicitly connected.

In the 1689 series celebrating Mary's conception Sor Juana links Mary's freedom from sin to her beauty when she writes:

> For his loving Mother
> he destined Mary,
> and *ab aeterno* he gazed
> at her, ever Clear, ever Lovely.[17]

Throughout the series Mary is described as "perfect" and "without blemish." Sor Juana will return to this theme of purity, original sin, and beauty in *El Divino Narciso*. The notion of the *imago Dei* as the state of being clear and unmarked, and the Marian connections of this idea, will also figure prominently in *Narciso*. Early in the series Mary is described as the means of restoring the world to its original perfection. Her conception is the ultimate complement to the intended purity of the world, whose imperfection ends upon her arrival.[18] Lest one accuse Sor Juana of elevating Mary to the position of divinity, she reminds us, "Mary is not God, but the one who most resembles God."[19] One must always remember the poetic license and baroque excesses of Sor Juana's *villancicos*. The exaggerated and extravagant language is characteristic of the writing of her era. Mary is seen as a site of contradictions. She is "too much woman to be Divine, too Celestial to be human."[20]

The first poem in Sor Juana's 1676 series of *villancicos* celebrating the Assumption of Mary begins with the earth and the heavens engaged in a competition: the earth because Christ descended upon it, heaven because Mary is rising to enter into it. The earth claims the greater beauty, for it is the site of the incarnation within Mary's womb.[21] Mary's beauty is thus dependent on, or a reflection of, Christ's glory within her. Her beauty is relational, constituted by her relationship with Christ. In a later poem in this series she writes,

> To brighten light itself,
> to enliven Glory,
> to enrich riches,
> and crown the crowns;
> to make a Heaven of the very Heaven,
> to make beauty more lovely,
> ennoble nobility,
> honor honor itself,
> she who is of the Heavens
> raises honor, riches, crown,
> light, loveliness, nobility,
> Heaven, Perfection and Glory.[22]

Mary makes beauty beautiful. She is perfection and glory. Mary, in fact, enriches and intensifies the glory of God. The *villancicos* in the 1690 series on the Assumption continue the theme of Mary as Beauty, grounding it Christologically in her role as mother and bride. "She ascends, to make Heaven, Heaven, for until her beauty adorns it, Heaven is without ornamentation."[23] For Sor Juana, the Assumption is grounded and described, in true baroque fashion, as Beauty entering into the heavens. Similar themes are found in her *Letras a la presentación de nuestra señora*, which contain another celebration of Mary's beauty. "If the Beauty of Mary is God's best seat, to which temple will God go, Mary being God's greatest Temple?"[24] As the Mother of God, Mary is supreme beauty.

Marian holidays and feasts are not the only place in Sor Juana's writing where one finds the theme of Mary as Beauty. In nine of the thirty-two poems written for the dedication of a new church for the Bernardine Sisters (1690) Sor Juana emphasizes Marian themes. This should not surprise us, for Sor Juana states in the first lines of the series, "If Mary is the best Temple of God, when one dedicates a Temple to God, it can only be in the name of Mary."[25] The twenty-fifth poem of the series offers one of the more creative images of Mary, where Sor Juana compares the womb of Mary to the harvest of the Eucharist. She continues by describing Mary's pregnant stomach as the monstrance of the Eucharist.[26] The beauty of her stomach is found in the divine presence filled with the host.

The Eucharist is central to the genre of the *auto sacramental* (allegorical drama) in general and *El Divino Narciso* in particular. Though the emphasis in this play is Christological, Marian themes also appear. Mary clearly holds a privileged role in Sor Juana's theology as the mother of God and consequently the reflection of Beauty. The source of her beauty is her motherhood. The ornate Baroque language that surrounds Sor Juana's depictions of Mary is grounded in a clear Christology. In fact, the beauty of Christ is the foundation of the *imago Dei* and the glory of all humanity.

El Divino Narciso

In this section I analyze the allegorical drama *El Divino Narciso*, with an emphasis on the theological aesthetics found therein. As

Sor Juana's most theological text, this play is an obvious choice for a study that strives to retrieve her theological voice. I begin with an introduction to the literary genre of the *auto sacramental* (allegorical drama), including a brief examination of the work of the Spanish dramatist Pedro Calderón de la Barca, considered by many the master of this genre. Since *autos sacramentales* are most likely an unknown literary vehicle to a modern theological audience, it is important to establish the genre and its theological function in Baroque literature. I then turn to *El Divino Narciso* itself, providing a two-part treatment of the play: first, an exploration of the plot of the *auto*, accompanied by a theological and philosophical analysis of the main play; second, a consideration of the theological and philosophical currents underlying the text, especially as they reflect the intellectual climate of Sor Juana's era.

El Auto Sacramental

Autos sacramentales were performed in Europe as early as the Middle Ages. Their history is tied to that of the Eucharist and the Feast of Corpus Christi. *Autos* were vehicles to instruct the people on their faith.[27] The *auto sacramental* began to flourish as a literary genre in the sixteenth century. The Church in Madrid supported their production and performance. The genre peaked in the seventeenth century with the work of Lope de Vega, Calderón, and Sor Juana.[28] Definitions of the *auto sacramental* vary, but most emphasize two fundamental elements: the significance of the Eucharist and the role of allegory. As defined by literary scholar Barbara Kurtz, "The *auto sacramental*, a play celebrated as part of the annual Corpus Christi festivities, is commonly defined as a one-act drama with scriptural or allegorical characters and the Eucharist as its ostensible subject matter; indeed, the conventional ending of the *auto*, the 'discovery' of a host and chalice, gives the play a quasi-liturgical status and function."[29] A historical definition of the *auto sacramental* is found in the work of Bruce W. Wardropper. Wardropper notes that according to Spanish dramatist Lope de Vega (1562-1635), an *auto sacramental* must have three elements: it must glorify the Eucharist; it must be a public spectacle; and it must combat heresy while simultaneously affirming dogma. Decades later, for Calderón de la Barca and his contemporaries, the function of the *auto* changed slightly. The *auto* became a means of instructing the laity regarding various basic theological and philosophical questions. Instead of combating heresy, they became weapons against the Christian public's ignorance of basic theological doctrine.[30] This pedagogical dimension of the *auto* operates in Sor Juana's writing. Calderón defines the *autos* as "Sermons written in verse, an idea representing questions about sacred Theology."[31] Calderón's understanding of his *auto*, as his definition suggests, accentuated its theological character, poetic nature, and public role.

The centrality of allegory in defining the *auto sacramental* is emphasized in the scholarship of Verónica Grossi. Grossi writes, "Allegory—the complex symbol that poses the epistemological possibility of finding analogues to transcendental, absolute truth in the temporal, material reality of language—is the rhetorical centerpiece of the *auto sacramental*."[32] In Sor Juana's *autos* (and in her poetry, too, for that matter) allegory abounds. Music, Human Nature, Religion, and Pride, to name a few, are incarnate on the pages of her writing and in the characters performed by actors. Grossi also highlights the complexity of the genre and argues for a comprehensive understanding of the *auto sacramental*, emphasizing the relationship between the *auto* itself and its larger catechetical function in colonial culture.[33] In the Latin American context, the *auto* functioned as a means of transmitting religious and political ideologies. As the following chapter will demonstrate, Sor Juana expounds a clear political agenda in her *autos*, carefully constructed to speak directly to her audiences. *El Divino Narciso* explores a particular colonial consciousness that distinguishes it from its Spanish contemporaries. In the very elements and characters of the play Sor Juana depicts an American consciousness. This is not only due to the presence of American characters, but also to the concerns transmitted and questions raised by the play itself.

Pedro Calderón de la Barca (1600-1681) is considered Spain's quintessential dramatist with regard to the *auto*. He authored over seventy *autos* is his lifetime, nine of these adapted from Greco-Roman mythology. In Calderón's era, the *auto* was a means of explaining scholastic theological and philosophical doctrines.[34] While the Eucharist is a central feature of the Calderonian *auto*,

it is not the sole emphasis. Refuting Alexander A. Parker's thesis
that the Eucharist is the fundamental theme of the *auto*, Donald
Dietz argues that the vision is much more complex. Dietz emphasizes the centrality of God's active presence in human history
through the Church and sacraments in the Calderonian *auto*. In
this theological vision, the Trinity, salvation history, and the
Church become significant aspects of Calderón's dramas.[35] The
three movements characterizing Calderón's *auto*—creation, fall,
and redemption—indicate that one must understand the significance of the Eucharist in light of the larger framework of the
auto. This framework is characterized by God's dramatic salvific
presence in human history. Sor Juana shares with Calderón a
dynamic view of humanity and its relationship with the divine.

Calderón's mythological dramas are of special concern for this
study, as *El Divino Narciso* falls into this genre. His allegorical
drama *El divino Orfeo* is one of the plays that influenced Sor
Juana's *El Divino Narciso*.[36] Mythology serves a dual function in
the Calderonian *auto*. On one level, myth functions as a narrative framework for his dramas. The well-known stories of Greek
and Roman mythology are a sure way to connect with his audience. Second, the use of myth to explore Christian themes is a
means of affirming the validity of non-Christian sources for Christian theological and philosophical reflection. In this sense,
Calderón's work must be situated in the larger corpus of Christian theology, which historically has struggled to resolve the tensions of non-Christian sources (especially philosophy) in Christian thought. Barbara E. Kurtz grounds Calderón's rhetorical
devices in Augustinian theology, specifically in his rationalization of pagan myth as a prefiguration of Christian doctrine.[37] This
is significant for the *auto* itself. "By explicitly thematizing the divine Word as source and guarantor of pagan myth, as well as of
language and (illuminated) interpretation, Calderón's plays embody a powerful allegory of the assumed divine origin and sacral
significance not only of myth, but also of the *auto* itself."[38] Calderón
thus simultaneously argued for the divine origin of the *auto* and
grounded mythology in a Christian framework.[39] With this strategy he sought to legitimize the *auto* as a Christian theological text.

Sor Juana's plays are not mirrors of Calderón's. She constructs
her own theological discourse drawing from a broader range of

sources, most notably from her context as a *criolla* living in New Spain. As Stephanie Merrim aptly writes, "Sor Juana Inés de la Cruz both bespoke, with a hyper- and self-consciousness, *and* transcended her milieu."[40] While emulating and drawing from the male literary canon, Sor Juana writes her own feminine discourse. This theme is emphasized by Judith A. Kirkpatrick when she writes, "Sor Juana, then, evidently adapts and reflects the works of previous male authors at the same time that she creates a new text."[41] The construction of this text, and the role of gender in it, will be a central aspect of chapter 4 of this study. Sor Juana also creates her own colonial discourse that reflects the context of New Spain. Rather than bowing down before the canonized Spanish male model, she subverts it, creating an entirely new genre of colonial Latin American writing.

Literary historical analysis of *El Divino Narciso* often introduces the play as one of her greatest achievements. Electa Arenal refers to *El Divino Narciso* and the *loa* preceding it as one of Sor Juana's dramatic masterpieces.[42] Building on Karl Vossler's assessment that *El Divino Narciso* is one of the most beautiful works in Spanish literature, Manuel Antonio Arango L. notes that it is "a work of universal quality, without equivalent, an extraordinary work of Spanish literature."[43] *El Divino Narciso* was first circulated as a separate edition in Mexico in 1690, and then published in the first volume of Sor Juana's collected works in 1691. Sor Juana wrote a total of three *autos sacramentales*, composing *Narciso* last. The origin of each drama is different: *San Hermenegildo* is historical; *El cetro de José* is biblical; and *El Divino Narciso* is mythological, theological, and liturgical.[44] As mentioned above, *El Divino Narciso* was published as an *edición suelta* (separate edition) in New Spain. This type of printing indicates that the play was written at the request of the Condesa de Paredes in order to be performed in Spain. Thus, the intended audience for the play were Europeans, who had little knowledge of culture and life in the Americas.[45]

Plot

The Divine Narcissus was inspired by the tale of Echo and Narcissus, as written by Ovid in the *Metamorphoses*.[46] Sor Juana transformed Ovid's myth into an allegory of Christ's passion, death and resurrection. As noted by Octavio Paz, "Sor Juana's originality lies in her transformation of the pagan myth: Christ does not, like Narcissus, fall in love with his own image, but with Human Nature, who is and is not himself. . . . In Sor Juana's *auto* knowledge does not kill; it resurrects."[47] In the context of the *loa*, the play is used for catechetical purposes. The use of a myth to tell the story of Christ reaffirms Sor Juana's belief that there is something redeemable in pre-Christian religions.

The main characters of the play are as follows: Gentilidad (Gentile), who represents the non-Christian world; Sinagoga (Synagogue), representative of the ancient Hebrew world; the celestial Narcissus, who is Christ; Naturaleza Humana (Human Nature); Eco (Echo); La Soberbia (Pride) and Amor Propio (Self-love), who accompany Eco; Gracia (Grace), who helps Human Nature find Narcissus. The play opens with Gentile and Synagogue conversing, the former praising humanity, the latter Divinity. Human Nature, their mother, overhears them and warns them of their mutual faults:

> And you, blind Gentile,
> mistaken, ignorant, dull,
> applauding in your praises
> a beauty long expired,
> and you, Synagogue, certain
> of the truths you hear
> from your Prophets, and to God
> you render venerations
> avoiding all reflection
> upon your opposition,
> how clear it is you err.[48]

She offers them the story of Narcissus as a means of explaining herself. Why use a non-Christian myth to explain a Christian truth? Because, Human Nature holds, these non-Christian myths have the ability to reveal Christian truth. "Because many times Divine and Human Letters conform, and they reveal that God puts even in the pens of Gentiles appearances that begin to show His high Mysteries."[49] Clearly, Sor Juana does not hold an explicit and radical separation between her Christian and non-Christian sources.

Human Nature begins her story by praising the divine Beauty of Narcissus, whom she adores. While she is created in his image, sin has corrupted this image in her. Sin has so clouded the image that Human Nature has become ugly, and she is sure that if Narcissus saw her, he would not recognize himself in her.[50] She has lost the ability to reflect Narcissus. The distortion of the image is unnatural to her intended state of being. Human Nature prays that she will one day find a fountain, free from sin, which will perfectly reflect Narcissus's Beauty. This fountain will be the site where Human Nature can cleanse her sins.[51] Human Nature is therefore proactive in attempting to renew her ability to reflect Narcissus. She is not a passive character.

The next scene opens with Echo, accompanied by Pride and Self-love. Echo notes the presence of Human Nature and her desire for Narcissus. Echo also mentions that through her combination of myth (form) with the Christian Mystery (content), Human Nature has come to name Narcissus God. "She calls Narcissus God, because His Beauty, is such that it has no equal, and no one deserves it."[52] Echo reaffirms beauty as the primary attribute of God, as seen in Sor Juana's Marian poetry. Echo describes herself as she who is beautiful, but in desiring to be even more so, was reduced to ugliness. Self-interest and arrogance clouded her beauty. Echo, Pride, and Self-love form an "unholy" trinity, motivated by egoism and self-gratification. Jealous of any other potential lovers for Narcissus, Echo's goal is to prevent an encounter of Narcissus and Human Nature. Echo is convinced that if Narcissus sees an unsullied image of Human Nature, he will recognize himself in her and fall in love. Human Nature, according to Echo, is created in God's image. "He will see his image in her and this will obligate His Divinity to incline himself to love her; because the similarity is so great there can be no one who is not drawn to it."[53] Humanity's resemblance to him would lead Narcissus to redeem humanity. Attraction and love are therefore central in Sor Juana's understanding of the Incarnation. In the play, salvation is defined as Narcissus seeing his beauty reflected in Human Nature and becoming incarnate in her. This in turn would lead to his passion, death, and resurrection. Echo proceeds to recount the various times when humanity has come close to reflecting the image of God, but has always ultimately failed. The figures of Abel and Moses, for example, are evoked. It is only through the incarnation of the Christ-Narcissus that humanity can hope to return to its original state of reflecting beauty. Following this section, Echo proclaims Narcissus the Son of God and source of salvation.[54] Echo's intention is to soil all the waters where Narcissus seeks his image in order to prevent him from seeing Human Nature in his reflection. In Sor Juana's play the particular character of Human Nature is representative of all of humanity. The corruption of the water represents sinfulness, leading many scholars to interpret Echo as representative of the devil.

Echo decides to go to Narcissus, who has been hiding on a mountaintop for forty days with no food or water. This is reminiscent of Jesus' temptation in the desert. Echo's intention is to torment and tempt him. She points out the riches of the world, claims them as her own, and demands that Narcissus bow down and worship her. Narcissus, however, rejects her. "Abhorred Nymph, do not let ambition deceive you, for only My Beauty is worthy of adoration."[55] Echo departs, warning Narcissus that he now faces her wrath, and that she will seek his death. Again, this imagery reinforces an interpretation of Echo as a demonic character whose sole purpose is to tempt Christ-Narcissus and corrupt humanity.

The next scene opens with Human Nature, searching for Narcissus, wandering the forest. Much of her speech, as George Tavard notes, is lifted from the Song of Songs.[56] She proclaims Narcissus's beauty and her similarity to him. "Oh, with what reason all adore you! But that the sun's intensity has marked me need not dismay you; Behold, though soiled, I am beautiful, because your countenance I bear."[57] Human Nature is on a quest for Divine Beauty, yet she is frustrated that she cannot find it. She also affirms the traces of beauty that remain in her, even though they are distorted by her sinfulness. At this point Grace arrives on the scene in order to help Human Nature directly. Grace reminds Human Nature of a time when they were once together, alluding to the Garden of Eden, though they have been separated since then. Human Nature asks to be embraced by Grace. Grace, however, pauses, for a certain condition must be met:

> It lies not in your hand,
> though the desire to attain it
> may be your eager errand;
> for human efforts lack
> what is needed to deserve it,
> though they beg for it in tears;
> Grace is a gracious gift,
> not something we are owed.[58]

Only with the gift of Grace can Human Nature reflect Christ-Narcissus. Human Nature then asks how she can acquire this disposition. Grace answers: in following her to a clear and crystal fountain that is the womb of living waters.

Human Nature understands that this is the fountain of She who is filled with Grace:

> Oh, Fountain divine,
> oh Well of living waters,
> preserved from the beginning
> from original pollution,
> from the transcendental stain
> that plagues all other Rivers:
> you return the clearest image
> of Narcissus's loveliness,
> for only you can portray
> with perfection all His beauty,
> without a blot His likeness![59]

Grace leads Human Nature to this fountain, of which Grace is the guardian, and tells Human Nature to hide in the trees and await Narcissus. When Narcissus arrives, Grace tells Human Nature to lean in so that her face may appear in the waters and Narcissus will see her reflection. Human Nature realizes that if Narcissus sees her image in this fountain, he will feel love and desire for her. Grace then hears Narcissus arriving, and tells Human Nature that they must sit together, for Human Nature accompanied by Grace will certainly attract him.[60]

Narcissus enters, dressed as a shepherd, searching for his lost lamb. Even though his lamb has become vain and full of pride, he searches for her. He arrives at the fountain, and as he peers in, is struck by the celestial beauty he beholds. He immediately falls in love. Narcissus falls in love with his image, Human Nature purified in the Divine Spring with the accompaniment of Grace. In recognizing that his beauty is shared with humanity, the Incarnation occurs. Sor Juana's Christology and consequently anthropology are based on this theme. The *imago Dei* is Beauty. Humanity shares in divine *hermosura* (loveliness). At this moment Echo enters the scene. She realizes that Narcissus has recognized his resemblance in Human Nature. The trauma of this realization renders Echo practically mute. She is only able to repeat the last words or syllables of others' statements. Pride and Self-love arrive, and find Echo tormented and in mourning. At the end of the scene, Echo is able to construct a sentence based on the echoing of Pride and Self-love's words. Though reduced to an echo, she is not rendered silent. The three depart off stage.

Narcissus remains at the fountain, yet his joy in being in love turns slowly to sorrow, for he realizes that he must die for his love. Echo returns, but as a shadow of her former self, exemplified by her shift from independent speech to mere restatement. Sor Juana's skill is evidenced by the construction of the dialogue, for when Echo's repetitions are strung together, they summarize the plot lines of the story. In fact, her echoes are clearer than Narcissus's statements. Thus, while she is reduced to echoing, hers remains a powerful voice. The climax of the play follows. Narcissus approaches the fountain and falls to his death. His last words are:

> Father! Why in this terrible trance
> do you forsake me? It has happened.
> Into Your hands I entrust My Spirit![61]

After his death, an earthquake is heard, followed by an eclipse. Listening to the turmoil of nature, Echo proclaims Narcissus to be the Son of God.[62] Echo decides to undo Narcissus's work now that he is gone. She will make sure that Human Nature forgets Narcissus.

Echo, Pride, and Self-love retreat to the side of the stage as a distraught Human Nature enters, mourning the death of Narcis-

sus. In her sorrow she is accompanied by the lamentations of all
of creation. Grace appears and asks her why she is mourning.
Human Nature informs her of Narcissus's death. Grace tells
Human Nature to stop weeping, for not only does Narcissus live,
he lives eternally. Narcissus then appears and asks Human Nature why she is sorrowful. She explains her sorrow surrounding
Narcissus's death, not realizing it is he with whom she speaks.
Like Mary Magdalene in the Gospels, at first Human Nature
does not recognize the risen Savior. When she does identify him,
he refuses her rush to embrace him because he states that he is on
His way to his Father's heavenly throne. Human Nature begs
him not to leave her; she is worried that Echo will try to tempt
her away from him. Echo, Pride, and Self-love emerge from the
sidelines, confirming Human Nature's fears. Grace refutes them,
promising to remain by Human Nature's side. Grace then recounts
the story of Narcissus's love for humanity:

> His own likeness was
> His loving attraction,
> for only God could be
> of God a worthy object.
> Blessed to enjoy that likeness;
> but when His adoration
> more lovingly pursued
> the magnet for which he yearned,
> to keep envy away
> from His well-deserved affection,
> the waters boldly intervened
> to prevent such a crime.
> And seeing that it was futile
> to achieve his desires
> (because even God in the World
> cannot find love without danger),
> He decided then to die
> in that necessary trial,
> to show the risk encountered
> in the search for excellence.[63]

Narcissus assures Human Nature that he is leaving her with
something to help her when her faith is faltering, the establish-

ment of the Church and the sacraments. In the true form of an
auto sacramental, the play ends with the Eucharist. The conclusion emphasizes the body and blood of Christ (Narcissus) as redemptive for all.

El Divino Narciso—*Analysis*

The complexity of Sor Juana's *auto* is demonstrated by the
plurality of sources Sor Juana weaves into the story. Octavio Paz
notes,

> In addition to Ovid and countless poems on the theme, Sor
> Juana was directly inspired by a mythological play of
> Calderón's, *Eco y Narciso*. Sor Juana's *auto*, however, is
> more complex and of greater intellectual and lyrical richness
> than the work of the Spanish poet. She also adapted from the
> Vulgate several fragments from the Song of Songs and others
> from Jeremiah, as well as the passage from the gospel of
> Matthew relating Jesus' temptation on the mountain (4:8-
> 11). The final verses are a translation of a hymn written by
> Thomas Aquinas. . . . Although *The Divine Narcissus* com-
> bines several styles and modes, this diversity in no way
> damages its unity or originality. . . . The *auto* converts
> Ovid's fable into an allegory of the passion of Christ and the
> institution of the Eucharist.[64]

While Paz exaggerates the influence of Calderón's *Eco y Narciso*
as opposed to *El divino Orfeo*, he nonetheless highlights the many
layers of Sor Juana's play. Her tapestry of sources demonstrates
her unique contribution. She preserves the three elements of the
Ovidian myth: Narcissus, Echo, and the fountain, adding the elements of Human Nature and Grace.

Two themes must be noted at this juncture, underlying the
entire play. The first theme, Sor Juana's engagement in the peren-
nial debate surrounding the One and the Many, is highlighted by
Mauricio Beuchot in his theological analysis of Sor Juana's three
allegorical dramas.[65] Beuchot observes that in transforming the
myth of Narcissus into an account of the incarnation and the
Eucharist, Sor Juana engages this recurring theme of classical and

medieval philosophy.[66] The Narcissus of mythology falls in love with himself as an individual. The new Narcissus, as the Son of God, falls in love with himself as a member of the human race, and consequently falls in love with humanity. It is through the encounter with the individual character of Human Nature that Narcissus falls in love with humanity in its entirety. In a similar manner, the act of the individual Narcissus has implications for the many.

The second significant theme is the role of theological aesthetics in Sor Juana's play. As the embodiment of divine beauty, Narcissus *is* Beauty, not a mere reflection of Beauty.[67] The play affirms beauty as the primary attribute of God. In a similar vein, as created in the image of God, Human Nature also embodies this beauty. The *imago Dei* is defined as Beauty, the incarnation a result of love and attraction. Echo's fear that Narcissus will see Beauty in the face of an unsullied Human Nature, a fear that is realized in the play, is based on the beauty of humanity. Humanity's beauty, however, is only complete with the Grace of God. It is only with the gift of God's grace that humanity's beauty fully comes forth.

In order to structure my theological analysis of the play, I focus on four elements or characters: Human Nature, Echo, the fountain, and Narcissus. I have chosen to center my remarks on these figures, instead of on explicit theological loci, for this is more in consonance with Sor Juana's writing. Sor Juana was not a systematic theologian. Therefore, to classify her writing under the heading of systematic theology (i.e., method, Christology) would falsely imply an intention on her part. Instead, through the study of these elements, aspects of her Christology, anthropology, and soteriology will emerge.

The character of Human Nature is in the image of Narcissus, though sin has clouded her beauty. Four aspects of Human Nature indicate the trajectories of Sor Juana's theological anthropology. The first is her depiction of Human Nature as the parent of both Synagogue and Gentile. In this gesture, Sor Juana emphasizes the universal nature of the character. That Human Nature is not merely Christian human nature, but the human nature all of humanity, is affirmed in her use of the myth of Narcissus. At a time when the very humanity of Indigenous and African peoples was being debated, Sor Juana's assertion of the full and equal humanity of Christian and non-Christian peoples is a clear response to the oppression of those dehumanized under the Spanish Crown. As Narcissus is also the savior of all of humanity, Sor Juana affirms Christ's universal salvific will. The universal nature of the character is linked to her depiction of natural and revealed religions, especially in light of the *loa*. As noted by Pamela Kirk, "Though maintaining the conventional primacy of revealed religion over natural religion on the surface, a shift from a clear primacy of revealed religion is introduced through the costuming of the allegorical figures, and through their described family relationships."[68] The second feature is closely tied to the first. I return to my emphasis on Sor Juana's transformation of the myth of Narcissus from a story of arrogant love of self (the one) to his redemptive love for all of humanity (the many). While Human Nature is one character, as an allegorical figure she is representative of the many. This reaffirms her character as symbolic of all of humanity.

The third feature is the role of the *imago Dei*. In the beginning of the play, Human Nature in its fallen state retains its resemblance to the Divine. The *imago Dei* continues to exist, though sullied by self-love and arrogance. Thus, though corrupt, humanity has not lost its ability to reflect the image of God. Humanity is distorted, yet not to the point of no return. With the gift of Grace, Human Nature will once again be able to find her beauty. The freely-given nature of grace is significant to note, for Sor Juana makes an explicit effort to emphasize the giftedness of Grace. Grace is not something owed to humanity. However, Human Nature must participate with God's Grace in salvation history. This is not a gift that is merely received; it evokes a response. Echo, on the other hand, can be interpreted as representative of those impulses in humanity that cloud the *imago Dei*. Echo is described as ugly; Human Nature is not yet at that extreme. As Beauty is the fundamental attribute of the *imago Dei*, the ugliness of Echo posits her as the allegorical representative of sin. Sor Juana juxtaposes the vision of humanity as created in the image of God with an understanding of the self as egocentric (Echo—Pride—Self-Love). Though not explicit in Sor Juana's drama, for she examines the human in light of the gift of God's grace, an inter-subjective and relational human is the modern-day opposite to the clouded image of humanity personified in Echo.

Finally, the dramatic nature of humanity's participation in salvation history is also an important feature of Human Nature's character. Human Nature begins the play by seeking Narcissus. She is an active agent in her own redemption. The introduction of the Eucharist and the affirmation of the Church and other sacraments demonstrate that Human Nature has a participatory role in salvation history. The image of the Divine Narcissus is not merely imprinted in Human Nature unconditionally, nor is it a fleeting moment. Instead, Human Nature is a dynamic expression of God's glory. Human Nature remains humanity at the end of the play, yet it is a humanity to whom the gift of God's grace and beauty has been revealed. Echo's pride and egoism can no longer conquer the human spirit. The "image" can no longer be "distorted" by the egocentricity that Echo represents. Christ-Narcissus's passion, death, and resurrection do not lead to a permanent and static salvation of humanity. Instead, Human Nature must participate in her own salvation. Human Nature has the potential to become distorted again, though through her engagement and remembrance of Christ-Narcissus, she can maintain her beauty and resemblance to Him.

The relationship between Human Nature and Echo is intriguing, for the main structure of the play is a triangle of two women (one "good" and one "evil") and a man; the man is the object of their desire. In addition, the two women have lost their *imago Dei* due to the sin of pride. They constitute a contrasting pair focused on the same object of desire, Narcissus, yet the manner in which they strive to attract him is oppositional.[69] Echo contains the mythological Narcissus within her, suffering from self-pride. This twist is worthy to note, as indicated by Stephanie Merrim, who writes, "It is interesting, and will prove telling, that Sor Juana actually builds the mythical identities of both Echo and Narcissus into her figure of Echo: unrequited and humiliated in her love, as was Echo, Sor Juana's devil-Echo nevertheless encarnates the self-pride traditionally represented by Narcissus, as evidenced by the counter-Trinity she and her companions, Soberbia and Amor Propio, together form."[70] Echo embodies the sins of the mythological Narcissus. Echo not only represents the

mythological Narcissus, her egocentric cohorts affirm this. Sin is
defined as self-love, pride, and arrogance throughout the play. The
contrast of Echo as dissimilarity and Human Nature as similarity
is a rhetorical device used throughout the play. Echo is the agent of
dissimilarity, motivating and activating the relationship between
Human Nature and Grace. She is placed in opposition to them in
order that Human Nature's true similarity can come to fruition.

Margo Glantz, in her analysis of the play, sees Mary (the fountain), Echo, and Human Nature as a feminine trilogy, representative of the caricatures of women in Sor Juana's era. Glantz also
sees Echo as, in a sense, representative of Sor Juana herself. "Echo
could impeccably represent a demon, but in a certain sense is Sor
Juana herself. Do not the echoes of sacred scripture, those of
Góngora, Calderón, Saint John of the Cross, and Jeremiah, Isaiah,
Micah, Esther, and the Song of Songs resonate in her work? But,
above all, was not Sor Juana condemned to silence?"[71] The thesis
that Echo is in fact representative of Sor Juana is an intriguing
avenue that has developed in feminist interpretations of this play.
Though Sor Juana would have no idea that later in her life she
would take a vow of silence, she would have been, by this time,
aware of the Church's disdain toward the popularity of her works.
In addition, Sor Juana uses the Spanish verb *borrar* in reference
to Echo sullying the waters, and uses the noun *borrones* (smudges
or scribblings) several places in her corpus to refer to her own
writing. Echo, as sin, while reduced to an echo, is not utterly
silenced in the play. Not only does she echo others, she is able to
construct her own sentences and ideas through her echoes. Therefore, sin is hampered, yet not silenced, by the incarnation. In a
similar vein, the presence of writing in her convent cell at the
time of her death testifies that while censured publicly, Sor Juana
was not silenced in the last years of her life.

Turning to the last element of Glantz's feminine trilogy, the
fountain is unanimously interpreted by Sor Juana scholars as representative of Mary, the mother of Jesus. Though Mary is not
portrayed by an actress in the play, she participates in its climax.[72] While the fountain is not a speaking character, it is an
important player in the drama. Without the fountain, there is no
reflection; without the unsullied fountain of Mary, Narcissus will
be unable to recognize the humanity in him. "Narcissus sees

Nature and Grace together, or, better, he sees Nature through Grace, as their reflected images now form only one beauty in the Virgin Mary."[73] Mary, as she who is held to be free from sin, is the vehicle for Narcissus's recognition. This theme resonates with the above discussion on the depiction of Mary in Sor Juana's *villancicos*. Again, the pure and unblemished nature of Mary is the subject of Sor Juana's theological exposition.

However, the fountain does not solely represent Mary. As Marie-Cécile Bénassy-Berling indicates, the fountain represents Immaculate Conception, Baptism, and Passion.[74] In describing the fountain as crystalline and free from sin, the references to the Immaculate Conception are fairly obvious. The baptismal aspects of the fountain are demonstrated by the references to it as living waters. In fact, in many ways the fountain as baptismal font is more obvious to the spectator of the play than the reader.[75] Finally, the fountain is the site of Christ-Narcissus's passion and death. He approaches the fountain as he gasps his last words. This could perhaps be interpreted as Narcissus returning to the place from which he came. In other words, his incarnation and passion emerge from and return to the same site. It is difficult to discern whether Sor Juana's placement of the Passion at the fountain was motivated by a theological rationale or by dramatic flair.

Unlike the Narcissus of the myth, Christ-Narcissus falls in love with the human dimension found within him. What Christology emerges from Sor Juana's Narcissus? George Tavard situates Sor Juana's Christological reflections in light of Scholastic theology:

> Juana does not side exactly with either of the two medieval answers to the question of the purpose of the incarnation. She does not, with Anselm, Bonaventure, and Thomas Aquinas, understand the incarnation as primarily remedial, chosen by God to undo the effects of sin by way of redemption. Juana comes closer to John Duns Scotus's idea: the purpose of the incarnation is that humankind should give God the highest possible glory. Yet her view cannot be identified simply with this. Rather, the purpose of the incarnation—identical to that of creation—is the ultimate union of two kinds of divine beauty: the beauty of the eternal Word and the beauty that has been given to creatures.[76]

A clear emphasis for Sor Juana is an understanding of Christ in terms of beauty and desire. Christ-Narcissus's incarnation is a result of this: his captivation with humanity's beauty as reflective of him, and his consequent desire for her as a result of it. However, humanity's beauty is impermanent and fragile, and will never truly reflect the divine perfectly. Narcissus articulates this in his realization that he must die for his love. While his love for Human Nature is great, and her beauty through her accompaniment by Grace is similar to his, it is not identical. Sor Juana bases the incarnation on Christ's desire for the human. However, this desire is rooted in an image of humanity accompanied by grace, as reflected in the perfect disciple Mary. The significance of the fountain as representative of a redeemed humanity is as vital as Grace's role in the redemption of Human Nature.

Some Sor Juana scholars have deemed problematic Christ-Narcissus's act of falling in love with Human Nature as the image of himself. Manuel Arrango L., for example, fears that Sor Juana has collapsed the divine reality into the human myth. She fails, he claims, to pay sufficient attention to divine Mystery. Jean Krynen contends that Sor Juana fails to hold the mystery of God's love in her play, and that the play reduces theology to myth. She also holds that Sor Juana collapses the first and second persons of the Trinity, as well as having divine Mystery create the object of its love in its image and likeness.[77] At the opposite end of the spectrum, Alexander Parker argues for the theological validity of Sor Juana's play. In a lengthy quote that merits full citation, he states:

> When Narcissus approaches, it is therefore not his own face he sees reflected but hers, and it is with her image that he falls in love. . . . The idea is surely a beautiful one: but it is made still more beautiful, theologically speaking, by two further touches. The first is that Human Nature's face is identical with that of Narcissus only when reflected in the pure waters of Grace: on her, disfigured as she is by sin, the likeness is obscured. Narcissus enamoured of his reflected image is therefore Christ so in love with Human Nature that he assumes it to his divine Nature in the Hypostatic Union. . . . The second additional symbolic touch that the imagery

discloses is that the immaculate water of the stream of Grace represents the Virgin Mary. She alone is sinless humanity, made in God's image; her face is therefore the face of his own sinless Humanity. The allegorization of the myth seems to me beautiful and successful, both poetically and theologically.[78]

Parker instead finds fault in the play's allegorization of the passion, for it does not in any way portray Christ-Narcissus as sacrificial victim. These scholars' critiques of Sor Juana's theology are worthy of serious consideration. They do not, however, in my eyes, devalue the importance of the play.

Philosophical and Theological Undercurrents

Framing the depiction of Christ-Narcissus are the theological and philosophical strands that underlie the entire play and were hallmarks of colonial Mexico. The theological and philosophical elements that inform *El Divino Narciso* are eclectic. They include Thomism, Neoplatonism, and hermeticism. Sor Juana was not a systematic thinker: she drew from various philosophical and theological streams in her writing. As noted by various *sorjuanistas*, one philosophical strand of special importance to a study of *El Divino Narciso* is hermetic philosophy.[79] Elena Granger-Carrasco holds that one cannot fully understand *El Divino Narciso* without examining the hermetic elements in the drama.[80] As noted by Octavio Paz, "Sor Juana's central allegory offers a truly extraordinary similarity to a passage from the *Pimander*, the first book of the *Corpus hermeticum*."[81] In this account Mind created Man in the image of the Father. This Man had absolute power over the world and mortals. Nature saw the beauty of Man and became enamored of Him. Man, in turn, saw his reflection in Nature and desired to dwell in it. And so Man and Nature became one, and this is why the human has a twofold nature. Paz notes similarities between the two, especially in the act of seeing and the role of love and desire. In the hermetic creation myth primordial man (son of the divine mind) sees his own image in the beautiful order of the cosmos and, falling in love with this order, descends. This is to say that he falls in love with his reflection of himself in nature. "But there is a fundamental difference, the great dividing line between Neoplatonic hermeticism and Christianity: while dwelling in Nature, the Man of eternal substance of the *Pimander* falls; Christ, in contrast, redeems Nature. Gnostic pessimism becomes Christian optimism."[82] Moreover, while the hermetic myth is a story of creation, Sor Juana's story is a tale of redemption. The hermetic myth is the story of a fall, while Christ's passion, death, and resurrection is the story of a return: the return of Christ from earthly existence and the return of humanity to its *imago Dei*.

Hermeticism embraces a pantheist and emanationist picture of the universe; the universe is an emanation of God, yet God is distinct from creation. Hermes believed that God must be understood through nature. The images of this world are metaphors of an unseen world.[83] This search ends with the inner quest for the divine light in all, which shows humanity that they are children of God. One begins with the study of the world, and from there applies what one has learned in personal self-discovery. "Nature is thus the mirror in which the human being looks at himself [*sic*] and discovers his [*sic*] own divinity with which inevitably he [*sic*] falls in love."[84] Hermetic cosmology, however, does not have a savior. In hermeticism each human being has the ability to become his or her own savior through self-reflection.

Turning to the Christian influences on Sor Juana's work, many scholars have attempted to decipher what the various sources were that informed her writing. Marie-Cécile Bénassy-Berling asserts that scholars today can be fairly certain that Sor Juana did not study Greek or Hebrew, though she read the Vulgate and was steeped in the Latin tradition of Christianity. It is through Latin eyes that she read of the Greek world, and this adds yet another layer to her hermeneutic. Also, Bénassy-Berling holds, Sor Juana most likely did not read Pascal or Newton.[85] Sor Juana's good friend, Carlos de Sigüenza y Góngora, knew Descartes' work. However, the Cartesian revolution did not begin in Mexico until the eighteenth century. While there is a possibility that Sor Juana read Descartes, or became familiar with Cartesian ideas through her friendship with Sigüenza y Góngora, this hypothesis cannot be proven through a study of Sor Juana's work.

Mauricio Beuchot stresses the Scholastic elements of *El Divino Narciso* in his writing. In the *loa*, for example, when Sor Juana indicates that the play was written in Mexico, though performed in Madrid, she is arguing for the transcendence of intellectual ideas.[86] Sor Juana does not see the transference of the play from one context to another as problematic. Beuchot also finds a Scholastic stamp on Human Nature's speech and theological arguments.[87] Sor Juana takes the idea that non-Christians can be inspired by the Holy Spirit from the Church Fathers, especially Clement of Alexandria. For Clement, the Holy Spirit inspired ancient philosophers such as Plato and Aristotle. One finds a similar strand in Augustine, as discussed in the above section on Calderón. Using the myth of Narcissus to explain a Christian mystery affirms Sor Juana's idea that non-Christian texts can inform Christianity. Beuchot also links Narcissus's falling in love with Human Nature, and his consequent love for the human race, to Scholastic philosophy. "It is a particular usage of the Scholastic doctrine of identity, that one was not only the individual, when things were indiscernible, but also there was an identity beneath a certain concept or nature, that is, a universal identity, whether it be species or genus."[88] Sor Juana's concern for the One and the Many can thus be situated within the Scholastic framework of colonial Mexican philosophy.

Beauty as Form and Content

The use of poetry and drama as a theological resource poses interesting questions for contemporary theology, especially in the area of theological method, and particularly with regard to theological aesthetics. Sor Juana's play demonstrates the tension between form and content. "It is true that the aesthetic form dominates, but that is also the form that beautifies the contents it touches. And those contents are very profound, taken from theology and Scholastic philosophy, and taken to a successful expression by the Mexican poetess."[89] In fact, the aesthetic form of Sor Juana's writing contributes to its theological content. The two are in organic unity. The literary expression does not weaken the strength of Sor Juana's theological and philosophical ideas.

Instead, they make them more appealing and accessible to a broader audience.[90] The aesthetic form contributes to the public nature of her theology. This strategy is in part a mark of Sor Juana's era and culture. Sor Juana's reaffirmation of the dramatic and poetic as a theological vehicle can be seen in *El Divino Narciso* in the initial comments by Human Nature, whose introduction of the allegorical and metaphorical affirms this medium.

Theater played a significant role in religious life in Sor Juana's era, especially as a means of evangelization. The mythological and theological unity of *Narciso*, as seen also in Calderón's *autos*, is also characteristic of baroque literature.[91] In a similar vein, *villancicos* were another public form of theological expression. "They were ideally suited to teaching a broad nonliterate audience and reflect the nun's connection with the elements of the 'popular religion' of her day."[92] The unity of humanism and religion, which is characteristic of the Baroque, adds to the complexity of interpreting Sor Juana's work. The ornamentation and intricacy of her baroque style are a challenging hurdle for the contemporary reader. Sor Juana must be studied in light not only of the complexity and eclecticism of her own philosophical and theological background, but also of the complexity and ambiguity of baroque expression.

Is Sor Juana's use of drama and poetry an intentional methodological gesture? At first glance, one might readily answer no. As Margo Glantz reminded us, Sor Juana's corpus was, for the most part, written on commission. Therefore, the decision to write a poem or a play was not her own. Also, as a woman writing in colonial Mexico, drama and poetry were a "safer" form of theological expression, less likely to be noticed by Church authorities. A passage in the *loa* for *El Divino Narciso*, however, sheds some light on this question. The use of the allegorical drama is introduced at the end of the *loa* as the best manner to explain the beauty and glory of the Christian God. The character called Religion decides to evangelize by presenting *El Divino Narciso*. She describes the *auto* as a vehicle for allegorical representation. "Let us go. For, through an idea that is metaphorical, dressed in rhetorical colors, represented to your eyes, I will show you."[93] Contained in the *loa* is a subtle argument for the use of drama as a theological resource. As Pamela Kirk writes, "All three of the one-act plays with which Sor Juana prefaces her sacramental dramas are designed to point up the limits of the 'discussion of the schools' in theological debate and to plead gracefully for drama as a more appropriate form for the communication of theological truths than rational discourse because of the very nature of 'divine things.' "[94] Religion's use of the *auto* as the appropriate device to explain Christian faith demonstrates the validity of this genre for kerygmatic discourse. Allegory and metaphor, Sor Juana contends, are more appropriate vehicles for the exploration and articulation of divine truths.

Sor Juana's literature offers an aesthetic contribution that contains Marian, Christological, anthropological, soteriological, and methodological implications for theology, emerging from a distinct Latin American context. While Sor Juana remained steeped in the theological debates and concerns of her era, her theology offers an alternative approach to addressing contemporary theological loci. A major emphasis in her Christological reflections is the primacy of Christ's universal salvific will. While this insight may sound dated to modern ears, in her explicit incorporation and emphasis on the Indigenous of the Americas, Sor Juana was a pioneer. She affirmed the very humanity of those who were systematically dehumanized and oppressed. Her Mariology and Christology are also marked by an aesthetic starting point and, consequently, so is her concept of God. Sor Juana's anthropology is relational and dramatic. She stresses human participation in the dramatic event of salvation history, in addition to her depiction of the human as constituted by relationships. For Sor Juana, relationship must be defined as right relations. This is seen in the *auto*'s "unholy trinity" of Echo, Pride, and Self-love. Sor Juana's *villancicos* echo the insights found in *Narciso*. The Marian language of beauty and glory echoes her aesthetic Christology. The beauty of Mary's pregnant womb and the glory of her place as the Temple of God emerge from the beauty of Christ. This also has implications, as indicated above, for Sor Juana's concept of God. However, perhaps the most "dramatic" contribution Sor Juana offers is the very form of her theology, poetry and a dramatic play.

Notes

[1]"Gocémonos, Amado, / y vámanos a ver en tu hermosura." Juan de la Cruz, San, "Cántico Espiritual," in *Obras Completas*, 5th ed., ed. Eulogio Pachi (Burgos: Editorial Monte Carmelo, 1997), 53.

[2]Beatriz Melano Couch, "Sor Juana Inés de la Cruz: The First Woman Theologian in the Americas," in *The Church and Women in the Third World*, ed. John C.B. Webster and Ellen Low Webster (Philadelphia: The Westminster Press, 1985), 54.

[3]While von Balthasar is not viewed as a "systematic" theologian, one cannot deny the systematic nature of the Trilogy, which was clearly planned out as an aesthetics (*The Glory of the Lord*), a dramatics (*Theo-Drama*), and finished with the *Theo-Logic*.

[4]Tavard, along with many other Sor Juana scholars, agrees with this claim. "The writing of Juana Inés de la Cruz that is, from a theological point of view, both the most ambitious and the most successful is undoubtedly *Divine Narcissus.*" George Tavard, *Juana Inés de la Cruz and the Theology of Beauty: The First Mexican Theology* (Notre Dame, IN: University of Notre Dame Press, 1991), 104.

[5]Juana Inés de la Cruz, Sor, *The Answer/La Respuesta: Including a Selection of Poems*, critical ed. and trans. Electa Arenal and Amanda Powell, 95. OC 4:469.1219-1220.

[6]Chapters 3 and 7 of Tavard's study are a helpful supplement for this section, as well as chapters 4 and 5 of Kirk's book. In addition see part II of Margo Glantz, *Sor Juana Inés de la Cruz: La comparación y la hipérbole* (México: CONACULTA, 2000).

[7]OC 3:463.384.

[8]OC 3:469-470.384.

[9]A *loa* is a short one-act play. Sor Juana wrote two types of *loas*, free-standing (such as this one) and attached to an allegorical drama (as in the case of *El Divino Narciso*).

[10]OC 3:486.79-82; 487.91-94.

[11]Augustine of Hippo, *Confessions*, trans. Henry Chadwick (Oxford: Oxford University Press, 1991), 65.

[12]Tavard, *Juana Inés de la Cruz*, 186.

[13]On Augustine, see Carol Harrison, *Beauty and Revelation in the Thought of Saint Augustine* (Oxford: Clarendon Press, 1992). "Order, in the sense of the ordered succession of history and time, Augustine often describes in terms of a beautiful song or poem, whilst the ordered beauty of Creation, he teaches, is maintained despite sin and evil because of God's just judgment and providential ordering." Harrison, *Beauty and Revelation*, 108.

[14]Pamela Kirk notes that "nearly all of the nun's religious poems are

connected to Mary in some form." Pamela Kirk, *Sor Juana Inés de la Cruz: Religion, Art, and Feminism* (New York: Continuum, 1998), 57.

[15]Ibid., 59. *Sorjuanista* Marie-Cécile Bénassy-Berling also emphasizes (the "problematic of") Sor Juana's strong Marian devotion. Marie-Cécile Bénassy-Berling, *Humanisme et religion chez Sor Juana Inés de la Cruz: La femme et la culture au XVIIe Siècle* (Paris: Éditions Hispaniques, 1992), 245-258.

[16]OC 2:21.227 (EC). As Tavard notes, it is not surprising that Sor Juana has an "incomplete" view of Mary's Immaculate Conception, as it did not become doctrine until 1854. Tavard, *Juana Inés de la Cruz*, 69.

[17]OC 2:104.279 (EC).

[18]OC 2:100.276.

[19]OC 2:211.349.

[20]OC 2:64.253.

[21]OC 2:4.217.

[22]OC 2:69-70.257.

[23]OC 2:156.308.

[24]OC 2:218.355.

[25]OC 2:182.323.

[26]OC 2:209.347.

[27]Donald T. Dietz, "Liturgical and Allegorical Drama: The Uniqueness of Calderón's Auto Sacramental," in *Calderón de la Barca at the Tercentenary: Comparative Views*, ed. Wendell M. Aycock and Sydney P. Cravens (Lubbock, TX: Texas Tech Press, 1982), 75-76.

[28]Alejandro López López, "Sor Juana Inés de la Cruz y la loa al *Divino Narciso*," in *Memoria del Coloquio Internacional: Sor Juana Inés de la Cruz y el Pensamiento Novohispano 1995* (Mexico: Instituto Mexiquense de Cultura, 1995), 221.

[29]Barbara E. Kurtz, " 'No Word without Mystery': Allegories of Sacred Truth in the Autos Sacramentales of Calderón de la Barca," *Publications of the Modern Language Association of America* 103:1 (Jan. 1988): 270, n.1.

[30]Bruce W. Wardropper, *Introducción al teatro religioso del siglo de oro (La evolución del auto sacramental: 1500-1628)* (Madrid: Revista de Occidente, 1953), 20-21.

[31]Ibid., 21, citing the *loa* of *La segunda esposa*.

[32]Verónica Grossi, "Political Meta-Allegory in *El Divino Narciso* by Sor Juana Inés de la Cruz," *Intertexts* 1:1 (Spring 1997): 92.

[33]Grossi critiques contemporary literary scholarship's homogenous and monolithic depiction of the unified structure of the *auto*, its emphasis on allegory and the exaltation of the Eucharist, and the *auto*'s performance on Corpus Christi. While these features are characteristic of seventeenth-century authors such as Sor Juana and Calderón, they do not address the plurality of the *auto* genre. Grossi lists various types of *autos* that include: the evangelizing *auto*, the court *auto*, the theological-sacramental *auto*, and the convent *auto*, to name a few. These various types of *autos* contain, in addition to the above-mentioned features, mythological, Scholastic, humanist, Baroque, and

prehispanic elements. Verónica Grossi, "La loa para el auto sacramental *El Divino Narciso* de Sor Juana Inés de la Cruz frente al canon del auto oficial," *Monographic Review/Revista Monográfica* XIII (1997): 124.

[34]For philosophical and theological studies of the Calderonian *auto* see, Donald T. Dietz, "Theology and the Stage: The God Figure in Calderón's *Autos sacramentales*," *Bulletin of the Comediantes* 34:1 (Summer 1982): 97-105; Ignacio Elizalde, "La Interpretación Teológica de los Autos Sacramentales," in *Varia hispánica: Homenaje a Alberto Porgueras Mayo*, ed. Joseph L. Laurenti and Vern G. Williamsem (Kassel: Edition Reichenberger, 1989), 147-161; Louise Fothergill-Payne, "The World Picture in Calderón's *Autos Sacramentales*" in *Calderón and the Baroque Tradition*, ed. Kurt Levy et al. (Ontario: Wilfrid Laurier University Press, 1985), 33-40; Kurt Reichenberger, "Calderón's Welttheater und Die *Autos Sacramentales*," in *Theatrum Mundi: Gotter, Gott und Spielleiter im Drama von der Antike bis zur Gegenwart*, ed. Frank Link and Gunter Niggl (Berlin: Duncker and Humbolt, 1981), 161-175.

[35]Dietz, "Liturgical and Allegorical Drama," 77.

[36]Historically, Sor Juana scholars have attributed inspiration for *El Divino Narciso* to Calderón's mythological drama *Eco y Narciso*. This is a thesis proposed, for example, by one of the editors of Sor Juana's *Obras completas*, Alfonso Méndez-Plancarte. In contrast, Alexander Parker, who has done a substantial amount of work on Calderón's *auto*, argues that Méndez-Plancarte exaggerated the influence of Calderón's *Eco y Narciso* on Sor Juana's play. "While *El Divino Narciso* and *Eco y Narciso* have the same plot in general outline, they are so dissimilar in theme that the former cannot be a *Kontrafaktur* of the latter. It is a *versión a lo divino* of the myth itself, not of Calderón's treatment of the myth." Parker asserts that Sor Juana drew from the Calderonian *autos* found in the first volume of his collected *autos* in writing *El Divino Narciso*. Alexander A. Parker, "The Calderonian Sources of *El Divino Narciso* by Sor Juana Inés de a Cruz," *Romanistisches-Jahrbuch* 19 (1969): 261.

[37]For Calderón, "Myth contains veiled, prophetic allusions to Christianity's eternal truths." Barbara E. Kurtz, *The Play of Allegory in the Autos Sacramentales of Pedro Calderón de la Barca* (Washington, DC: The Catholic University of America Press, 1991), 76. For more on the Augustinian theology of Calderón's allegorical dramas see Hans Flasche, "Ideas agustinianas en la obra de Calderón," *Bulletin of Hispanic Studies* LVI (1984): 335-342.

[38]Kurtz, *The Play of Allegory*, 66.

[39]The *loa* of Calderón's *auto sacramental El divino Orfeo* demonstrates his use of mythology as a vehicle for transmitting Christian truth. The *loa* presents a competition between divine and human letters. The human letters represent ancient and pagan writing. The divine letters represent Christian writing and the Church Fathers. The eleven characters in the *loa* (five young women, five young men, and an older man) enter on stage carrying placards with letters on them. The letters are scrambled and merely spell EAUICTHSAIR, which is

gibberish. The characters then begin a dance, and when they finish their letters spell out EUCHARISTIA (Eucharist). As mentioned above, the Eucharist is a key element in allegorical dramas. The characters then dance again, and when they stop their letters spell CITHARA IESU (the lyre of Christ). This last spelling indicated that Orpheus' mythological lyre is being transformed into the figure of Christ.

[40]Stephanie Merrim, *Early Modern Women's Writing and Sor Juana Inés de la Cruz* (Nashville: Vanderbilt University Press, 1999), xi.

[41]Judith A. Kirkpatrick, "The Word and the Woman: Creative Echoing in Sor Juana's *El Divino Narciso*," *Hispanofila* 122 (Jan. 1988): 57.

[42]Electa Arenal, "The Convent as Catalyst for Autonomy: Two Hispanic Nuns of the Seventeenth Century," in *Women in Hispanic Literature: Icons and Fallen Idols*, ed. Beth Miller (Berkeley, CA: University of California Press, 1983), 171.

[43]Manuel Antonio Arango L., *Contribución al estudio de la obra dramática de Sor Juana Inés de la Cruz* (New York: Peter Lang, 2000), 16.

[44]In this chapter, I will be using the terms allegorical drama and *auto sacramental* interchangeably. While I am aware that allegorical drama is the common English designation for *auto sacramental*, since some of the secondary authors I cite use the term *auto sacramental* (even in English literature), I use both terms to avoid confusion.

[45]Interestingly, Alexander A. Parker has noted that the play was most likely not performed there. Having examined records of the *autos* performed in Madrid from 1688 to the end of the century, there is no record of *El Divino Narciso*'s presentation. Parker hypothesizes that this was perhaps due to the fact that after Calderón's death, it was very difficult to stage an *auto* that was not one of his own. Parker, "The Calderonian Sources of *El Divino Narciso*," 259.

[46]Due to space constraints and familiarity, I felt it was unnecessary to include the story of Echo and Narcissus as told by Ovid. For a complete account of Ovid's myth see Ovid, *Ovid's Metamorphoses*, trans. Charles Boer (Dallas: Spring Publications, Inc., 1989).

[47]Octavio Paz, *Sor Juana: Or, The Traps of Faith* (Cambridge, MA: Harvard University Press, 1988), 352.

[48]OC 3:25.62-71 (EC). All translations of *El Divino Narciso* are my own except those translated for this book by Ellen Calmus, indicated by (EC). While the *auto* and its *loa* have been recently published into English in its entirety, I find some of the alterations made to the text in order to improve its readability for a modern English-speaking audience to be problematic. Sor Juana Inés de la Cruz, *The Divine Narcissus – El Divino Narciso*, trans. and annotated by Patricia A. Peters and Renée Domeier (Albuquerque, NM: University of New Mexico Press, 1998).

[49]OC 3:26.125-130.

[50]OC 3:31.232-240.

[51]OC 3:31.269-271.

[52]OC 3:34.339-342.

[53]OC 3:37.460-466.

[54]OC 3:41.601-607.

[55]OC 3:47.803-806.

[56]Tavard, *Juana Inés de la Cruz,*120.

[57]OC 3:50-51.1036-1040 (EC).

[58]OC 3:53.1105-1112 (EC).

[59]OC 3:54.1137-1148.

[60]OC 3:56.1209-1216 (EC).

[61]OC 3:78.1703-1705.

[62]OC 3:81.1760 (EC).

[63]OC 3:93.2111-2130.

[64]Paz, *Sor Juana,* 351.

[65]Mauricio Beuchot, "Los autos de Sor Juana: Tres lugares teológicos," in *Sor Juana y su mundo: Una mirada actual,* ed. Sara Poot Herrera (México: Universidad del Claustro de Sor Juana, 1995), 353-392.

[66]Ibid., 362-363.

[67]I would like to thank my former advisor and colleague, Alejandro García-Rivera, for this insight.

[68]Pamela Kirk, "Christ as Divine Narcissus: A Theological Analysis of 'El Divino Narciso' by Sor Juana Inés de la Cruz," *Word & World* XII:2 (Spring 1992): 148.

[69]Stephanie Merrim, "*Mores Geometricae*: The 'Womanscript' in the Theater of Sor Juana Inés de la Cruz," in *Feminist Perspectives on Sor Juana Inés de la Cruz,* ed. Stephanie Merrim (Detroit: Wayne State University Press, 1991), 115-116.

[70]Stephanie Merrim, "*Narciso Desdoblado*: Narcissistic Stratagems in *El Divino Narciso* and the *Respuesta a Sor Filotea de la Cruz,*" *Bulletin of Hispanic Studies* 64:2 (April 1987): 113.

[71]Glantz, *Sor Juana Inés de la Cruz,* 105.

[72]As George Tavard highlights, "It is one of the more notable features of *Divine Narcissus* that although the Virgin Mary is not represented by an actress she is nonetheless present at the climax of the play: she is the well with clear water. Bent over it, looking into it, Narcissus will see his perfect image." Tavard, *Juana Inés de la Cruz,* 121.

[73]Ibid., 125.

[74]Marie-Cécile Bénassy-Berling, *Humanisme et religion,* 403.

[75]Ibid., 403.

[76]Tavard, *Juana Inés de la Cruz,* 118.

[77]Jean Krynen, "Mito y teología en *El Divino Narciso* de Sor Juana Inés de la Cruz," in *Actas del Tercer Congreso Internacional de Hispanistas,* ed. Carlos H. Magis (México: El Colegio de México, 1970), 505.

[78]Parker, "The Calderonian Sources of *El Divino Narciso,*" 270.

[79]See Aída Beaupied, *Narciso hermético: Sor Juana Inés de la Cruz y José*

Lezama Lima (Liverpool: Liverpool University Press, 1997); Marie-Cécile Bénassy-Berling, "Sobre el hermetismo de Sor Juana Inés de la Cruz," in *La creatividad feminino en el mundo barroco hispánico: María de Zayas – Isabel Rebeca Correa – Sor Juana Inés de la Cruz,* ed. Monike Bosse et al. (Kassel: Edition Reichenberger, 1999), 629-639; Elena Granger-Carrasco, "La fuente hermafrodita en *El Divino Narciso* de Sor Juana," in *Y diversa de mí misma en vuestras plumas ando: Homenaje internacional a Sor Juana Inés de la Cruz,* ed. Sara Poot Herrera (México: El Colegio de México, 1993), 237-246; Octavio Paz, *Sor Juana.*

[80]Granger-Carrasco, "La fuente hermafrodita en *El Divino Narciso,*" 240.

[81]Paz, *Sor Juana,* 352.

[82]Ibid., 353.

[83]Beaupied, *Narciso hermético,* 4.

[84]Ibid., 4.

[85]Bénassy-Berling, *Humanisme et religion,* 110.

[86]Beuchot, "Los autos de Sor Juana," 359.

[87]Ibid., 360.

[88]Ibid., 364.

[89]Ibid., 368.

[90]Ibid., 356.

[91]Arango L., *Contribución al estudio de la obra dramática,* 182.

[92]Kirk, *Sor Juana Inés de la Cruz,* 58.

[93]OC 3:17-18.401-405.

[94]Kirk, *Sor Juana Inés de la Cruz,* 38.

Chapter 4

The Good

You foolish men, who denounce women in unjust remonstrance, not seeing you yourselves are cause of that which you accuse us of.[1]
—Sor Juana Inés de la Cruz

The most recent surge of secondary scholarship on Sor Juana's corpus has been clearly marked by the concerns and hermeneutic of feminist philosophers, theorists, and literary scholars. The question of the role and function of gender in Sor Juana's life and writing is a lively topic in academic studies of her work. This applies to the gender coding of Sor Juana's corpus and to the manner in which her biological sex affected her relationship with ecclesial authorities, especially in relation to the subject matter of her writing. Underlying this increasing concern for gender is the broader emphasis on the presence of the Other in Sor Juana's writing. Not only do women find a voice in the pages of her writing, but also Black and Indigenous peoples. As mentioned in chapter 2, these groups were at the bottom of the social hierarchy in New Spain. They are the forgotten, at the margins of Mexican colonial society. Sor Juana's intentional creation of Indigenous and Black characters, who are given a voice to articulate and denounce the injustices inflicted upon them, is a hallmark of her work. The voiceless, whether they are women, the Indigenous, or Africans, are given a voice through Sor Juana's literature.

This chapter will explore the function of the Good, or justice, in Sor Juana's work, with special attention to the role of gender, race, and ethnicity. Sor Juana's defense of those at the margins of society is a central and theologically grounded feature of her writing. For Sor Juana, denouncing injustice was always a Christian claim. This chapter is divided in two parts: the first examining gender, the second exploring the construction of Indigenous and African peoples in Sor Juana's writing. Section one is notably longer, for gender concerns saturate Sor Juana's writing. Though the same cannot be said of her writing on Indigenous and African peoples, they still remain an important aspect of her work.

Sor Juana: Precursor to Liberation Theologies?

Accompanying the emphasis on gender in Sor Juana's corpus is the modern categorization of her work as feminist or protofeminist. This tendency has also crossed over to the few theological reflections on her writing, labeling her the first feminist theologian of the Americas.[2] While acknowledging that in Sor Juana's corpus there is a clear defense of women's rights, I do not agree with categorizing a seventeenth-century figure in the terms and paradigms of modern scholarship. In other words, while Sor Juana was aware that she was excluded from various activities based on her sex, this does not correspond to feminism as scholars understand it today.[3]

Sorjuanistas are very clear in stating that Sor Juana's recognition of the social construction of gender is what distinguishes her from other Baroque figures. José González Boixo emphasizes that what sets Sor Juana apart from other great Baroque poets (e.g., Lope de Vega, Góngora, Quevedo) is her conviction of the intellectual equality of men and women. While González Boixo is wary of scholars who label Sor Juana a feminist and ignore her historical context, he nonetheless feels feminism is the most adequate term to denote the struggle for the equality of men and women in her work.[4] González Boixo is hesitant, and rightly so, to project a feminist ideology onto Sor Juana's writing. However, he highlights the fact that she was very conscious of the society and world view that defined her role as a woman. Electa Arenal and Amanda Powell, in their introduction to a feminist rereading and translation of *La respuesta*, depict Sor Juana as a protofeminist. "Because she wrote as a woman aware of her gender status and because she intended her arguments to be applied on behalf of other women *as women*, she is certainly a precursor to world views and activities we call feminist."[5] Arenal and Powell make a persuasive point. Sor Juana does, at times, argue not only on her own behalf, but on behalf of all women. This is seen in her *Respuesta*. However, Sor Juana does not have either the systemic analysis or the link with a broader social movement that defines feminism. With some hesitancy, therefore, I will refer to her writing as protofeminist. This is a heuristic device, for the term protofeminist borders on implying a continuity of thought between the writing of Sor Juana and contemporary academic feminists today.

In addition to the emphasis on gender, the growing body of scholarship exploring the function of Indigenous and Black peoples in Sor Juana's corpus links this emphasis to both her context as a *criolla* and her concerns for social justice. Yolanda Martínez-San Miguel, for example, sees Sor Juana's writing as constituting a discourse with a concern for subjectivity, especially with regard to a feminine, colonial, and *criolla* consciousness.[6] Sor Juana, Martínez-San Miguel contends, fashions an "American" subject at the intersection of gender and colonial society.[7] Sor Juana's writing creates an alternative discursive space in a discourse that is otherwise exclusively masculine. Her writing is also a point of intersection between epistemology, gender, and the colonial condition. Martínez-San Miguel sees *La respuesta* and the poem *Primero sueño* as two places where Sor Juana defines rationality as a human capacity, not a gendered one, thus refuting the male philosophical constructs of her day. She simultaneously argues against women's marginalization. "Far from self-marginalizing herself through the creation of 'feminine writing' or in the postulation of a world of knowing that was specifically feminine, Sor Juana leans towards amplifying the intellectual space of her era through the inclusion of women in the epistemological and theological debates in the University, religious centers, and other educational and intellectual institutions in New Spain."[8] This is a significant point to highlight. Sor Juana did not argue for a particular space for women's contributions. Instead, she wanted the discourse of her era to be expanded in order to include women's voices. Sor Juana was not critical of masculine discourse; she was critical of her exclusion from it.[9] She did not argue, for example, that women would somehow make a different sort of contribution. Instead, she held, women and men should be playing on the same field in the constructs of knowledge of her day.

The intention of this study is not to posit Sor Juana as a seventeenth-century liberation theologian. Contemporary liberation theologians have very little awareness of Sor Juana's existence, much less of her theological voice. Defining Sor Juana in such a manner would imply the existence of a certain body of literature embracing the concerns defined by contemporary scholars and imposing those constructions upon the past. In a similar vein, to define Sor Juana in contemporary categories is to imply an evolution in thought, thus making her work older, less progressive, and therefore less relevant. In the spirit of Gustavo Gutiérrez's retrieval of Bartolomé de Las Casas, I am hesitant to present Sor Juana as a liberation theologian, since that would be to imply that our current era is the pinnacle of Christian social justice. In addition, such a label is unnecessary for this project. As Gutiérrez indicates, regarding Las Casas, "It does not seem to us to be appropriate, or even necessary, for an expression of our appreciation of his theological work and witness. That work and witness transpired in a context very different from today's, at the social level as at the theological."[10] Sor Juana should be appreciated as a historical voice whose contributions can inform some of the questions being explored by contemporary theology. Also, her voice bears witness to a theological and philosophical tradition in colonial Latin America that has been erased from the history books of those very disciplines. Last, her writing demonstrates that some of the concerns of liberation theologies are not new ones, but rather sites of resistance and struggle that have marked the Americas for centuries.

Gender

Turning to Sor Juana's writing, I would like to examine five themes / rhetorical practices in relationship to the centrality of gender in Sor Juana's corpus. These are: her cataloguing of women to justify women's intellectual endeavors; her emphasis on women known for their intellectual gifts; her critique of the construction of silence and authority imposed upon women; her theological anthropology; and her defense of women's right to education. I draw from a variety of her writings, including poetry, prose, and drama. A centerpiece in this section is *La respuesta* (*The Answer*), which is the most well known of her texts and considered to be Sor Juana's most explicitly "feminist" text. Her biological sex ignited the controversy that led to the writing of *The Answer*. As Jean Franco has explained through the critique of a clergy member's writing in the *Carta atenagórica*, "Sor Juana Inés de la Cruz . . . not only trespassed, at least symbolically, on clerical terrain, but directly defied the clergy's feminization of ignorance."[11] In doing so she transforms the very nature of the male discourse into which she boldly enters.

A Litany of Women

The rhetorical construction of a catalog of women in order to justify women's intellectual pursuits is not unique to Sor Juana. Sor Juana's list of illustrious women must be situated within a tradition of early women writers who used this rhetorical device. As Stephanie Merrim argues, *The Answer* did not emerge *ex nihilo*: "Listened to carefully, Sor Juana herself articulates an awareness that she writes in a tradition of feminist debates: in her catalog of illustrious women mentioned above, Sor Juana employs the *brevitatis* formula and states that she will omit further names of women 'to avoid relaying what others have said.' "[12] Sor Juana herself writes that she constructs her litany in *The Answer*, "without mentioning others, whom I omit so as not merely to copy what others have said (which is a vice I have always detested)."[13] In two of her most important texts Sor Juana utilizes a litany of women in order to justify her intellectual endeavors: in the above-cited *Answer* and in the poem *Primero sueño* (*First Dream*).

The catalog found in *The Answer* includes women from a variety of eras, both Christian and non-Christian: Old Testament, Antiquity, New Testament, Early Church, Medieval, and contemporary. Of particular interest are the women of Antiquity, especially Aspasia of Miletus, Hypatia, and Leontium. Nina Scott in her thoughtful analysis of the women included in this list notes, "All three of these Greek women were models of great intellect who approached the men of their time on a near-equal footing, and two of them paid the price for so doing."[14] Sor Juana also makes explicit references to Christian women, who are the centerpiece of her argument for the legitimacy of her own writing. Sor Juana draws on a history of women, especially including women in the Church, in order to justify her intellectual life. Mary is referred to as "Mother of the Word" and the "Queen of Wisdom." Special importance is given to the scholarly women who surrounded Saint Jerome, the founder of her order. Saint Paula, friend and devotee of Saint Jerome, is of particular interest to her, as the namesake of her convent. Sor Juana constantly reminds the reader of the intellectual abilities of these women and the legitimacy of their writing within the Church. In addition Sor Juana includes aristocratic women and women in government.

However, the rhetorical purpose of this list remains the justification of Sor Juana's own writing as a Christian woman religious. As Scott notes, "To Sor Juana the central issue remained that of the legitimacy of writing by women religious, and based on the examples cited above Sor Juana concluded that the Church indeed sanctions writing by both canonized and noncanonized women."[15] Evoking them with the verb *a ver* ("to see"), Sor Juana created a collectivity of women of great power and intellect. The women in the litany mirrored Sor Juana's hopes and aspirations, and shared her own intellectual pursuits. Sor Juana "saw" herself in the lives of these women. In a lengthy quotation Scott connects these two strands:

> The characteristic verb "I see" with which she referred to women she considered her role models does not seem to me a random choice nor does it perform a solely dramatic function: in the figures of her elected foremothers and in the particular characteristics she chose to see there Sor Juana created for herself a gallery of mirrors that reflected many of her own aspirations: the freedom to learn, to teach, and to

write in public; social and political power; iconoclasm; intellectual competition free from constraints of gender.... In the desperate solitude of her intellectual struggle Sor Juana took strength from that network of women who accompanied her in spirit.[16]

The women in *The Answer* not only represent Sor Juana's ambitions; they also defend her right to have these ambitions.

The second list of women is found in Sor Juana's most complex poem, *First Dream*. Instead of offering a textual account of this complex and lengthy poem, I would instead like to focus on Sor Juana's uses of feminine mythological characters in the poem. Chapter 5 of this study will examine *First Dream* in more detail, focusing on its epistemological implications. In *First Dream* Sor Juana created a world of feminine mythological characters that constitute the collective feminine "I" of Sor Juana's poem.[17] In other words, the poem is permeated with feminine characters that represent and participate in the epistemological journey that constitutes the poem.

These mythological characters are female, and they are transgressive of the male norms that dominate their culture and lives. The characters are Nyctimene, Ascalaphus, and the daughters of King Minyas. Nyctimene seduces her father; Ascalaphus is turned into an owl for defying Persephone; the Minyas sisters are punished for refusing to honor Dionysus. These characters are feminine figures that transgress male authority. In Sor Juana's quest for knowledge, these women accompany her in her defiance of male normativity with regards to rationality. As Electa Arenal has indicated, "Despite punishments against their intelligence, grace, and beauty, resisting women, throughout the poem, persevere."[18] In a similar fashion to the list of women found in *The Answer*, Sor Juana again evokes a collectivity of women in her support in *First Dream*. However, in contrast to the women included in *The Answer*, women who are revered and praised in Church history and philosophy, here the women are subversive, standing in solidarity with Sor Juana's intellectual project. Thus Sor Juana constructs a community of women who are both revered and condemned for their voices and for their autonomy.

Intellectual Women

Linked to Sor Juana's catalogs of illustrious women is her emphasis on women renowned for their intellectual abilities. This emphasis is found in three areas of her writing: *The Answer*, her *villancicos* to Saint Catherine of Alexandria, and Sor Juana's Marian poetry. Regarding *The Answer*, the women known for their intellectual gifts constitute a community with which Sor Juana sought to identify and justify her writing. In addition to offering this catalog, Sor Juana argues in *The Answer* that her intellect was in fact a divine gift. A key feature of Sor Juana's justification of her study and writing is grounded in her belief that her desire to study was in fact a gift from God, which she must utilize in order to serve.

> For ever since the light of reason first dawned on me, my inclination to letters was marked by such passion and vehemence that neither the reprimands of others (of which I've received many) nor reflections of my own (there have been more than a few) have sufficed to make me abandon my pursuit of this native impulse that God himself bestowed on me. His Majesty knows why and to what end He did so, and He knows that I have prayed that He snuff out the light of my intellect, leaving only enough to keep His Law. For more than that is too much, some would say, in a woman; and there are even those who say that it is harmful. His Majesty knows too that, not achieving this, I have attempted to entomb my intellect together with my name and to sacrifice it to the One who gave it to me.[19]

In *The Answer* she also describes her intellect as something proceeding from a force beyond her. In a thoughtful study of the rhetorical practices of *The Answer* and its connections to the accepted forms of Christian women's writing, especially Teresa de Avila's *Vitae*, Kathleen Meyers says that Sor Juana both adopts and revises the tradition of women's spiritual autobiography.[20] This is especially seen in her revision of the call to vocation reinterpreted as a call for intellectual study. "Sor Juana extends this to include the highest authority, God, as she weaves it together with the convention of the Divine call. Sor Juana locates the need for her writing and the desire to pursue intellectual life in God's will."[21] The religious vocation is transformed to include an intellectual vocation. Through this rhetorical strategy, Sor Juana defends her intellectual pursuits as motivated by a divine force beyond her control.

These affirmations of the divine origin of her intellect are juxtaposed with the moments when she ponders whether this particular calling is a gift or a punishment. On numerous occasions Sor Juana reminds readers of *The Answer* that her writing was always compelled by exterior forces: either by the God-given gift of intellect or by the demands of the Church or the viceregal court. She even describes her intellect as a *"negra inclinación"* (wicked inclination). It would appear that Sor Juana had an ambivalent relationship with her intellect. "My greatest enemy is my inclination to study, which I know not whether to take as a Heaven-sent favor or as a punishment."[22] The uncontrollable desire to study is likened to gunpowder, uncontrolled even by her religious exercises. On the one hand, Sor Juana views it as a gift of God, on the other a curse. A closer reading of her work, however, reveals that she sees her knowledge as a curse only when it results in her persecution by others. In fact, she even states that she is a martyr for her gift: "A strange martyrdom, indeed, where I must be both martyr and my own executioner!"[23] In using the gift of her intellect, Sor Juana is aware that she puts herself in danger of persecution or marginalization. However, like the martyrs, she is willing to suffer the consequences in order to follow God's will.

The second example, and perhaps the most engaging for this study, is Sor Juana's *villancicos* to Saint Catherine of Alexandria.[24] Sor Juana's *villancicos* to Saint Catherine were sung in 1693 at the Cathedral of Oaxaca, not in Mexico City or Puebla. This is significant, for the *villancicos* are in part autobiographical, and were written and performed during the controversial later years of her life. Also key to understanding these eleven poems is that, as Pamela Kirk states, "It is generally admitted that they represent a 'second' *Response [Respuesta].*"[25] Many of the "feminist" themes found in *The Answer* are expressed in these poems.

Saint Catherine is the patron saint of women students, philosophers, and wheelwrights, among others. Accounts of her life emphasize her learning. She has also been the patron saint of the University of Mexico since Sor Juana's lifetime. In 1672 a work was published on Mexico entitled "La Rosa de Alexandría," which describes Catherine's intellect as masculine inclinations or a male principle within her, thus negating the notion of female reason or intellect. Elías Trabulse has highlighted that Sor Juana's *villancicos* were perhaps written in response to this very work.[26]

Saint Catherine is held by Sor Juana to be a model of an intellectual woman. *Villancico* 317 is a defense of the intellectual rights of women and the spiritual equality of both sexes. The first lines highlight St. Catherine as someone who overcame adversity with her knowledge. Sor Juana writes, "The learned men of Egypt, by a woman have been vanquished, to demonstrate that sex is not the essence of intelligence."[27] In the story of Saint Catherine, the Egyptian emperor Maximus summons fifty wise men to convince her to abandon her Christian faith.[28] The second verse recounts her being challenged by these fifty philosophers. The miracle is not that she convinced them that she was right, but that they admitted to it. As Sor Juana continues in verse nineteen, Saint Catherine's female reason triumphs over the men who come to challenge her. "How well we see that they were wise in admitting they were beaten: it is a triumph to concede the supremacy of reason."[29] Later in the poem Sor Juana also states that biological sex has no role in one's intellect. In the sixth stanza Sor Juana claims that God intended women to serve the Church through their intellect. She writes, "She studies, and disputes, and teaches, and thus she serves her Faith; for how could God, who gave her reason, want her ignorant?"[30] Saint Catherine's intellect is a gift of God, not a flaw in her nature, Sor Juana continues: "God wished through her to honor womankind."[31] This poem is thus an example of Sor Juana's public denunciation of the role society and the Church had assigned her. Like Saint Catherine, Sor Juana saw herself as a woman whose intellect was a gift from God, yet whose biological sex had turned this into a curse within her gendered societal constraints. In their public performance at the cathedral, Sor Juana was able to voice her "protofeminist" concerns to a large public. Sor Juana argued for an understanding of

rationality that is asexual. She was advocating an abstract understanding of knowledge free from the influences of biological sex.
This theme resurfaces in a later section on Sor Juana's theological
anthropology.

The last genre of writing that demonstrates Sor Juana's emphasis on intellectual gifts is her Marian poetry. In addition to
depicting Mary as God's beauty and glory, Sor Juana also describes Mary as a sage theologian. The third poem in the 1676
series of *villancicos* on the Assumption begins, "The sovereign
Doctora of divine Schools, from whom all the Angels gather wisdom."[32] Mary is described as the doctor of the heavens. Because
she participates most closely with God, Sor Juana contends, Mary
is capable of reading the supreme science of theology. Sor Juana
then goes on to describe Mary as mastering the various tools
necessary for the theology studied at the university. The fourth
poem opens describing Mary as the "Divine Teacher of the Supreme Classroom."[33] In describing Mary as doctor, teacher, and
theologian, Sor Juana is presenting an image of the Mother of
God as a deft intellectual, not solely an object of adoration. In
addition, these descriptions of Mary are coupled with Sor Juana's
repeated description of Mary as Mother of the Word. This is
seen, for example, in the first pages of *The Answer*. Also in *The
Answer* Mary is deemed "Queen of Knowledge." In fact, Sor
Juana uses Mary's authorship of the *Magnificat* to defend her
own right to write poetry. As noted by Jean Franco, this also
affirms Mary's wisdom. "Sor Juana's celebration of the Virgin
allows her to envisage female power and intellect. She describes
Mary as the Mother of the Word. When this is taken literally, it
means that the female body is the matrix that gives birth to the
logos."[34] Mary as scholar affirms Sor Juana's own intellectual
efforts, which were regulated by the male ecclesial hierarchy.

Silence and Authority

The polarities of silence and voice, submission and authority,
dominated the daily lives and overall structure of religious life
for women in colonial Mexico. Convent life was highly regimented, and while each convent had a governing body, in the end
the male clergy had control over the lives and activities of women

religious throughout New Spain. Silence and authority dominate Sor Juana's story. She struggled against the ecclesial authorities that tried to silence her voice, and she also sought to legitimize her authority through the various rhetorical strategies discussed in this chapter. As her writing demonstrates, Sor Juana was aware of the gendered construction of silence and authority in her era, and attempted to subvert them.

El Divino Narciso offers a fruitful, albeit unexpected resource for an exploration of the gendered construction of silence and authority in Sor Juana's writing. The main thrust of my analysis of the role of gender in this play concerns the figure of Echo. Traditionally, analyses of Echo have addressed her role in the play as representing Satan. Literary scholar Jean Kirkpatrick, while not refuting this claim, expands the understanding of Echo as it relates to feminist discourse. She notes that in Sor Juana's play, both Echo and Satan share a common fate, for they are both voices that have been silenced and marginalized by dominant Christian discourse.[35] Both are robbed of their voices in the face of authority. Kirkpatrick does not interpret Echo, and consequently Satan, as essentially negative figures in the play. Instead, "Eco and Satan are joined by the mutual bond of having been silenced by men and through the necessity of discovering a way to speak in spite of that control. Eco's primary 'sin' is that of being a woman in a culture dominated by men."[36] Echo, after all, is silenced in the face of Narcissus' love for Human Nature.

One cannot reject that there is evidence of the function of Echo as devil-temptress in the play. The scene where Echo tries to tempt Narcissus when he has been in the wilderness for forty days is a clear allusion to the Gospels. I am not denying this claim. However, in her ever-ingenious manner, Sor Juana offers Echo as a subtle and more complex figure than the devil. Perhaps it is her Baroque sensibility, or her desire to employ a protofeminist subtext in the play, but Sor Juana's Echo cannot be reduced to merely the representation of evil. Or can she? In a patriarchal society that constrained the voices and intellects of women, is not a voice that strives to rupture this dominant paradigm a threat to authority? Has not the Church historically marginalized transgressive voices that contest its authority, deeming them heretical? As Verónica Grossi indicates, "It is important to note that both in

Primero sueño and in *El Divino Narciso*, the mythological figures associated with the transgressive and liminal space of writing are for the most part feminine figures who are persecuted and castigated by the authorities."[37] The silencing of Echo can be interpreted as the silencing of women and their authoritative voices.

While Echo loses her voice in the play, she is not reduced to silence. Instead, she loses control over her speech, incapable of authority over her own voice. She is reduced to repeating fragments from the speech of others in order to convey meaning.[38] Through her subversion of the voices of others, Echo claims a narrative voice. Her reduced speech begins by expressing her own views, but is then used to reveal to Narcissus the meaning of his words. Through her echoing, Echo uncovers the underlying significance of Narcissus's words. Though reduced to echoing the speeches of others, Echo in fact ends up guiding Narcissus through her narrative authority. While the sight of him renders her incapable of her own speech, she subverts and transcends this state. Kirkpatrick sees this as a distinct "feminist" move in Sor Juana's play. "Sor Juana has, in *El Divino Narciso*, effectively converted feminist theory into practice. She gives the woman the word and the power to tell the story. She also discovers the means to recover the female voice, in spite of the restrictions placed upon her in a patriarchal society."[39] Sor Juana's use of Echo as narrator, even while reduced to echoing, can be interpreted as embodying women's attempts to subvert dominant patriarchal paradigms in order to find a space for their own voices.[40] Another feature of *El Divino Narciso* is the fact that women serve as the storytellers in the play and its *loa*: first Religion, then Human Nature, and lastly Echo. Women hold the narrative authority

In addition to subverting the gendered paradigms of silence and authority in her era, Sor Juana also utilized the available means of feminine speech in order to defend her intellectual pursuits. This is most clearly seen in her use of humility in *The Answer*. The first paragraph is filled with belittling language, where she states, "I am unable to say anything worthy of you," and describes her writing as "drafts and scratches."[41] She then describes herself as "a poor nun, the slightest creature on earth and the least worthy of drawing your attention," and "an ignorant woman."[42] Traces of this are found in the above-referenced passages where Sor Juana defends her intellectual abilities as a gift from God. This language continues throughout the letter. In order to defend herself Sor Juana degrades herself.

Sor Juana uses self-deprecating language to describe herself, refuting any accusation of arrogance and pride. This is not new to Christian women's writing. Teresa of Avila, for example, used humility as a form of self-defense.[43] Stephanie Merrim has noted that various aspects of Sor Juana's *Answer* can be connected with Teresa of Avila's *Vitae*: writing as obedience, *vos me coegistis*, imitation of Christ, Holy Ignorance, self-vilification, and the self-effacing woman. Sor Juana's use of humble language, Merrim notes, is explicit. "Sor Juana *contrives* to write like a meek woman."[44] Sor Juana's use of humility is an intentional rhetorical device used as a defensive mechanism in the face of the public censure of her last years.

In addition to her use of rhetorical humility as a means of defending her right to study and write, Sor Juana also, at times, inserts feminine discourse explicitly into her writing. While disagreeing with Pamela Kirk's close correlation of Sor Juana's writing with that of contemporary feminists, I find that many of Sor Juana's rhetorical mannerisms do reveal an explicit concern with gender. For example, as Kirk indicates, in one of Sor Juana's poems on the Incarnation of the Word she explicitly uses the feminine word *palabra* instead of the masculine *verbo* (which is customary) to describe the Word.[45] As a result of this, the pronoun to refer to the Word becomes *Ella* (feminine) instead of the customary masculine *El*. This is an intentional move on Sor Juana's part that leads to the divine being spoken of in terms of the feminine.[46] This echoes, in part, other examples of women's mystical speech about God which use feminine word forms.[47]

Unlike Teresa and other women in Christian spirituality, however, Sor Juana does not use mystical experience to legitimize her voice. Instead, she uses her vast knowledge, claiming authority in the manner of her male peers. Pamela Kirk notes that this clearly sets Sor Juana's writing apart from other women religious. "Whereas most women religious writers like Maria of Agreda and Teresa of Avila drew their authority from mystical experience, Sor Juana writes with an authority that comes from her intellectual and literary talents. Neither does she need to appeal to the mystical experience of the reader as a basis for understanding what she writes."[48] In fact, while Sor Juana presents a tradition of learned women to defend herself, she simultaneously argues for an asexual understanding of the intellect and the soul to legitimize her entry into male theological and philosophical discourse. Sor Juana played with the gender of her voice, either emphasizing the female authorship of her work or adopting a male voice. Franco understands this as revealing the problem of constituting women's subjectivity and authorship in Sor Juana's era. "Because certain discourses, for instance the sermon, were authorized only when spoken by qualified subjects, Sor Juana was constantly forced to seek alternative forms of authorization (for example, obedience to the command of a superior) or to deploy disguises."[49] Underlying the fluid nature of Sor Juana's ability to move from female to male voice is her theological anthropology, which held the mind and soul to be in essence without gender, and highlighted the social construction of gender roles in her culture.

Theological Anthropology

Sor Juana's theological anthropology must be situated in the theology of her era, which was dominated by Augustinian and Scholastic theology. Sor Juana's writing is, in part, a reaction to the constructions of women that eclipsed their voice and full humanity. Before examining her reaction, one must briefly explore the philosophy and theology to which she responded. Sor Juana simultaneously affirmed and challenged the reigning philosophy of her era, arguing for women's full and unconditional humanity.

Sister Prudence Allen has performed the enormous task of tracing historical, philosophical, and theological reflection on the human being, with special emphasis on gender. Allen notes that for the Scholastics, the two Genesis accounts were a source of tension and rigorous reflection, for they paradoxically revealed a notion of a humanity as created equally in God's image and a notion of woman as somehow subordinate or secondary to man. In light of the incarnation of Christ as a male, the question of gender was further complicated. Because of their theological prominence, I will focus on the thinking of Augustine and Aquinas.

My depiction of gender in their anthropology is not exhaustive. Instead, I offer it as a window to the type of theological construction of gender Sor Juana reacts to and critiques in her writing.

While Augustine held that in heaven and in the highest functions of the mind there existed a sex complementarity, he maintained that in the corporeal world the male held some supremacy over the female.[50] This is based on his understanding of woman as symbolic of the terrestrial or embodied dimension of humanity. Man, on the other hand, represented the higher, intellectual plane. This rule, however, applied only to the temporal existence of humanity. With regard to the spiritual and heavenly existence of the human being, male and female were equal. However, with his reduction of the female to a symbol of the terrestrial, Augustine's theology resulted in the subordination of women. Allen notes, "As a consequence of his symbolic use of woman to represent the temporal orientation of human existence, Augustine fell into sex polarity in which man was superior to woman because man could represent the image of God by himself while woman could not."[51] Woman thus becomes inferior to man, and is seen as his helpmate. Her destiny is to obey, while man's is to rule. "While man by himself represents the image of God, woman, as helpmate to man, does not represent that image, particularly in the generative activity of temporal life."[52] Augustine's temporal subordination of women led to their theological marginalization. Turning to Aquinas, one finds that created man and woman both reflect the image of God. However, this image was present "imperfectly" in women. "For Thomas, grace did not overturn or destroy human nature. He believed instead that grace built on or perfected nature. Therefore, woman was able to achieve the full perfection of her 'imperfect' nature."[53] Women are somehow deficient. Men are the "more perfect" image of God, while women are derivative. This leads Aquinas to the same conclusions as Augustine: men being more perfect, must rule, while women must obey and be subordinate.

Returning to *El Divino Narciso*, the character of Human Nature, as a female figure, clearly transgresses Augustinian and Thomist understandings of the feminine as secondary to creation. I find it extremely significant that Narcissus falls in love with a female character. Unlike the hermetic myth that informs the play, where primordial man falls in love with creation in its entirety, here we have Narcissus falling in love with his image in a female figure. Tracing the development of the *imago Dei* in Scholastic theology, Kari Elisabeth Børreson has noted that for the most part there existed a spiritual gender neutrality, though because of his "exemplary" sex man was *especially* God-like.[54] Sor Juana, therefore, subverts this paradigm with a female-gendered Human Nature.

The fountain as symbolic of Mary is also significant for Sor Juana's theological anthropology. As noted in the previous chapter, the fountain is also simultaneously representative of baptism, the Immaculate Conception, and Jesus' passion, death, and resurrection. At this juncture, one could ask if there is an intentional relationship between these three interpretations of the fountain and their theological weight. Marie-Cécile Bénassy-Berling emphasizes that this is not an arbitrary association. Instead, it is an intentional emphasis on the feminine as a locus for redemptive action. The fountain makes possible the encounter between Christ/Narcissus and Human Nature. The feminine becomes the mediator between humanity and divinity, male and female. Mary as Mediatrix (a belief that remains controversial in Roman Catholicism today) counters a view of Mary as an empty vessel, passively filled by divine (masculine) grace.[55] George Tavard has in fact criticized Sor Juana's work on this very theme. "Her emphasis on Mary's privileges, whether merely given or also, in some sense, merited, conveys the impression of taking away the uniqueness and exclusiveness of Christ as the one 'Mediator of the new covenant' (Hebrews 8:6)."[56] Mary as the fountain is given an active and participatory role in the play, even though Mary is not a speaking character. In addition, one way to interpret the role of Mary is to see her as exemplary of Christian discipleship. In other words, Narcissus fell in love with the image in the fountain because it reflected humanity in its most Christ-like state. The fountain does not necessarily have to be viewed as mediating the divine, but instead as mediating to the human the manner in which he or she can reflect the image of God within him or herself.

Existing in tension with Sor Juana's intentional rhetorical foregrounding of women is her understanding of the soul and the mind as gender-neutral. This is most clearly seen in Romance 48.

This poem is in reply to a man from Peru who wrote to her saying that she should become a man. Her poem is in order to "be rid of those who inquire whether I am a woman or not."[57] She goes on to argue that in Latin married women have a gender, while virgins have no sex. She concludes her argument by stating, "Of one thing I'm sure: that my body, disinclined to this man or that, served only to house the soul—you might call it neuter or abstract."[58] Sor Juana claims herself to be neuter. As we shall see in the next chapter's examination of *First Dream*, Sor Juana often retreats to language of the gender-free mind or soul in her epistemological reflections. Denying her sexuality is one strategy through which Sor Juana attempts to justify her intellectual capabilities and her right to read and write theology. Does this poem perhaps imply that Sor Juana is Augustinian in her anthropology? George Tavard believes so: "Juana defines herself by reference to her soul, not her body. Female in her body, she is simply and totally human in her soul. This had been, in substance, St. Augustine's anthropology."[59] That could perhaps be the case. Like Augustine, Sor Juana makes a distinction between embodied existence and what she sees as the more spiritual or intellectual dimension of human life. In requiring marriage to be the mark of womanhood and contrasting it to virginity, Sor Juana creates a criterion for women's identity based on embodied sexual activity. This is contrasted to the gender-neutral abilities of reflection and devotion, and here we find echoes of Augustine. There is an interesting twist and tension in her work, for while having argued that knowledge is neutral, Sor Juana must depend on her litanies of women in order to justify her writing and scholarship. However, unlike Augustine, who saw embodied women as secondary in creation, Sor Juana blames the negative attributes ascribed to women on the men who depict them in this manner.

Accompanying Sor Juana's view of the soul as being without sexual distinction is an awareness of the nature of gender as social construction that is surprising to read in the writing of a seventeenth-century figure. This is clearly seen in Sor Juana's most well known poem, the philosophical satire "*Hombres necios*" ("Foolish Men"). Her critique of male constructions of women's identity is astonishing. She begins, "You foolish and unreasoning men who cast all blame on women, not seeing you yourselves are cause of the same faults you accuse."[60] These early lines reveal the paradox of being a woman. Always the object of male construction, they can never escape the male caricature of their identity. Women are trapped: "why require them to do well when you inspire them to fall?"[61] In other words, women are victim to the negative male misrepresentations that always describe them as the negative contrast to male supremacy. This paradox is clearly stated when Sor Juana writes, "Women's good favor, women's scorn, you hold in equal disregard: complaining if they treat you badly; mocking, if they love you well."[62] Men can never be satisfied with the negative projection of women they have created. "Once you've caused them to be bad, you want to find them as good as saints."[63] Here we find the paradoxical dualism of the virgin-whore, or in Christian language Eve-Mary.

Throughout the poem Sor Juana emphasizes that women are always constructed as the objects of male desire. In the latter half of the poem, she demands of the reader: Who is worse: "she who falls to constant pleading, or he who pleads with her to fall?"[64] The answer is, of course, the man who constantly tries to encourage the woman to fulfill his worst expectations of her for his own pleasure. The last lines of the poem are astounding, for Sor Juana turns the tables and objectifies man: "We have devil, flesh, and world: a man."[65] As noted by Marie-Cécile Bénassy-Berling, "Discreetly, but firmly, the woman religious creates a small Copernican revolution in the last verse by attributing to man, in his own right, the role of object, object of desire, object of sin, object of scandal."[66] Sor Juana takes the very words that are often used to describe women and makes them the attributes of men. The negative attributes so often associated with women become the characteristics of the very men who caricature women. As Stephanie Merrim affirms, " 'Hombres necios' turns the table on men and their 'sin razón' or lack of reason by attributing to them the negative qualities that misogyny imputes to women. Men are, she concludes, 'carne, Diablo y mundo' [the flesh, the devil and the world]. No other love poem or poem on love of Sor Juana's so explicitly defends women per se against men's constructions of them."[67] Through her clear awareness of not only the male construction of gender but the power relationships implicit in the subjectivity of he who is able to define both genders, Sor Juana expresses a level of gender analysis that rings eerily and appreciatively familiar in the ears of modern feminists.

Women's Right to Education

Building on the arguments explored above, Sor Juana concludes *The Answer* with an argument for the right to women's education. The center of this claim is Sor Juana's refutation of the claim that the passage in 1 Corinthians "*Mulieres in Ecclesiis taceant, non enim permittitur eis loqui*"(1 Cor 14:34) suggests that women should not be able to study and write privately. Citing seventeenth-century Mexican Scripture scholar Juan Díaz de Arce to support her claim, Sor Juana notes that this maxim applies to women's public, not private, activities. Dr. Juan Díaz de Arce was a theologian and university professor at the Pontifical University of colonial Mexico. His interpretation of 1 Corinthians 14:34 was that the maxim applied to the university and the pulpit, but that study and private instruction were permitted, if not encouraged, for women. Sor Juana continues by arguing that not all women should be allowed to study, only those who have intellectual gifts. She also indicates that the same should be true of men. "[F]or there are many who study only to become ignorant, especially those of arrogant, restless, and prideful spirit, fond of innovations in the Law (the very thing that rejects all innovation). . . . For them, more harm is worked by knowledge than by ignorance."[68] She cites Arius, Pelagius, and Luther as examples of the harmful effects of knowledge placed in the wrong hands. Sor Juana is suspicious of the feeble state women are kept in by those who prefer that they remain uneducated. She is also wary of what she sees as unintelligent and ignorant men, who become ever more ignorant the more they study. One can only wonder if this is a veiled allusion to certain men who criticized Sor Juana's work or in some way attempted to silence her voice.

As a solution to the problem of women's lack of education, Sor Juana proposes that older women teach young women. Sor Juana sees the education of women by men as problematic, a factor that prevents families from allowing their daughters to become educated. She does not hold the education of women by women to be in conflict with the Corinthians decree. Not only is this a suggestion for private study, but also, in a move that mirrors modern day biblical interpretation, Sor Juana argues that one must view this biblical passage in light of its context. "There can be no doubt that in order to understand many passages, one must know a great deal of the history, customs, rituals, proverbs, and even habits of speech of the times in which they were written, in order to know what is indicated and what alluded to by certain sayings in divine letters."[69] She then proceeds with a litany of Scripture passages in light of their contextualization. Sor Juana proposes two alternatives for the interpretation of the above cited 1 Corinthians passage: it is either a condemnation of women's public preaching (which she agrees with) or it is a command to silence all women in the Church. "And if they understand it in the second extent and wish to extend the Apostle's prohibition to all instances without exception, so that not even in private may women write or study, then how is it that we see the Church has allowed a Gertrude, a Teresa, a Brigid, the nun of Argueda, and many other women to write?"[70] Clearly, Sor Juana argues, a Church that has saintly women such as Teresa of Avila does not interpret this passage in the latter light. Therefore, Sor Juana concludes, there is no reason to object to women's private study. In addition, Sor Juana emphasizes, the Church has also permitted writing by women who are not saints, even in Sor Juana's era. Historically, Teresa herself was writing before she was canonized, and Maria de la Antigua, a contemporary of Sor Juana, was also encouraged to write. These women, however, did not attempt, as Sor Juana did, to enter the male theological discourse of their eras.

This argument, with its emphasis on the reduction of women's intellectual pursuits to a solely private domain, may seem dated to modern ears (as it is, in fact). However, *The Answer* was written as a response to Sor Juana's public critique of a sermon. Sor Juana's adamant insistence that she is solely interested in private study should not be surprising. Sor Juana does not restrict the material that she feels women have the right to explore. Due to her desire to study theology, Sor Juana clearly wants to continue her pursuit of sacred letters. She wants to remain in the realm of male discourse, philosophy and theology, and is willing to concede a tangential status in the private realm. Her awareness of the restrictions of her sex force her to maneuver the rhetorical devices available to her in order to argue for her intellectual rights and the rights of other women.

Is protofeminist an accurate label of Sor Juana's writing? Georgina Sabat de Rivers says, "I think that we may say that the whole of her literary production is permeated by her feminine consciousness of her society's patriarchal character and of her exceptional status as a female writer and intellectual. . . . Born a woman and an intellectual, what she did do was to assert herself and demand the same rights that were conceded to enlightened men."[71] Jean Franco, who argues that Sor Juana had an awareness of gender as a social construction, gives a similar depiction.[72] Stephanie Merrim, however, gives us a word of warning. "Her script, however, does not enunciate the overtly 'feminist' message that Sor Juana's pronouncements in the *Respuesta* regarding women would lead us to expect. The *Respuesta*, we cannot forget, is a response to an act of persecution."[73] While I agree with Merrim's assertions that both *The Answer* and the *villancicos* to Saint Catherine were written during a time of turmoil in Sor Juana's life, this does not negate their protofeminist import. Nor does this rule apply to the earlier *First Dream* or the other places in Sor Juana's corpus that demonstrate a consciousness of female marginalization. In the end, I am most comfortable with maintaining Sor Juana's work as protofeminist. Exhibited in her writing is an awareness of marginalization and oppression on the basis of gender. There is not, however, a systemic critique that is characteristic of contemporary feminist writing. In addition, the term feminism is associated with modern social movements, thus Sor Juana's work cannot be defined in this manner. Sor Juana wrote in isolation. Though she was not the only woman writing in New Spain, she is the only woman treating the theological and philosophical themes that characterize her corpus. Yet another distinguishing mark of her scholarship is the function of race and ethnicity in her writing.

Race and Ethnicity

Sor Juana's arguments for the intellectual rights of women are not the only place where one finds a defense for the marginalized in her corpus. In her writing on Indigenous and Black peoples, Sor Juana also expresses an advocacy for the oppressed that was progressive for her era. In this section I explore the function of race and ethnicity in Sor Juana's thought through an examination of the *loa* preceding *El Divino Narciso* and her *villancicos*. As the more succinct and theological articulation of her position, this *loa* will be the subject of the majority of this section.

All three of Sor Juana's allegorical dramas are preceded by *loas*. As defined by Octavio Paz, a *loa* is "a brief theatrical piece played as prologue to a principal play, often in praise of visiting or newly arrived dignitaries or for royal anniversaries."[74] The four main characters of *Narciso's loa* are Occidente (Occident), América (America), Celo (Zeal), and Religión (Religion). Occident, a male, and America, a female, are both *indios*. Zeal (a male) represents the Spanish military force, and Religion is Roman Catholicism, represented by a Spanish lady. America and Occident are celebrating the feast of the *dios de la semillas* (god of the harvest), their pagan god. America praises their god: "Moreover, his protection of us is not limited to bodily sustenance from that which we eat, but more, feeding us with his own flesh (having been purified before of every corporeal stain), he purifies our soul from every stain."[75] Sor Juana has the voices of the Indigenous use language that is clearly analogous to Christianity to describe their pre-Christian beliefs and practices. Zeal and Religion arrive during the festivities. Religion attempts to introduce them to Christianity, but they do not listen to her and continue with their ritual. This enrages Zeal, who, as the self-proclaimed wrath of God, states, "I am Zeal. Does that surprise you? For when Religion is depreciated by your excesses, then Zeal will arise in vengeance chastising your insolence. I am the minister of God."[76] He attempts to instigate a battle with America and Occident, who retreat from him. Zeal's efforts in the conquest and "conversion" of the Indigenous are reduced to military force.

Religion, however, has a different tactic. She pleads with Zeal to withdraw his force, so that she can reason with America and Occident. "In order to subdue them you used your strife, but now it is time for my mercy in order to conserve life: because to defeat them by force was your effort, but to yield them with reason is mine, with my gentle persuasion."[77] Her goal is not forced aggression or murder; instead, she wants to convert them to Christianity. In an interesting gender twist, the female Religion is depicted as rational, while Zeal is portrayed as irrational and emotional. She first asks America and Occident about the god they worship, *el dios de las semillas*. After listening to Occident, she despairs at the thought that they are attributing features of the Christian God to their deity. She informs them that they are worshiping a false idol, and that the works they attribute to *el dios de las semillas* are in fact the works of the Christian God: "those portents that you exaggerate, attributing their effects, to your false gods, works that are of the True God, and of His Wisdom are effects."[78] America then asks if there is an idol of the Christian God, similar to the ones made of human blood for *el dios de las semillas*. Religion answers by informing her that while the Christian God is infinite and unbound, this God resembles humanity. Occident then asks if there is a sacrifice in Christianity similar to the one they offer their gods. Religion replies that the sacrifice is found in the Mass, where the bread and wine are transformed into the flesh and blood of Christ, whose offering on the cross redeemed the world.[79]

America and Occident then ask to see the Christian God. Religion assures them that they will, once they are baptized. After having baptism described to them, Occident notes that the practice resembles one of their purity rituals. "I already know that before I arrive at the rich table, I must bathe, for that is my ancient custom."[80] Religion finally convinces the two *indios* that their god is but an anticipation of the Christian God. Both America and Occident want to know more about the Christian God. The *auto* is then offered as an allegorical, catechetical, and theological device to explain the Christian mystery.

In the *loa*, Sor Juana manages to give historical information on the Spanish conquest, argue for the establishment of the Eucharist, and enter her work in the Spanish canon of allegorical dramas while adding elements of the culture and context of New Spain. The internal plot of the *loa* revolves around the instruction of the Indigenous concerning Catholic doctrine. However, based on the intended performance of this *loa* in Madrid, as noted in its closing scene, this *loa* was also intended to demonstrate to the Spanish audience the dignity and complexity of Indigenous peoples, through its exposition of their history and customs. *El Divino Narciso* was written for performance in Spain, not in colonial Mexico. As Pamela Kirk has noted, "Though the fiction at the preface of the play is that the sacramental drama, *El Divino Narciso*, will teach the Indians the mysteries of the Catholic doctrine of the Eucharist, it is again clear that the play is really intended to convince the audience at the Spanish court of the dignity and piety of the Indians and of the complexity of their history, customs, and religion."[81] While the *loa* seems to address the evangelization of Indigenous peoples, it is in fact the Spanish audience that will be "evangelized" by Sor Juana's *loa*.

One of Sor Juana's primary sources on Indigenous culture and practices was the chronicle of Juan de Torquemada entitled *Monarquía indiana*. In Octavio Paz's analysis of this *loa*, he notes that one of its major themes is that "early pagan rites contained signs that, although encoded and allegorical, foreshadowed the Gospel."[82] This is clearly seen in Religion's declaration to Occident and America that their god of the seeds is prefigured in the Christian God. Sor Juana, having knowledge of an Aztec ritual that is characterized by the creation and eating of a figure of the god Huitzilopochtli, links this as a precursor to the Eucharist. In addition, Sor Juana presents an Indigenous ritual analogous to baptism. She is making connections between the practices of the Aztecs and those of the Spanish. This suggests the question: If Indigenous rituals contain a prefiguration of Christianity, then does this mean that their theology and beliefs also contain that prefiguration?

Sor Juana establishes an analogous relationship between Indigenous religious practices and Christian sacraments. Also, through the *loa*'s relationship with the *auto*, Indigenous beliefs are given an authority similar to that of classical Western literature, philosophy, and religion. The use of the Ovidian myth in the main drama parallels the use of Aztec ritual and religious belief in the *loa*. Comparing Sor Juana to Bartolomé de Las Casas, Pamela Kirk highlights Sor Juana's suggestion that Indigenous religions are of equal merit to that of Greek and Roman sources as vehicles for divine truths.[83] In a similar vein, Sor Juana creates a space where marginalized truths are able to enter into the discourse of Christian truth. This is exemplified in the *auto*'s intended performance in Europe.

Carmela Zanelli has grounded Sor Juana's argument that Indigenous beliefs could be understood as anticipations of Christianity in both the theology of the Jesuits and hermetic philosophy, especially in the writing of Athanasius Kircher, S.J. Kircher was one of the first to connect the Indigenous culture of the Americas to classical Greek culture.[84] Zanelli links Sor Juana's expression, through the voice of Religion, of the idea of the universality of the divine salvific will with the Jesuit intellectual climate of her era, which sought to understand Indigenous belief systems and religions. The presence of the Indigenous of the Americas mirrors Kircher's efforts to present Egyptian hermetic texts as prefigurations of Christianity.

Through her *loa*, Sor Juana attempts to validate the Indigenous people's religious practices. This was a dangerous endeavor, for Aztec rituals were greatly feared and condemned by the Church. The most recent Roman Catholic beatification of Juan Bautista and Jacinto de Los Angeles, martyred in 1700 for their role as Oaxacan "attorneys general" overseeing the population's religious practices, demonstrates that the Indigenous population, in spite of being heavily monitored, continued their own religious practices. Bautista and de Los Angeles, Indigenous converts to Christianity, were killed by a group of *indios* whose pre-Christian ritual they disrupted, accusing them of idolatry. Sor Juana addresses this struggle directly. The description of non-Christian sources as prefigurations of Christianity is not original to Sor Juana; this is seen even in the genre of the allegorical drama, as demonstrated in Calderón's work. Sor Juana's novelty is found in her application of this in the American context. As Margo Glantz has noted, "Her great novelty resides not in her use of analogy that relates Christianity to other religions, which was systematic and almost canonical in Calderón; it resides in the fact that she sought to add pre-Hispanic religion as another antecedent."[85] Through her inclusion of Indigenous voices, Sor Juana adds their world view to the "acceptable" canon of prefigurations of Christianity.

The influence of Bartolomé de Las Casas, the great defender of the Indigenous, underlies Sor Juana's text. Gustavo Gutiérrez has written that Las Casas's point of departure is found in his "conviction that in the Indian, as the poor and oppressed one, Christ is present, buffeted and scourged."[86] In *Del único modo de atraer a todos los pueblos a la verdadera religión*, Las Casas argues for the peaceful evangelization of the Indigenous of the Americas. This idea resonates in the arguments put forth by Religion in the *loa*. Religion rejects military Zeal. This is echoed in yet another of Las Casas's texts, *De unico vocationis modo*: "The central thesis of that book is one we know well. There is only one way to evangelize: by peaceful means, that is, by persuasion and dialogue. All use of force is radically to be excluded."[87] Gutiérrez indicates that Las Casas also argued for God's universal salvific will, that God's grace is offered to all. This resonates once again with the ideas put forth in Sor Juana's *loa*.

This defense of the Indigenous is not exclusive to the *loa* of *Narciso*. In the *loa* for the allegorical drama *El cetro de José* (*The Scepter of Joseph*), the character of Idolatry, an Indigenous woman, accuses the Christian allegorical characters (Faith, Law of Grace, Natural Law, and Nature) of wreaking havoc and violence on the Americas. "You introduced tyranny, your dominance in my Empires, preaching the Christian law."[88] This statement contains a veiled critique of the unity of the cross and the sword in the Spanish conquest. For Idolatry, evangelism and violence come hand in hand. In addition, Sor Juana also critiques the effectiveness of the religious conquest of the Americas. Idolatry proclaims that though Christians have been able to destroy the symbols (i.e., altars) of Indigenous beliefs, they cannot so easily wipe out the belief system behind them. "Though almost all of my people . . . embrace your Dogmas . . . your strength is not enough, that it can all at once remove the radical relics of my customs."[89] In other words, Sor Juana implies that the "evangelization" of the Indigenous has perhaps only occurred at a superficial level. In both *loa*s Sor Juana presents two levels of the conquest: spiritual and temporal. The physical, or temporal, military arm of the conquest may have been successful, but the outcome of the spiritual conquest is yet to be revealed.

As noted in the *loa* for *Narciso*, Sor Juana had an awareness of some Indigenous practices and beliefs. Her inclusion of these rites, along with African cultural symbols, is yet another way Sor Juana includes marginalized voices. Her *villancicos* offer a literary device for this endeavor. While these poems do not include the kind of systematic analyses one finds in the *loas*, in their use of Indigenous and Black voices Sor Juana creates a space for their experiences and concerns. In addition, as poems sung and performed publicly, they offer a public theology that allowed Sor Juana to share her world view with a broad audience, including the educated elite and the larger population.

In contrast to the dominance of Indigenous concerns in her *loas*, the presence of African voices occurs more frequently than Indigenous voices in Sor Juana's poetry. Marie-Cécile Bénassy-Berling grounds the privileging of Black voices in the Spanish literary tradition of the early seventeenth century. The originality of Sor Juana's thought lies in her valuing and defending Blacks in her writing. This includes, for example, adopting typically African themes in her poetry.[90] In the ninth poem of the 1686 series of *villancicos* written in celebration of Mary's Assumption, Sor Juana includes African dialect as the language of over half the poem. This language can be juxtaposed to the Latin of the earlier poems in the series. By incorporating their voices and even their language, Sor Juana creates a public forum for African concerns.

In addition to African language, this poem even goes so far as to describe Mary as a *"Nenglita beya."* In describing Mary as a beautiful Black woman, this *villancico* is in sharp contrast to the white European theology of the colonial clergy. This is not an isolated incident. In the 1689 *villancicos* on Mary's conception, Mary is described as "Negra, la Esposa." and "Morenica."[91] By providing imagery of Mary as nonwhite, Sor Juana sets a high value on the humanity of those peoples at the very bottom of the social hierarchy of her era. Her 1676 *villancicos* on the Assumption include sections sung by Indigenous and African voices. The Indigenous section is written in Nahuatl, the language of the Aztecs, and includes an Aztec ritual dance as part of the poem's performance.[92] Yet another *villancico* includes Nahuatl and Spanish words interlaced together.[93] It is interesting to note that many instances of her inclusion of African and Indigenous voices occur in her Marian poetry. Also, in her *Ejercicios de la encarnación* Sor Juana encourages her audience to pray the *Magnificat*.[94] One can perhaps find a connection in her work, therefore, between Mary and social justice.

What was the source of Sor Juana's awareness of Indigenous and Black peoples? Noemí Atamores hypothesizes that it was during her childhood years living on her family's hacienda that she came in contact with and learned the languages of Indigenous and African peoples.[95] This is perhaps a piece in the puzzle. Sor Juana would have most likely come in contact with people from various backgrounds growing up on the hacienda. Linking the personal with the intellectual, her friendship with Carlos Sigüenza y Góngora, known for his scholarship on the Indigenous, would also have been a resource. Bénassy-Berling situates Sor Juana in the tradition of Las Casas in her defense of Indigenous people's moral right to practice and defend their religion.[96] Regardless of their origin, the frequency of their inclusion, as well as the more refined arguments presented in her *loas* demonstrate that Sor Juana protested the injustices she saw around her. As Jean Franco notes, "She was uneasy about Black peonage, and her poems written in Nahuatl suggest a respect for Indigenous culture that others certainly did not share."[97] Sor Juana could not protest in a straightforward and outright manner. Such a thing would have made her the object of criticism and ridicule. The conquest was a recent memory in the minds of colonial Mexicans. However, in her own subtle manner, Sor Juana gently revealed her discomfort with some of the practices of her government. Subtlety is perhaps the best word to characterize Sor Juana's writing on marginalized peoples. Her texts dealing with gender were understandably more direct and passionate at times, fueled by her own personal persecution in light of her biological sex. These concerns would spill over into her understandings of truth, knowledge, and rationality. As the following chapter demonstrates, in her theological and philosophical reflections Sor Juana was constantly pushing against the intellectual walls in which her culture, her society, and her Church constantly attempted to enclose her.

Notes

[1]"Hombres necios que acusáis a la mujer sin razón, sin ver que sois la ocasión de lo mismo que culpáis" (OC 1:228.92) (EC).

[2]See Beatriz Melano Couch, "Sor Juana Inés de la Cruz: The First Woman Theologian in the Americas," in *The Church and Women in the Third World*, ed. John C.B. Webster and Ellen Low Webster (Philadelphia: The Westminster Press, 1985), 51-57; George Cruz-Martinez, "Sor Juana Inés de la Cruz: Mother of Latin American Feminist Theology," *Apuntes* 12:2 (Summer 1992): 30-32; Pamela Kirk, "Sor Juana Inés de la Cruz: Precursor of Latin American Feminism," *Journal of Hispanic/Latino Theology* 5:3 (1998): 16-38.

[3]In simplest terms, I understand feminism as a belief in the right to political, social, cultural, intellectual, and economic equality of the sexes, and as the social movements organized around this belief.

[4]José Carlos González Boixo, "Feminismo e intelectualidad en Sor Juana," in *Sor Juana Inés de la Cruz*, ed. Luis Sáinz de Medrano (Rome: Bulzoni Editore, 1997), 34.

[5]Electa Arenal and Amanda Powell, "Preface," in *The Answer/La respuesta*, critical ed. and trans. Electa Arenal and Amanda Powell (New York: The Feminist Press at CUNY, 1994), ix.

[6]Yolanda Martínez-San Miguel, *Saberes Americanos: Subalternidad y epistemología en los escritos de Sor Juana* (Pittsburgh: University of Pittsburgh Press, 1999), 13.

[7]Ibid., 14.

[8]Ibid., 51.

[9]As Stephanie Merrim writes, "Sor Juana militantly defends a woman's right to education and, by implication, participation in the male order. All of this together, added to the example of her own literary life, but substantiates the obvious: that—as is entirely natural in view of the context in which she wrote—rather than asserting or projecting women's 'difference,' both ideologically and literally Sor Juana sought to *negate* their difference, to introject or appropriate the masculine realm for the feminine and to place them on the same continuum. For Sor Juana, to write with the words of the ruling order may well have entailed claiming the woman's equal rights to write in that world." Stephanie Merrim, "Toward a Feminist Reading of Sor Juana Inés de la Cruz: Past, Present, and Future Directions in Sor Juana Criticism," in *Feminist Perspectives on Sor Juana Inés de la Cruz*, ed. Stephanie Merrim (Detroit: Wayne State University Press, 1991), 22-23.

[10]Gustavo Gutiérrez, *Las Casas: In Search of the Poor of Jesus Christ*, trans. Robert R. Barr (Maryknoll, NY: Orbis, 1993), 8.

[11]Jean Franco, *Plotting Women: Gender and Representation in Mexico* (New York: Columbia University Press, 1989), 23.

[12]Stephanie Merrim, *Early Modern Women's Writing and Sor Juana Inés de la Cruz* (Nashville: Vanderbilt University Press, 1999), xiv.

[13]Sor Juana, *The Answer/La respuesta*, 95. OC 4:462.902-904.

[14]Nina Scott, "'La gran turda de las que merecieron nombres': Sor Juana's Foremothers in 'La respuesta a Sor Filotea,'" in *Coded Encounters: Writing, Gender, and Ethnicity in Colonial Latin America*, ed. Francisco Javier Cevallos-Candau et al. (Amherst, MA: University of Massachusetts Press, 1994), 209. Aspasia, while celebrated by Socrates, became the object of criticism by Athenian intellectuals. Hypatia was the Neoplatonic philosopher who was killed by a mob of Christian monks. For full descriptions of the women cited in Sor Juana's essay, see the appendix of Scott's article.

[15]Ibid., 211.

[16]Ibid., 213.

[17]Georgina Sabat de Rivers, *En busca de Sor Juana* (Mexico: UNAM, 1998), 45.

[18]Electa Arenal, "Where Woman Is Creator of the Wor(l)d. Or, Sor Juana's Discourses on Method," in *Feminist Perspectives on Sor Juana Inés de la Cruz*, 128.

[19]Sor Juana, *The Answer/La respuesta*, 47. OC 4:444-445.188-200.

[20]Kathleen A. Myers, "Sor Juana's *respuesta*: Rewriting the *vitae*," *Revista Canadiense de Estudios Hispánicos* XIV: 3 (Spring 1990): 459-469.

[21]Ibid., 463.

[22]Sor Juana, *The Answer/La respuesta*, 51. OC 4:447.283-287.

[23]Ibid., 63. OC 4: 453.522-523.

[24]A recent study contests the authenticity of the *Villancicos a Santa Caterina*. In her book, *Los Villancicos de Sor Juana*, Martha Lilia Tenorio suggests that the complete set of villancicos are perhaps not written by Sor Juana, but instead were written in part by León Marchante. Tenorio finds the directness and explicitness of the *villancicos* problematic. As this is a fairly recent hypothesis, which will undoubtedly open up debate and discussion, it is worthy to note. However, I remain in agreement with the larger community of *sorjuanistas*, who do not (as yet) question these poems' authenticity. Martha Lilia Tenorio, *Los Villancicos de Sor Juana* (Mexico: El Colegio de México, 1999), 141-142.

[25]Pamela Kirk, *Sor Juana Inés de la Cruz: Religion, Art, and Feminism* (New York: Continuum, 1998), 143.

[26]Elías Trabulse, "*La Rosa de Alexandría*: ¿Una querella secreta de Sor Juana?" in *Y diversa de mí misma entre vuestras plumas ando: Homenaje internacional a Sor Juana Inés de la Cruz*," ed. Sara Poot Herrera (Mexico: El Colegio de México, 1993), 209-214.

[27]Sor Juana, *The Answer/La respuesta*, 161. OC 2:171.317.

[28]The reader may note the similarities between Catherine's story and Calleja's account of Sor Juana's intellectual debate with Mexican scholars when she was living in the court.

[29]Ibid., 161. OC 2:171.317.

[30]Ibid., 161-163. OC 2:171.317.

[31]Ibid., 162. OC 2:172.317.

[32]OC 2:6.219.

[33]OC 2:7.220.

[34]Jean Franco, *Plotting Women*, 52.

[35]Jean Kirkpatrick, "The Word and the Woman: Creative Echoing in Sor Juana's *El Divino Narciso*," *Hispanofila* 122 (Jan. 1998): 62-63.

[36]Ibid., 62.

[37]Verónica Grossi, "Political Meta-Allegory in *El Divino Narciso* by Sor Juana Inés de la Cruz," *Intertexts* 1:1 (Spring 1997): 97.

[38]Kirkpatrick, "The Word and the Woman," 63.

[39]Ibid., 66.

[40]Merrim, "*Narciso Desdoblado*: Narcissistic Stratagems in *El Divino Narciso* and the *Respuesta a Sor Filotea de la Cruz*," *Bulletin of Hispanic Studies* 64:2 (April 1987): 113-114.

[41]Sor Juana, *The Answer/La respuesta*, 139. OC 4:440.12,14. It is interesting to note that this is one of the places where Sor Juana uses the word "*borrones*" to describe her texts, the same word used to describe Echo's clouding of the waters in *El Divino Narciso*.

[42]Ibid., 41 and 83. OC 4:441.36-37; 4:463-464.977-978.

[43]For an excellent study of the role of humility in Teresa's *Life*, see Alison Weber, *Teresa of Avila and the Rhetoric of Femininity* (Princeton, NJ: Princeton University Press, 1990). On this rhetorical practice in Hildegard of Bingen see Rosemary Radford Ruether, *Women and Redemption: A Theological History* (Minneapolis: Fortress Press, 1998), 81-92.

[44]Stephanie Merrim, *Early Modern Women's Writing and Sor Juana Inés de la Cruz* (Nashville: Vanderbilt University Press, 1999), 169.

[45]OC 2:222-223.359.

[46]Kirk, *Sor Juana Inés de la Cruz*, 59-60.

[47]This is seen, for example, in the writing of Julian of Norwich.

[48]Kirk, *Sor Juana Inés de la Cruz*, 65.

[49]Franco, *Plotting Women*, 29.

[50]Augustine, *The Trinity*, trans. Edmund Hill, O.P. (New York: New City Press, 1991); *The Literal Meaning of Genesis*, 2 vols., trans. John Hammond Taylor, S.J. (New York: Paulist Press, 1982).

[51]Sister Prudence Allen, R.S.M. *The Concept of Woman: The Aristotelian Revolution, 750 B.C.-A.D. 1250* (Grand Rapids: William B. Eerdmans Publishing Co., 1985), 222.

[52]Ibid., 225.

[53]Ibid., 385.

[54]Kari Elisabeth Børresen, *Subordination and Equivalence: The Nature and Role of Woman in Augustine and Thomas Aquinas* (Washington, DC: University Press of America, 1981; reprint, Kampen: Kok Pharos Publishing House, 1995).

[55]See Elizabeth A. Johnson, "Mary as Mediatrix," in *The One Mediator,*

the Saints, and Mary: Lutherans and Catholics in Dialogue VII, ed. H. George Anderson et al. (Minneapolis: Augsburg Fortress, 1992), 311-326.

[56]George Tavard, Juana Inés de la Cruz and the Theology of Beauty: The First Mexican Theology (Notre Dame, IN: University of Notre Dame Press, 1991), 99.

[57]Sor Juana Inés de la Cruz, A Sor Juana Anthology, trans. Alan S. Trueblood (Cambridge, MA: Harvard University Press, 1988), 31. OC 1:138.48.

[58]Ibid., 31. OC 1:138.48.

[59]Tavard, Juana Inés de la Cruz, 185-186.

[60]The Answer/La respuesta, 157. OC 1:228.92.

[61]Ibid., 157. OC 1:228.92.

[62]Ibid., 157. OC 1:228.92.

[63]Ibid., 159. OC 1:229.92.

[64]Ibid., 159. OC 1:229.92.

[65]Ibid., 159. OC 1:229.92.

[66]Marie-Cécile Bénassy-Berling, Humanisme et religion chez Sor Juana Inés de la Cruz: La femme et la culture au XVIIe siècle (Paris: Éditions Hispaniques, 1982), 277.

[67]Merrim, Early Modern Women's Writing and Sor Juana Inés de la Cruz, 66.

[68]The Answer/La respuesta, 81. OC 4:462-463.933-936, 939-940.

[69]Ibid., 87. OC 4:466.1062-1067.

[70]Ibid., 91. OC 4:467.1133-1137.

[71]Georgina Sabat de Rivers, "A Feminist Rereading of Sor Juana's Dream," in Feminist Perspectives on Sor Juana Inés de la Cruz, 144-145.

[72]"The importance of Sor Juana is that she defended the rationality of women and was able to do so because the slippage between her devalued status as a woman and her empowerment by writing led her to understand gender difference as social construction, and interpretation as a rationalization of male interests." Franco, Plotting Women, xv.

[73]Stephanie Merrim, "Mores Geometricae: The "Womanscript' in the Theater of Sor Juana Inés de la Cruz," in Feminist Perspectives on Sor Juana Inés de la Cruz, 95.

[74]Octavio Paz, Sor Juana: Or, The Traps of Faith, trans. Margaret Sayers Peden (Cambridge, MA: Harvard University Press, 1988), 513.

[75]OC 3:5.59-68.

[76]OC 3:8-9.141-146.

[77]OC 3:11.210-217.

[78]OC 3:14.302-307.

[79]OC 3:16.356-369.

[80]OC 3:17.384-387.

[81]Kirk, Sor Juana Inés de la Cruz, 50.

[82]Paz, Sor Juana, 346.

[83]Pamela Kirk, "Christ as Divine Narcissus: A Theological Analysis of 'El Divino Narciso' by Sor Juana Inés de la Cruz," *Word & World* XII:2 (Spring 1998): 153.

[84]Carmela Zanelli, "La loa de 'El Divino Narciso' de Sor Juana Inés de la Cruz y la doble recuperación de la cultura indígena mexicana," in *La literatura novohispana: Revisión crítica y propuestas metodológicas*, ed. José Pascual Buxó and Arnulfo Herrera (Mexico: UNAM, 1994), 190.

[85]Margo Glantz, *Sor Juana Inés de la Cruz: ¿Hagiografía o autobiografía?* (Mexico: UNAM, 1995), 164.

[86]Gutiérrez, *Las Casas*, 18.

[87]Ibid., 154.

[88]OC 3:192.238-241.

[89]OC 3:193.247-255.

[90]Bénassy-Berling, *Humanisme et religion*, 298-299.

[91]OC 3:105.281.

[92]OC 2:14-17.224.

[93]OC 2:39-42.241.

[94]Kirk, *Sor Juana Inés de la Cruz*, 71

[95]Noemí Atamoros, *Sor Juana Inés de la Cruz* (Toluca, Estado de México: Instituto Mexiquense de Cultura, 1995), 18.

[96]Bénassy-Berling, *Humanisme et religion*, 328.

[97]Franco, *Plotting Women*, 51.

Chapter 5

The True

"If Aristotle had been able to cook, he would have written a great deal more."[1]

—Sor Juana Inés de la Cruz

Attempting to gather an author's statements concerning what she considers to be true or views as Truth, and finding a way to discern that Truth is a daunting task when one is dealing with an author as unsystematic as Sor Juana. In some instances, Sor Juana's writing on this matter seems to fit more appropriately under the modern-day heading of philosophy than of theology. However, such distinctions did not apply for our seventeenth-century nun. For Sor Juana, philosophy and theology were intertwined. This was perhaps not only due to the nature of her era, but also because philosophy, while still a male terrain, was the "safer" route of reflection. As a woman, her philosophical claims, at times vague and contradictory, were not as controversial as any sort of direct theological inferences. It was one thing to trespass into the academy, quite another to intrude on the pulpit.

In her theological and philosophical texts Sor Juana set herself apart from other women religious writing in seventeenth-century Mexico. Far from expounding mysticism, Sor Juana's writing was carefully researched and studied, in conversation with the academic questions and concerns of her contemporaries. For example, Sor Juana wrote a work on logic that is lost today. The writing of such a treatise, which was in Latin, was an anomaly for a woman.

However, while engaging the "canon," Sor Juana simultaneously challenged and expanded the reigning understanding of the sources and norms of theological and philosophical reflection. This was seen, for example, in her intellectual eclecticism that broadened the pre-existing sources of normative discourse. In a lengthy quote, Mauricio Beuchot reminds us of the contours of Sor Juana's intellectual climate:

The main current of Mexican colonial philosophy was Scholasticism. A strong current of Renaissance humanism was present in sixteenth-century Mexican thought, sometimes in its pure form, sometimes in a mix of Scholastic humanism. . . . In the seventeenth century, one notes the presence of hermeticism, above all in the work of the Jesuit Atanasio Kircher. The society of Jesus practiced quite effectively a certain syncretism that created a favorable atmosphere for the mestizaje and the Baroque. In this way, in addition to a type of humanist Scholasticism, there was also a baroque Scholasticism, with touches of hermeticism and other currents of the period, and even some pure hermeticism (if one can speak of such a thing).[2]

Modern philosophy arrived at the end of the seventeenth century but did not flourish until the latter half of the eighteenth century. In her incorporation of daily life and American concerns, as well as her reaction to the gender-coded discourse that constrained her, Sor Juana both challenged and affirmed the assumptions operating in her time.

This chapter offers an organized presentation of Sor Juana's unsystematic writing on Truth and epistemology. In approaching this chapter, as well as chapters 3 and 4, I am reminded of Jesús García Alvarez's comment, "It is useless to search for a system in Sor Juana's thought. One can make a synthesis of her ideas and try to discover the visions she had of the world; no more."[3] In the spirit of his remarks, and in a vein similar to my previous chapters, I have chosen to organize this chapter thematically. My comments will be gathered under the following headings: daily life; the universal nature of truth; knowledge as contextual; the role of theology; the use of myth, metaphor, and allegory; lo americano;

and epistemology. Due to the significance of these works in light of Sor Juana's understanding of Truth, I will be drawing substantially from *The Answer* and the poem *First Dream*. Discussion of these works will be supplemented by insights drawn from other sections of her corpus.

Daily Life

Cloistered for most of her adult life, Sor Juana did not have much outside of her books and her visitors in the locutory as conversation partners and intellectual peers. The loneliness she must have felt is clear when she writes, "My only teacher was a mute book, my only schoolfellow an unfeeling inkwell."[4] Despite these hindrances, Sor Juana's passion for learning fueled the continuation of her studies. "I persevered in my studious task . . . of reading and more reading, of study and more study, with no other teacher than the books themselves. How hard it is to study those soulless characters, without the living voice and explanation of a teacher; yet I endured all that labor most gladly for the love of learning."[5] Almost entirely self-taught, the limitations of Sor Juana's life also created the freedom for her to explore and engage non-traditional sources for her musings.

The books lining the shelves of Sor Juana's library were her companions. Thus, we cannot imagine her dismay when we learn, about halfway through *The Answer*, of a time when the Inquisition forbids her from reading for three months. She does not explain why this occurred, only blaming the prohibition on the initiative of her mother superior.[6] The most likely explanation, however, was that the nature of her reading caught the attention of Church authorities. While preventing her study of texts, the prohibition was not capable of ensnaring Sor Juana's mind. As she writes, "I obeyed her (for the three months or so that her authority over us lasted) in that I did not pick up a book. But with regard to avoiding study absolutely, as such a thing does not lie within my power, I could not do it. For although I did not study in books, I studied all the things that God created, taking them for my letters, and for my book all intricate structures of this world."[7] In this passage we find two important details. First, Sor Juana again emphasizes that her intellect emerges from a force beyond her. She is unable to control it. This resonates with the theme explored in chapter 4 regarding Sor Juana's presentation of her intellect as a gift from God, a source of both joy and torment. Throughout this passage of *The Answer* Sor Juana describes her intellect as a "madness," even an "annoyance," something out of her control, which is even "tiring." However, she wavers in her depiction of her intellect as gift when she writes, "This trait, whether a matter of nature or custom, is such that nothing do I see without a second thought."[8] Sor Juana introduces the possibility that her intellectual passion is partly her own doing, due to her own cultivation of it.

Second, and more important to this chapter, is Sor Juana's expansion of her intellectual sources due to her punishment. For Sor Juana, all of God's creation was a suitable object of study, down to the minutest creature, for it revealed God's greatness and glory. What, then, did Sor Juana study? She observed the world around her, within the convent. She studied daily life. The next few pages of *The Answer* continue with an account of the objects of her scrutiny during that three-month period. The very people she encounters become a source of inspiration, "Whence could spring this diversity of character and intelligence among individuals all composing one single species?"[9] Here we return to the theme of the One and the Many. How, Sor Juana ponders, can one humanity contain such diversity? The premise that daily life can be a source for philosophical and theological reflection transforms the nature of these disciplines. As Jean Franco observes, "For when Sor Juana argues that she can pursue learning without books, she is by no means praising the mystics who abhorred practical life, but rather showing that the experiences that are supposedly feminine can enlarge the field of learning. In the struggle for interpretive power, women are forced to bring practical life into the realm of knowledge."[10]

Sor Juana utilized experiments as a means of learning. This experimentation perhaps contributed to her silencing. Irving A. Leonard argues that Sor Juana's use of observation and scientific experimentation reveals her suspicions concerning the Scholasticism of her era. He also posits that it is this hesitancy, in part, concerning Scholasticism that caught the attention of ecclesial authorities.[11] Her study of the architecture of the dormitories led to lessons on geometry. Noting that visual perspective does not always produce a geometrically accurate depiction of the planes where walls and ceiling meet, Sor Juana wondered if these "delusions of the eye" led to the incorrect assumption that the world was flat. In this passage, Sor Juana is implicitly expressing that human experience can mold and shape reality. In other words, human truth claims are subject to human limitations and error.

The pleasure of watching two girls spinning a top was interrupted by "this madness of mine," and Sor Juana turned the exercise into a scientific experiment with flour to see whether the top moved in circle or spirals. This led to her experiments in the kitchen. Cooking with eggs, she found, led to a wealth of knowledge. On these culinary experiments she writes, "What can women know if not philosophies of the kitchen?"[12] With this question, Sor Juana is sarcastically challenging the caricature which represents activities gender-coded as women's as somehow thoughtless and lacking in intellectual value. In the context of Sor Juana's describing the knowledge she gleaned from the kitchen, this question has almost a mocking tone. This comment is closely followed by perhaps the most delightful statement in Sor Juana's corpus, "If Aristotle had been able to cook, he would have written a great deal more."[13] Sor Juana expresses her subtle humor when she wonders if Aristotle's philosophy would not have benefitted from the "women's work" of cooking. Common experience becomes a source of philosophical reflection. Within this statement is a veiled critique of traditional understandings of the subjects and sources of philosophy, as well as an argument for the domain of the private as worthy of philosophical speculation.

What is the significance of these anecdotes Sor Juana shares about her daily life? Through her experimentation Sor Juana explored alternative sources of knowledge, especially in the sphere traditionally attributed to women, and thus not considered a source of wisdom. As Josefina Ludmer explains by equating the knowledge acquired in the private women's sphere to that of the great philosophers and theologians she read extensively, Sor Juana constitutes the woman's private arena as a space for rational reflection. While not offering a systematic critique of women's place in society, Sor Juana transforms the very significance and meaning of that place.[14] Ludmer writes:

Those regional spaces that the dominant culture has extracted from the realms of the daily and the personal and has constituted as separate fields (politics, science, philosophy) exist for women precisely in the realm of the personal and are indissociable from it. And if the personal, the private, the quotidian are included as points of departure and perspectives in other discourses and practices, they cease to be merely personal, private, and quotidian.[15]

Sor Juana transformed the discourse of philosophy through her philosophical reflection. Far from imitating the work of male contemporaries and historical voices, Sor Juana transcended these voices. As Veronica Grossi indicates, "Sor Juana's rhetorical piece *Respuesta a Sor Filotea* also establishes a clear semantic link between feminine writing, knowledge, and transgression. Writing and the acquisition of knowledge are subversively associated with the conventional feminine domestic activities of cooking, weaving, and gossiping."[16] Sor Juana inserted the private sphere of the feminine into the public sphere of philosophical discourse. In addition, as the sphere that is restricted to the feminine, the privacy of daily life is a wellspring of philosophical insight from which men are excluded.

Truth as Universal

Emerging from these sources is an understanding of truth which is universal, in an almost Neoplatonic sense, existing behind the various contextualized expressions in which it is manifest. For Sor Juana, Truth, though perhaps inaccessible in its entirety to the human intellect, existed. However, as the following section will demonstrate, Sor Juana attempted to maintain an understanding of universal truth in tension with her emphasis on its historical, human construction. Sor Juana's musings on truth are found prominently in her opus, the lengthy and complicated poem *First Dream*. Her thoughts on truth also surface in her construction of allegorical characters in her poetry and plays, and the manner in which they are able to translate their messages into various contexts.

First Dream is a *silva* (a poem with no fixed rhythm), with nine hundred seventy-five verses. The title in the original Spanish is complex, though this is not obvious for the English reader. The Spanish word *sueño* has multiple meanings: sleep, dream, vision. Therefore, the translation of *sueño* to the English dream limits the meaning of the title. In addition, though the title includes the word "First," Sor Juana never wrote a second dream. Whether she ever intended to write a "second" or "third" dream is unknown to us today. The poem is an account of a soul, freed from bodily restraints, on a quest for divine knowledge. Without exploring the intricacies of Sor Juana scholarship surrounding the division of the poem, I agree with those scholars who categorize the poem into three blocks: the arrival of sleep and night; the intellectual voyage of the night world; and the arrival of day awakening.[17] The poem is symbolic of the many nights Sor Juana spent researching and writing. The soul of the poem is impersonal, with no gender. This reinforces Sor Juana's view of the soul as genderless, as explored in chapter 4.

Numerous *sorjuanistas* have speculated on the meaning of the poem, whose dense and opaque language and imagery make it difficult to interpret. The poem contains hermetic elements, as well as Platonic thought and Aristotelian categories. Jean Franco eloquently summarizes the poem when she writes:

> The *Primero sueño* is usually read as the flight of this soul that has been released from its bodily impediments by sleep, its attempt to attain absolute knowledge of the world through intuitive panoptic ("Platonic") vision, and, when this fails, its attempt to attain the same end by orderly progression through the Aristotelian categories. The second search is halted because the soul cannot understand the simplest phenomenon of nature although its will to knowledge persists. With daylight and the awakening of the self, the shadowy inner world of disembodied fantasy dissolves in the "more certain" light of day.[18]

The soul, liberated from the body, embarks on a shadowy quest to find the clarity of Truth. The poem thus embraces the distinctiveness of the body and soul. The soul is depicted as trapped in the body. This results in a harsh polarity between the soul and the body. While this dualism has existed throughout the history of Christian thought, and even predates it, Sor Juana poses it in a sharp and radical manner. Why would Sor Juana attempt to downplay the importance of the body? This could be, in part, based on the very limitations placed upon Sor Juana's life because of her (female) body. Denying the link between soul and body also reinforced her notion of the soul as genderless.

In addition to the soul-body dualism, another dimension of the poem that continues to engage scholars is its very nature. Is *First Dream* a philosophical or religious poem? Is it about a spiritual journey? Octavio Paz posits the poem as not only irreligious, but arguing against religion. He writes, "The poem is the account of a spiritual vision that ends in nonvision."[19] In other words, the dissatisfaction of the awakened soul at the end of the poem, unable to attain the Truth she so desires, is an argument against the presence of revelation. Paz continues, "The theme of the voyage of the soul is a religious theme and is inseparable from revelation. In Sor Juana's poem not only is there no demiurge, there is no revelation. . . . It denies revelation. More precisely, it is the revelation of the fact that we are alone and that the world of the supernatural has dissipated."[20] In the poem Sor Juana does not speak of God, but instead of a Supreme Being. In describing the Soul, she does not refer to it as created, but instead as a "spark of divine fire," demonstrating the influences of hermeticism and Neoplatonism. The hermetic and Neoplatonic strands intersect with Scholastic influences in Sor Juana's understanding of the human as microcosmos. "Man is, in sum, the greatest marvel posed to human comprehension, a synthesis composed of qualities of angel, plant, and beast, whose elevated baseness shows traits of each of these."[21] Another Scholastic hallmark of Sor Juana's work is her understanding of metaphysics as aiding in the human quest for knowledge.

While affirming the interpretation of *First Dream* as a poem that is not mystical in the traditional sense, I disagree with Paz's assertion that this leads to an interpretation of the poem as antireligious. The soul in *First Dream* does not want mystical union with God; instead, it wants to contemplate the First Cause. However, mystical union with God is not the sole avenue for expressing religious faith. The subject of the poem, the soul, is described as "immaterial," with a "lovely essence." It is also, as mentioned above, a result of the divine spark. However, Sor Juana also uses the language of the soul as created in the image of the divine: "all her immaterial being and lovely essence contemplated, communicant of the highest being, that spark, so like herself."[22] This signals a theological anthropology in which the immaterial soul of the *Dream* participates in her likeness to Good through her intellectual contemplation of God.

The poem is, in essence, an account of humanity's limitations and thus its inability to fully contemplate the divine. The last line of the poem is, "the World illuminated, and me awake."[23] Contemporary scholars place great emphasis on this last line, for it contains two key elements of the poem. First, the "I" of the poem is revealed as a woman, given the feminine ending to the adjective awake in the original Spanish. Thus, scholars conclude, the "I" of the poem was Sor Juana herself. This gendering also signals the return of the soul to the body. The soul, no longer neuter, is awake and trapped in its feminine body. Second, this line is major in that the awakening of the soul signifies the failure of the *sueño*. The soul, unable to achieve ultimate knowledge, is awakened, instead. For Paz, this is the foundation of his interpretation of the non-revelation of the dream. But is this the case? Did revelation not occur, or was Sor Juana's soul merely unable to grasp it in its entirety? Created in the image of God, the human being reflects God, but is not God. Therefore, divine Truth is accessible, yet only in a fragmentary way. The failure of the soul to attain this Truth does not challenge its existence. The theme of human arrogance, especially, regarding intellectual pursuits is a recurrent theme in Sor Juana's corpus, seen when she writes, "Learning is one more vice. Unless deterred, its ambition, when the ambitious least expect, will lead them straight to perdition."[24] *First Dream* can be interpreted as embodying Sor Juana's own struggles with the arrogance accompanying her success as a thinker and author.

While *First Dream* recounts the failure of the soul's attempt to contemplate this world, Sor Juana still holds that certain human constructions are able to capture the broader essences of universal concepts. This is seen prominently in her dramas, where characters such as "Faith," "Music," and "Human Nature," for example, inhabit the pages of her writing as individuals that embody these broader concepts. Human constructions are able to capture some essence of Truth, though not in its entirety. This is perhaps best seen in the closing section of the *loa* for *El Divino Narciso*. In the last scene of the *loa* the character of Zeal asks Religion how it is possible that something written in Mexico will be performed in Madrid. Religion answers with a question: "Have you never seen something that is made in one place to serve in another?"[25] The character then continues by noting that because the characters are abstractions they are easily transported to Spain. In other words, Sor Juana contends, it is possible to abstract from essences universal characteristics that can be embodied in allegorical constructions. However, these symbolic representations never fully embody the essences they claim to contain.

Knowledge as Contextual

The various places in Sor Juana's corpus where she appears to argue for the contextuality of all human knowing are scattered. They are also in a sense contradictory to the above claims of her belief in universal Truth and her use of allegory as representative of broader universal concepts. However, in a sense these passages where one finds an argument for the contextual can perhaps be viewed as sites where Sor Juana is arguing in a defensive mode for her own right to intellectual writing and study. In other words, as a means of undermining the gender codes of her era Sor Juana presents the limitations of human abilities to access and construct truth claims concerning the world around them.

In the first of her *romances* classified by modern editor Alfonso Méndez Plancarte as philosophical, Sor Juana explores the inability of philosophers to establish authentic truth claims. "The world is full of opinions of what is or is not true; whatever is black for one will be white in another's view. What one man finds attractive will make another recoil; while what brings one man relief, another rejects as toil."[26] Knowledge is reduced to a matter of taste or opinion. One can have, Sor Juana notes, contesting opinions about a matter, in fact opposite ones, and still both opinions may be entirely wrong. Of Democritus and Heraclitus she writes, "Those two old thinkers of Greece were always of opposite cheer: what split the one with laughter reduced the other to tears. The centuries since their time have echoed their difference of view, but no one can ever decide which opinion is false, which is true."[27] The two philosophers are presented as having opposing views and the inability to discern which of the two understands Truth demonstrates the sheer powerlessness of humans when posed with questions of ultimate value.

Even the very act of human reasoning was subject to Sor Juana's critique. Reason, for Sor Juana, was political. "Reason, just like a sword, can be wielded at either end: the blade, to wound to the death; the hilt, to provide defense."[28] In other words, reason can be manipulated to serve whatever purpose it desires. Humans are able to mold their limited view of reality in order to justify their own needs and causes. This comment, linked with the verses above, demonstrates Sor Juana's skepticism regarding questions of ultimate value. Reason is simply used to rationalize and justify actions.

The political motivations underlying rational constructions are also found in two pieces studied in chapter 4: The poem "Hombres necios" and *The Answer*. The poem contains Sor Juana's argument regarding the social construction of gender and the way gender functions politically to subject women to the desire and fancy of men. Through her emphasis on gender as a construction, Sor Juana challenges the caricature of women as in any way normative. This normativity is merely based on the political power of the men who are able to control the discourse of the academy and society. The poem describes ways in which men exploit and demean women, demonstrating the weak foundation upon which the image of woman as a temptress, a seductress, and inferior to man is built. Through her inversion of negative attributes traditionally associated with women, Sor Juana creates her own gender construction where men become the objects of the female gaze. This gesture reinforces her argument and also, in a broader sense, demonstrates the fragility of all human interpretations of the world around us.

In a similar vein, Sor Juana emphasizes the role of context on human rationality in her refutation of the broad application of the Pauline maxim silencing women in churches. Sor Juana argues for an interpretation of scripture that takes its culture and context under serious consideration. She holds that the text is wedded to its context, and cannot be ahistorically removed from it. Her explanation of Paul's statement is that "Furthermore, that prohibition applied to the case related by Eusebius: in the early Church, women were set to teaching each other Christian doctrine in the temples. The murmur of their voices caused confusion when the apostles were preaching, and this is why they were told to be silent."[29] Sor Juana attempts to undermine the ahistorical authority of the Pauline maxim in order to argue for her own right to study and write. Following this statement she proceeds into a long litany of instances where she holds that study of culture and history will illuminate the true meaning of biblical passages. "Do not many passages by the Apostle [Paul] on the aid and comfort of widows refer to the customs of his times?"[30] Again, the purpose of Sor Juana's example is to demonstrate that biblical texts are limited by their historical context and cannot be decontextualized as abstract maxims that are authoritative throughout the ages.

The Role of Theology in Her Corpus

The flexibility Sor Juana favors regarding the interpretation of scripture is curiously juxtaposed with the high reverence she holds for the discipline of theology. In *The Answer* she even writes of her unworthiness regarding the ability to reflect theologically, "My having written little on sacred matters has sprung from no dislike, nor from lack of application, but rather from a surfeit of awe and reverence toward those sacred letters, which I know myself to be so incapable of understanding and which I am so unworthy of handling. . . . How should I dare to take these up in my unworthy hands, when sex, and age, and above all our customs oppose it?"[31] Displaying a sense of humility that is characteristic of this letter, Sor Juana expresses her unworthiness before the theological task.

In the autobiographical section of *The Answer*, Sor Juana says that the ultimate goal of all of her studies was the study of theology. "Being a Catholic, I thought it an abject failing not to know everything concerning the divine mysteries that can be achieved in this lifetime through earthly methods."[32] This statement, defending her pursuit of both secular and sacred letters, contains a weighty message concerning the limits of human reason regarding matters of the divine. Sor Juana emphasizes the limitations that will hinder all human quests for ultimate truth. In addition, by limiting her scholarship to "earthly methods," Sor Juana leaves open the door for other means of informing humanity's knowledge of God, such as faith.

One must recall the irony of *The Answer*. Though Sor Juana is responding to a letter from a bishop in which he chastises her for her pursuit of secular letters, the censure had come in response to her *Carta atenagórica*, the example of Sor Juana's writing which most mirrors the male theological voice. Sor Juana is therefore being chastised for writing theology. She is encouraged to write in a manner more suitable for a woman religious, to imitate Teresa of Avila in her style and topics.[33] In fact, both her secular and sacred texts appear to have angered Church authorities. Her secular writing appears to have infuriated her confessor, Antonio Nuñéz de Miranda. In the recently discovered and authenticated letter that reveals Sor Juana's dismissal of her confessor, Sor Juana defines his anger toward her as stemming from her secular verses. "The basis, then, for the anger of Y.R. (most beloved Father and dear sir) has been none other than those miserable verses granted me."[34] This statement is followed by a litany of justifications for the various public texts Sor Juana produced over the years. The letter implies that Nuñéz de Miranda disapproved of these texts and was publicly critical of Sor Juana's authorship. Interestingly, Sor Juana describes an aversion to her non-religious texts: "there was the natural repugnance I have always felt in writing them, as all those who know me can attest."[35] As a result of this, as well as other factors, Sor Juana dismisses this powerful Jesuit as her confessor. Sor Juana therefore existed in the paradox of being criticized for both her secular pursuits and her theological writing. Church authorities sought to control the style and content of her elaborations. Essentially, they wanted her writing to mirror the spiritual and mystical writing of other women religious. Theology remained inappropriate territory for Sor Juana's pen. However, playing along with the baroque banter of her era, in *The Answer* Sor Juana attempts to justify and legitimize her pursuit of worldly letters while simultaneously pleading a case for theology.

Sor Juana begins the defense of her writing by evoking the parentage of her order and convent, Saints Jerome and Paula. She must study, she argues, as the "daughter" of these two great minds, "for it would be a degeneracy for an idiot daughter to proceed from such learned parents."[36] She admits, however, that this may have been one of her ways to encourage her "inclination." While conceding that she is in part self-motivated in her studies, Sor Juana holds steady in using language that implies that this is something natural to her being. Her studies, she argues, were always geared to "the summit of Holy Theology; but it seemed to me necessary to ascend by the ladder of the humane arts and sciences in order to reach it."[37] Theology is the queen of sciences, the ultimate subject of the human intellect. Sor Juana places theology above all other forms of study. At the same time, other disciplines are tools that one can use when one finally reaches the zenith of theological studies. Though limited, they still aid in understanding the theological task. "For who could fathom the style of the Queen of Sciences without knowing that of her handmaidens?"[38] In a style reminiscent of today's arguments in support of interdisciplinary studies, Sor Juana proceeds to demonstrate the need for logic, rhetoric, physics, geometry, architecture, history, and music, among other subjects, within the theological task.

These disciplines, while helpful, are not sufficient for the study of theology. "And once each science is mastered (which we see is not easy, even possible), She demands still another condition beyond all I have yet said, which is continual prayer and purity of life, to entreat God for that cleansing of the spirit and illumination of the mind required for an understanding of such high things. And if this be lacking, all the rest is useless."[39] This statement is often overlooked by *sorjuanistas* who downplay Sor Juana's sense of vocation or Christian commitment. For while she does not say it explicitly, Sor Juana is arguing here for the importance of faith in the theological task. As Anselm noted, theology is "faith seeking understanding." Without faith, theology is useless. The secular sciences can only take you so far. In the end, they will never lead you to ultimate Truth. The soul in *First Dream* which sought to attain that Truth without the light of faith, failed miserably in its arrogance. Echoing the theology of Thomas Aquinas, Sor Juana holds that the gift of faith perfects human knowledge. Without it, one can never approach the Queen of Sciences.

Sor Juana proceeds by citing the words of Aquinas, who once wrote of the need for prayer and the divine gift of knowledge that came from a force that was not his own. Shifting into the rhetoric of humility, Sor Juana asks, "How then should I, so far from either virtue or learning, find the courage to write?"[40] While Sor Juana employs the feminine code of humility, she still poses the question in light of male theological discourse. She continues, apologetically, elaborating on the eclecticism and superficiality of her self-taught education. Unlike the desire she had to write theology, she describes her pursuit of secular letters as haphazard, "having no inclination toward any one of them in particular." Instead, topics were chosen based on the availability of books, not her own desire. Sor Juana underscores the interconnectedness of all topics, and their common link as proceeding from God. In a statement that rings of Neoplatonism she writes, "All things proceed from God, who is at once center and circumference, whence all lines are begotten and where they have their end."[41] This rationale is used to justify, in yet another way, her secular studies.

Myth, Metaphor, and Allegory

Linked to her understanding of the secular and informing the sacred letters of theology is the role of the symbolic in Sor Juana's writing. The use of myth, metaphor, and allegory as avenues of theological and philosophical reflection is one of the great hallmarks of her corpus. Underlying this methodological gesture is, as Jesús García Alvarez highlights, a critique of the ability of reason to adequately express Truth. "The use of novels and theater as philosophical expressions responds to this conviction: the essence of life and of the world cannot be captured or expressed through pure reason."[42] The aesthetic form of Sor Juana's writing has methodological implications for what is deemed the most appropriate means of theological expression. For Sor Juana, the world of myth, metaphor, allegory, and symbol are the most appropriate avenues for theology, revealing as they conceal the mysteries of God. Mythology and symbol permeate Sor Juana's corpus, in her dramas, poetry, and prose.

In the *loa* of *El Divino Narciso*, the figure of Religion presents Sor Juana's argument for the privileged place of the symbolic in her corpus through the justification of the *auto* as the most appropriate means of evangelizing the Indigenous characters. The character of Religion describes the *auto* as "a metaphoric idea, dressed in rhetorical colors," and its effectiveness is ascribed to the fact that "you are inclined towards visible objects, by which faith whispers in your ear: and so you are best served through your eyes, for through them you will receive faith."[43] The symbolic becomes the privileged means for the reception of the mysteries of faith. The verbal and the visual are the privileged avenues of theological expression. Dramatic and symbolic performance is privileged over rational exposition. One might assume that this was a remark geared toward the Indigenous characters in the *loa*. However, the reader must remember that the intended audience of the play was the elite of Madrid. Therefore, it is their eyes and ears that benefit from the allegorical drama.

Also in the play, the use of the myth of Narcissus demonstrates Sor Juana's belief that myth can provide both theological insight and a thematic paradigm for Christian expression. Sor Juana explicitly chooses myth as a means of explaining the story of Jesus Christ's passion, death, and resurrection, as well as the establishment of the Eucharist. The same preferential role is given to mythology in Sor Juana's poetry—*First Dream* comes to mind—and in her texts written for public events. In *First Dream*, Sor Juana creates a pantheon of mythological women to support women's intellectual pursuits. These women accompany her in the same manner as the flesh and blood women of Christian history cited in *The Answer*. In terms of her more public writing, which was not only published but performed, *Neptuno alegórico* (*The Allegorical Neptune*) stands as a strong example of the privileged position of myth in her writing. This was Sor Juana's first significant commission. Her task was to write an allegory that was to accompany the arch built to welcome the newest viceroy to Mexico. The arch itself was to mirror the content of the allegory through the images painted upon it. Sor Juana's good friend, Carlos Sigüenza y Góngora, was commissioned to create a second arch and allegory. In contrast to Sigüenza y Góngora, who used Aztec imagery in his allegory, Sor Juana resorted to traditional Greco-Roman mythology. The longest of Sor Juana's texts, this piece demonstrates in a very public way the privileged place of mythology in Sor Juana's body of work.

Mythic figures saturate Sor Juana's corpus. Through her use of myth Sor Juana blurs the lines between imagination and reality, creating a space similar to the *sueño* that her soul experienced in that ill-fated quest for absolute knowledge. Her use of myth, allegory, and metaphor underlie the centrality of aesthetics in Sor Juana's corpus. The aesthetic becomes the privileged expression of theology and philosophy. "Philosophy for her [Sor Juana] was not simply a rational explanation of things: it was an experience that could be communicated only through symbols and images."[44] The limitations of human language require the use of the symbolic as a means of accessing those topics of ultimate concern. The heavy use of mythology in *First Dream*, which Sor Juana claims is the only poem she wrote by her own volition, demonstrates the significance of myth as an avenue to the opening of epistemological horizons for human understanding. Poetry, however, like every form of human expression, has its limits. "What is it to see all the tired metaphors that have overtaken the Muses? There is no science, art, or profession, that with strange vice the poets, with vain subtlety, have accommodated to beauty; and thinking that they paint the heavens, they make altarpieces of their sufferings."[45] Like every human endeavor, poetry is open to the same human arrogance that can corrupt its ability to speak of Beauty.

Mauricio Beuchot argues that Sor Juana's philosophical and theological ideas gain a particular energy in the accessibility to a broader audience as a result of their "literary clothing." As stated in chapter 3, this does not happen at the expense of the ideas themselves.[46] The unity of Scholasticism and verse is found in the *loa* to the allegorical drama *El mártir del sacramento, San Hermenegildo*. The *loa* consists of a debate among students, written in verse, that mirrors the method of Scholastic disputations. The inclusion of poetry as a form of theological expression is, in part, due to Sor Juana's baroque sensibilities. Also, with her belief in the interconnectedness of all knowledge at the service of theology and her confessed talent for writing in verse, it is not surprising that Sor Juana preferred symbolic language. Reinforcing many of the ideas of chapter 3, the privileged position of aesthetic form in Sor Juana's theology demonstrates the privileged position held by Beauty in her corpus, and her belief in the aesthetic as the most appropriate means of theological expression.

Lo Americano

Sor Juana was just as much a child of the Baroque as of the colonial context in which she lived and wrote. A growing area of research among contemporary *sorjuanistas* is an appreciation of her work as expressive of an American consciousness that is distinct both from Europe and from the Indigenous populations. As Magdalena Galindo emphasizes, this privileged place is due to the historical moment in which Sor Juana was alive and writing in the Americas as well as to her own personal story.[47] The *criollo* population of New Spain was beginning to grow, as was their sense of entitlement as they emerged from the secondary status they'd had compared to the ruling European-born elite. The marginalization of these people, who were full-blooded Spanish, demonstrates the importance of place in defining one's identity in colonial Mexican culture. These factors lead Galindo to claim, "Sor Juana's poetry and thought . . . represent a privileged moment in the establishment of a nationality and a cultural terrain. Starting with this poet, one can speak without reservation of a Mexican literature."[48] Sor Juana's presence in both the convent and the court contributed to her ties to the colonial consciousness of New Spain. Through her political, intellectual, and ecclesial connections Sor Juana was privy to the socio-cultural colonization of the Americas. However, as a *criolla*, Sor Juana was at the crossroads of the European power-base and the Mexican-born and Indigenous populations. Her childhood on the hacienda may also have contributed to this. While a *criolla*, her role in the court and her reputation as a scholar inserted her into the discourse of the elite; yet her background kept her at the fringes of this society.

Relations towards the Indigenous remained hostile in seventeenth-century Mexico, and Sor Juana was one of a handful of scholars who depicted Indigenous culture in any sort of positive light. Sor Juana's writing demonstrated her background in Indigenous cosmology, poetry, and mythology.[49] More importantly, however, Sor Juana's incorporation of Indigenous voices and sources affirmed their validity as sources of theological insight. The previous chapter examined how these voices were presented and the political implications of this gesture. Adding to this claim, through her incorporation of American sources Sor Juana created an American subject in her texts. This subjectivity holds in tension European, *criollo/a*, and Indigenous concerns in such a manner that the mixture of theses voices constituted a new subjectivity, one that contained and transcended the diversity that informed it.

At various moments in her corpus, Sor Juana expresses an awareness of the fusion permeating her texts. She asks, "What magical infusions from the Indian herbariums of my native land, have poured their charms into my letters?"[50] In her ever-graceful and poetic manner, Sor Juana recognizes the presence of the Indigenous in her writing. When she speaks of this process, it is often in terms of desire and attraction. "But where does my native land and my sweet affection for it carry my thoughts and divert me from my intention?"[51] In these statements, Sor Juana's fondness for her native lands and its Indigenous populations rings clear. She is aware of the distinguishing marks of the America that comprise her corpus.

Sor Juana's use of American culture not only creates a particularly American discourse, but also increases the accessibility of her work in New Spain. As Pamela Kirk emphasizes, "Because she draws on both intellectual and on devotional traditions, her religious writing is open to the educated reason of the elite, as well as to the imaginative intuitive understanding of the uneducated populace."[52] Her incorporation of popular culture and popular practices, such as Indigenous song and dance, are clear markers to a broader populace that did not have Sor Juana's intellectual background. When approaching the significance of the inclusion of marginalized voices, the context in which the *villancicos* were sung must always be kept in mind. In her essay on the racial diversity of Sor Juana's *villancicos*, Georgina Sabat de Rivers evokes the image of the parishioners in the cathedrals of Mexico City, Puebla, and Oaxaca, singing the languages of Africans, Indigenous, and Spanish, bearing witness to the complexity of the culture of New Spain.[53] In an interesting twist, Sabat de Rivers informs us, only the Indigenous people sitting in the churches would have most likely been able to understand their language.[54] In a subversion of the societal power structure, the voices of the oppressed become the central discourse in a Catholic ecclesial setting. In addition to the language, certain *villancicos* included the rhythm of African and Indigenous languages; the style of the song straying from the dominant Spanish and conforming to the rhythm of the oppressed.[55] In the same *villancico* celebrating Mary's Assumption, two Africans go so far as to defend the superiority of people of color over whites.[56] Through the incorporation of these elements in a public manner, especially in her *villancicos*, Sor Juana reaches an audience significant in size and diversity. The diversity mirrors the multiracial nature of the Spanish colonies, and stamps her corpus with a clear American character, distinct from the Spanish European tradition.

Epistemology: Gendered or Neutered?

One cannot explore Sor Juana's understanding of Truth without emphasizing the gender code of her writing and its relationship to epistemology. Sor Juana's use of daily life is one example of her privileging women's "ways of knowing" as a resource for a philosophical and theological reflection that excluded men. However, even with her emphasis on the feminine, Sor Juana essentially argues that due to the genderless nature of the mind and soul, both men and women had an equal opportunity to explore the larger questions on Truth, Beauty, and Goodness. After all, for Sor Juana, human reason represents the ultimate freedom of the human. "There is nothing freer than human understanding;

For what God does not distort, why must I distort it?"[57] That
freedom is exemplified in *First Dream*, where her soul frees itself
from the confines of its body and is able to reflect unencumbered.

Always in a protective mode, Sor Juana defends her right to
study based on her shared humanity with men. "Am I not a person? Am I not animated by the rational form? Don't I descend,
like all, from Adam in a straight Line?"[58] Interestingly, Sor Juana
claims her lineage from humanity's first parents through the male.
This should not surprise us. In placing herself in the line of Adam,
Sor Juana undermines the negative caricature of woman as temptress and legitimizes her intellectual voice. Since gender is insignificant to rationality, it is the human soul that is valued, not its
material body. In Sor Juana's thought, humanity is defined by its
rationality, its ability to contemplate the divine and the created
world. This same line of argument appears in *La respuesta*, where
Sor Juana again evokes her common humanity in order to defend
her right to criticize a clergy member's sermon:

> If my crime lies in the "Letter Worthy of Athena," was that
> anything more than a simple report of my opinion, with all
> the indulgences granted me by our Holy Mother Church?
> For if She, with her most holy authority, does not forbid my
> writing, why must others forbid it? It is bold of me to oppose
> Vieira, yet not so for that Reverend Father to oppose the
> three holy Fathers of the Church? Is my mind, such as it is,
> less free than his, though it derives from the same source?[59]

Noting that since Vieira critiques the findings of the Church Fathers in his sermon without censure, Sor Juana questions why
her critique of him would be so scandalous. Sor Juana once again
places herself on equal ground with men around her. In addition
to attempting to coexist on a par with men, it also appears that
Sor Juana felt her voice was treated differently from that of other
women. In her dismissal of her confessor she asks, "Then why do
you find wicked in me what in other women was good? Am I the
only one whose salvation would be impeded by books?"[60] Sor
Juana probably knew very early in her life that she was different
from other women, based on the subjects which she studied. Ar-

guing that her studies do not conflict with her salvation, she writes later in the same letter, "Is not God, who is supreme goodness, also supreme wisdom?"[61] In her pantheon of defining God as Good, True, and as we saw earlier, Beautiful, Sor Juana echoes the three transcendentals that constitute the body of my study of her theology. God as Wisdom, in Sor Juana's eyes, validates her desire to continue her studies, especially in the area of theology. The intellectual life for her is the path of devotion.

Sor Juana simultaneously emphasizes and downplays gender depending on her rhetorical strategy. Both *El Divino Narciso* and *First Dream*, for example, contribute to an epistemology that takes gender seriously and privileges the voices of women. Veronica Grossi emphasizes that *El Divino Narciso* can be interpreted as arguing for the validity of a feminist epistemology:

> By proclaiming the positive values and the undefeatability of cognitive audacity, intellectual ambition, and disobedience, the *auto* can be read both as an imaginary authorization of a feminine epistemological and political space and as a disputation of the absolute authority of institutional dogma, defined as the rules and prohibitions that sought to discipline and control a religious woman's thinking and writing—her political agency—at a particular socio-historical moment, in this case, seventeenth century New Spain.[62]

In this play, through the character of Echo, Sor Juana demonstrates a manner in which women can subvert inherited dominant male speech in order to find their own voice. The narrative authority of the female characters throughout the *auto* and *loa* affirms the importance of the plays as a discursive space marked by women's voices. Throughout *First Dream* there is an abundance of feminine characters, primarily mythological, and nouns that rhetorically code the poem as women's speech. God is described at one point as a Wise and Powerful Hand, hand being a feminine noun in Spanish. The First Cause is also gendered as feminine. In addition to the characters studied in chapter 4, three mythological goddesses—Hecate, Diana, and Proserpina—open the poem. With the combination of the three, one has the earth, the sky, and the underworld dominated by female deities.[63] Sor

Juana creates a pantheon of the feminine that saturates the voices and imagery of the poem. The subject of the poem, the neuter soul of the dream, is in fact the feminine word "*alma*" thus affirming the primacy of women's presence. The soul is simultaneously neuter and feminine. In many ways, this image exemplifies the tension in Sor Juana's work of constantly emphasizing and negating the role of gender in epistemology.

Given her status as a woman writing in colonial Mexico, the simultaneous emphasis and rejection of gender in Sor Juana's corpus is not surprising. Her writing is heavily marked by the world in which she attempted to negotiate her voice while not being vilified or exploited for it. As noted by Jean-Michel Wissmer, "A body, 'neutral' or 'abstract', an intelligence without sex, here is Sor Juana's defense, her third way, that which allows her to escape—even superficially—the prototypes both masculine and feminine. For she refused to be considered as being like a man, and she also refused to be admired simply because she was a gifted woman. She did not want to be a sideshow curiosity, a *Monster*, as she revealed in her poems."[64] Sor Juana was never allowed to define herself freely, and was constantly mindful of the ways in which others depicted her. The convent walls did not protect her from the comments of others concerning her intellect, success, and fame. "Women feel that men surpass them, and that I seem to place myself on a level with men; some wish that I did not know so much; others say that I ought to know more to merit such applause; . . . and one and all wish me to conform to the rules of their judgment; so that from all sides such a singular martyrdom as I deem none other has ever experienced."[65] Sor Juana highlights the secondary status imposed on women, the arrogance many felt she had due to her studies, and her helplessness before her inability to conform to society's norms. Due to her culture and studies, gender becomes arguably the greatest hallmark of Sor Juana's thought. Georgina Sabat de Rivers holds that a hallmark of Sor Juana's corpus is her concern for women's status: "I think that we may say that the whole of her literary production is permeated by her feminine consciousness of her society's patriarchal character and of her exceptional status as a female writer and intellectual."[66] One cannot fully appreciate Sor Juana's writing and its societal impact without understanding the function of gender in them. For Sor Juana, however, gender was a social construction.

What then, does Sor Juana offer in terms of Truth? Through her inclusion of daily life as a resource for theological and philosophical reflection, Sor Juana opens up the private world of women as a fruitful space of insight. Similarly, the world of the African and the Indigenous mark her corpus, creating an American body of work that integrates the three cultures constituting the culture of New Spain. Through her emphasis on the contextual nature of knowledge, Sor Juana reminds us of the limitations of human words and constructions as transmitters of Truth. The metaphorical, mythological, poetic, and symbolic become privileged means of speaking of those matters that are of ontological importance. The symbolic, for Sor Juana, best captures the presence and absence of Truth in human discourse. Theology reigns as the Queen of Sciences in her corpus. This is not only due to its divine subject matter, but also to the dimension of faith that accompanies the theological task. Understanding will never be achieved without the gift of faith. While Sor Juana denies humanity's ability to understand the fullness of Truth, she does not deny its existence. Instead, it lies simultaneously revealed to and concealed from humanity.

This chapter concludes my analysis of Sor Juana's corpus. The remainder of the book will examine its significance for contemporary theology. As a historical figure, Sor Juana is a significant Latin American voice that contributes to efforts in Latin American, Latino/a, and feminist theologies to retrieve the lost voices of history that have been written out of the "canons" of theology. My study could end there; however, it does not. Following the step of retrieval is a revisionary moment, when the ways we do and think about theology are transformed by the inclusion of this new voice. In Sor Juana's case, given the aesthetic form and content of her theology, as well as the presence of Beauty, Truth, and Goodness in her corpus, her contribution is of special importance for theological aesthetics. Long forgotten by theology, Beauty is slowly shaking off the dust and re-entering contemporary theology. Her departure and return, and the manner in which Sor Juana's corpus can contribute to this homecoming, are the focus of the remainder of this text.

Notes

[1]"Si Aristóteles hubiera guisado, mucho más hubiera escrito" (OC 4:460.814-815).

[2]Mauricio Beuchot, O.P., *The History of Philosophy in Colonial Mexico* (Washington, DC: The Catholic University of America Press, 1998), ix.

[3]Jesús García Alvarez, *El pensamiento filosófico de Sor Juana Inés de la Cruz* (León, Gto.: Centro de Estudios Filosóficos Tomás de Aquino, 1997), 205.

[4]Sor Juana Inés de la Cruz, *The Answer/La respuesta: Including a Selection of Poems*, critical ed. and trans. Electa Arenal and Amanda Powell, 59. OC 4:450-451.443-443.

[5]Ibid., 53. OC 4:447.290-297.

[6]Ibid., 73. OC 4:458.736-738. In their notes to the translation of *La respuesta*, Arenal and Powell speculate that this prohibition was the result of the nature of Sor Juana's studies. They cite the work of María de San José, who recounts a tale of being chastised for crossing herself in Latin, as an example of the clergy's paranoia regarding women's entry into any sort of intellectual discourse.

[7]Ibid., 73.OC 4:458.738-745.

[8]Ibid., 75. OC 4:459.775-776.

[9]Ibid., 73. OC 4:458.753-743.

[10]Jean Franco, *Plotting Women: Gender and Representation in Mexico* (New York: Columbia University Press, 1989), 47.

[11]Irving A. Leonard, *Baroque Times in Old Mexico: Seventeenth-Century Persons, Places, and Practices* (Ann Arbor, MI: University of Michigan Press, 1959), 183.

[12]OC 4:459.811-812.

[13]Sor Juana, *The Answer/La respuesta*, 75. OC 4:460.814-815.

[14]Franco, *Plotting Women*, 93.

[15]Josefina Ludmer, "Tricks of the Weak," in *Feminist Perspectives on Sor Juana Inés de la Cruz*, ed. Stephanie Merrim (Detroit: Wayne State University Press, 1991), 93.

[16]Verónica Grossi, "Political Meta-Allegory in *El Divino Narciso* by Sor Juana Inés de la Cruz," *Intertexts* 1:1 (Spring 1997): 98.

[17]See Stephanie Merrim, *Early Modern Women's Writing and Sor Juana Inés de la Cruz* (Nashville: Vanderbilt University Press, 1999), 204; Octavio Paz, *Sor Juana: Or, The Traps of Faith*, trans. Margaret Sayers Peden (Cambridge, MA: Harvard University Press, 1988), 357-386.

[18]Franco, *Plotting Women*, 32.

[19]Paz, *Sor Juana*, 367.

[20]Ibid.

²¹Sor Juana Inés de la Cruz, *Poems, Protest, and a Dream: Selected Writings*, trans. Margaret Sayers Peden (New York: Penguin Books, 1997). Unfortunately, due to the complexity of the poem, *First Dream* is an extremely difficult piece to translate. Therefore, I will be offering the original Spanish when referring to lengthier citations and alternate between the two most readily available translations.

²²Sor Juana Inés de la Cruz, *A Sor Juana Anthology*, trans. Alan S. Trueblood (Cambridge, MA: Harvard University Press, 1988), 178. OC 1:343.216 (EC). "toda convertida a su inmaterial ser y esencia bella, aquella contemplaba, participada de alto ser, centella que con similitud en sí gozaba."

²³Sor Juana, *Poems, Protest, and a Dream*, 129. OC 1:359.216. "el Mundo iluminado, y yo despierta."

²⁴*A Sor Juana Anthology*, 93. OC 1:7.2.

²⁵OC 3:19.446-448.

²⁶*A Sor Juana Anthology*, 91. OC 1:5.2.

²⁷Ibid., 91-92. OC 1:5-6. 2.

²⁸Ibid., 93. OC 1:6.2.

²⁹Sor Juana, *The Answer/La respuesta*, 87. OC 4:465.1055-1060.

³⁰Ibid., 87. OC 4:466.1071-1073.

³¹Ibid., 45. OC 4:443.131-136; 151-154.

³²Ibid., 53. OC 4:447.301-304.

³³The letter from "Sor Filotea" (the bishop) is reprinted in the appendix of volume 4 of the *Obras completas*.

³⁴Paz, *Sor Juana: Or, The Traps of Faith*, 496. An English translation of the letter appears in the appendix.

³⁵Ibid., 496.

³⁶Sor Juana, *The Answer/La respuesta*, 53. OC 4:447.305-307.

³⁷Ibid., 53. OC 4:447.312-315.

³⁸Ibid., 53. OC 4:447.314-316.

³⁹Ibid., 53-54. OC 4:449.376-382.

⁴⁰Ibid., 57. OC 4:44.338-339.

⁴¹Ibid., 59. OC 4:450.421-424.

⁴²García Alvarez, *El pensamiento*, 211.

⁴³OC 3:17-18.401-412.

⁴⁴García Alvarez, *El pensamiento filosófico*, 211.

⁴⁵OC 1:322.214.

⁴⁶Mauricio Beuchot, "Los autos de Sor Juana: Tres lugares teológicos," in *Sor Juana y su mundo: Una mirada actual*, ed. Sara Poot Herrera (Mexico: Universidad del Claustro de Sor Juana, 1995), 356.

⁴⁷Magdalena Galindo, "Fundación de la nacionalidad: Sor Juana y la patria mexicana," in *Sor Juana y su mundo: Una mirada actual*, ed. Sara Poot Herrera (México: Universidad del Claustro de Sor Juana, 1995), 65-72.

⁴⁸Ibid., 72.

⁴⁹Some scholars have hypothesized that the poem *First Dream* has a five-

fold structure that mirrors Aztec cosmology. See Ludwig Pfandl, *Sor Juana Inés de la Cruz: La décima musa de México* (Mexico: UNAM, 1963); Robert Savukinas, "Las influencias indígenas, barrocas y gongorinas en la poesía de Sor Juana Inés de la Cruz," in *De texto a contexto: Practicas discursivas en la literatura española e hispanoamericana*, ed. Silvia Nagy-Zekmi (Barcelona: Puvill Libros, 1997), 9-15.

[50]OC 1:160.51.

[51]OC 1:103-104.37.

[52]Kirk, *Sor Juana Inés de la Cruz*, 65.

[53]Georgina Sabat de Rivers, "Blanco, negro, rojo: Semiosis racial en los villancicos de Sor Juana Inés de la Cruz," in *Critica semiológica de textos literarios hispanicos. Vol. II de Las Actas del Congreso Internacional Sobre Semiótica y Hispanismo Celebrado en Madrid los dias de 20 al 25 de Junio de 1983*, ed. Miguel Angel Gallaro (Madrid: Consejo Superior Investigaciones Científicas, 1986), 247-255.

[54]Ibid., 250.

[55]See, for example, Sor Juana's eighth *villancico* in the 1676 series on Mary's Assumption. OC 2:14.224.

[56]See OC 2:15.224.

[57]OC 1:3.1.

[58]OC 1:120.41.

[59]Sor Juana, *The Answer/La respuesta*, 91-92. OC 4:468.1165-1173.

[60]Paz, *Sor Juana*, 496.

[61]Ibid., 500.

[62]Grossi, "Political Meta-Allegory," 100.

[63]Georgina Sabat de Rivers, "A Feminist Rereading of Sor Juana's *Dream*," in *Feminist Perspectives on Sor Juana Inés de la Cruz*, 146.

[64]Jean-Michel Wissmer, *La religieuse mexicainse: Sor Juana Inés de la Cruz ou le scandale de l'ecriture* (Geneva: Editions Metropolis, 2000), 77.

[65]Paz, *Sor Juana*, 497.

[66]Sabat de Rivers, "A Feminist Rereading of Sor Juana's *Dream*," 144.

Chapter 6

The Organic Unity
of Beauty and Justice

❦

"The poor also want Beauty."[1]
—Rubem A. Alves

In the mid-twentieth century a group of European Roman
Catholic theologians began rediscovering historical Christian
sources and exploring their implications for contemporary theology. Years later, across the Atlantic, liberation theologians in the
Americas began their own projects of historical retrieval, though
they were motivated by concerns that were very different from
those of their European counterparts. While European theologians sought to *rediscover* traditional Christian sources, liberation theologians struggled to *discover* the voices of forgotten and
marginalized people in Christian history. Theirs was not merely a
return to established historical sources, but an active rewriting of
Christian history and theology. For feminist theologians such as
Rosemary Radford Ruether, this project entails retrieving the theologies of marginalized women throughout Christian history, with
special attention to the United States.[2] For Black liberation theologian Dwight Hopkins, this involves a recovery of slave narratives as a vital theological resource for contemporary theology.[3]
Liberation theologians situate their *ressourcement* of historical
sources in light of their preferential option for the oppressed and
marginalized throughout history. Surprisingly to some, many of

the resources that have appeared as a result of this historical research are aesthetic. Literature, music, and art become theological interlocutors in the recovery of marginalized voices. The implications of this historical research for contemporary theology involve a transformation of the manner in which one views Christian history and the nature of the theological task. History is not innocent, and cannot be viewed innocently. In a similar manner, the narrow and oppressive paradigms that exist in contemporary theology must be named and challenged.

European theologians assumed that through the critical assessment of historical sources, contemporary theology would be altered. However, they did not foresee the revolutionary upheaval that would result from the historical contributions of liberation theologians. It is in the spirit of this epistemological break that emerges from the method and sources of liberation theologies that this present study on Sor Juana can be situated. A retrieval of Sor Juana's work is to liberation theologies what *ressourcement* was to Yves Congar, Hans Urs von Balthasar, Karl Rahner, and their contemporaries. A Latin American *ressourcement* emerges in the spirit of the *ressourcement* movement in theologies from marginalized contexts. However, the project of *ressourcement* is not merely historical retrieval; it is also critical engagement with the current situation in light of the lessons of the past.

In this chapter I situate my retrieval of Sor Juana's theology in light of two interrelated strands of contemporary theology: liberation theologies and theological aesthetics. Some liberation theologians incorporate aesthetic resources in their historical research, uniting their preferential option for the marginalized with an emphasis on aesthetic theological expressions. While not all of these thinkers label their work as aesthetics, the resources and the implications of their sources result in a methodological shift in their theologies that privileges the aesthetic. There are those thinkers who explicitly examine the intersection of aesthetics and justice, arguing for the organic unity of the two. In addition to the liberation theologians I examine, I have also included the work of European and Euro-American theologians who are shaping the field of theological aesthetics. We find in these authors a concern for aesthetics that at times downplays the importance of ethics, though they also make connections similar to those established by their colleagues. A hasty interpretation of aesthetics can lead to perceiving its focus as downplaying or obscuring the significance of ethics and social justice.[4] However, an emphasis on Beauty does not have to be at the expense of the Good, and can in fact inform one's commitment to social justice.

The Fall of Beauty

One cannot entertain modern theological aesthetics without acknowledging that over the centuries Beauty has fallen on some hard times. Once at the center of theology, Beauty is given only a marginal place in contemporary theology. The current surge in theological aesthetics often begins with a lament for Beauty's demise in academic circles. Even in the twentieth century, while theologians such as Karl Rahner and Karl Barth treated the theme of Beauty, these texts consist of a fraction of their work. Rahner, for example, declares art to be central to the theological task, but he does not offer a sustained reflection on art in his own theology. Religious art, for Rahner, touches "the depth of existence where genuine religious experience takes place . . . even if it is not religious in its thematic, objective content, [religious art] nevertheless confronts a person in his total self in such a way as to awaken in him the whole question of existence."[5] Rahner's theology, however, offers little reflection on religious art or aesthetics. In Protestant circles, an emphasis on aesthetics is starkly lacking.[6] Hans Urs von Balthasar stands alone as a twentieth-century theologian who maintained Beauty as central to the theological task. For contemporary Euro-American theologian Edward Farley, a feature linking all contemporary theologies is a disinterest in Beauty.[7] This does not deny the existence of theological aesthetics in contemporary theological circles, but Beauty remains at the margins. This has implications not only for academic theology, but also for the role of the arts in churches. Art has become increasingly seen as irrelevant for religious institutions. As Amos N. Wilder notes, "When we speak of the cleavage between religion and the arts, we usually have in mind the whole modern period, and we contrast this period with the Middle Ages, when the arts were the handmaidens of the church."[8] In describing the cleavage between religion and the arts Wilder is not arguing that religious art is no longer produced or commissioned by churches, but that art has lost its place at the center of theology.

Accompanying the lament for Beauty's demise are the negative implications this has for theology and churches. As Wilder writes, "The church today has widely lost and all but forgotten the experience of glory which lies at the heart of Christianity."[9] Wilder correlates the loss of Beauty with the loss of glory. Rahner highlights the lack of poetic theology as a defect in contemporary theological elaborations.[10] Cuban-American theologian Roberto S. Goizueta links the demise of aesthetics to the growing irrelevance of theology to the churches and lives of Christians. In its effort to become an academic discipline, he says, theology has lost its ability to speak to people in a meaningful manner, and thus also loses its ability to deliver the Christian message: "A theology that fails to thus move and motivate cannot claim to be speaking of the liberating God of the exodus or the crucified God of Calvary."[11] The loss of aesthetics has resulted in rendering the Christian message unattractive and undeliverable. Perhaps no one in the twentieth century grieves the demise of aesthetics more than Hans Urs von Balthasar when he writes, "How could Christianity have become such a universal power if it had always been as sullen as today's humourless and anguished Protestantism, or as grumpy as super-organized Catholicism is?"[12] For von Balthasar, what makes Christianity attractive and desirable, what calls one to Christianity, is the aesthetic. With the demise of Beauty Christianity has lost its ability to convey the Christian message.[13]

Various contemporary theologians have attempted to hypothesize on this demise of Beauty. We are reminded that for great figures such as Augustine and Aquinas, Beauty was central to the theological task. In Aquinas's theology, God is the source of all beauty. As John Navone emphasizes, Beauty is central to understanding creation in Aquinas's theology:

> Aquinas, in his commentary on the *Divine Names* of Pseudo-Dionysius, claims that divine beauty is the motive of creation. Because God loves the divine beauty, God wishes to share it as much as possible by communicating this likeness to creatures. God is the cause of their radiance. Each form

imparted to a creature is a beautifying participation in the divine radiance; and since being (*esse*) comes from form, Aquinas affirms that beauty is the course of the existence of all things. Out of love for divine beauty God gives existence to everything, and moves and conserves everything. God has created the universe to make it beautiful for God's self by reflecting this same beauty. God, Beauty Itself, intends everything to become beautiful in the fullness of the divine beauty.[14]

For Edward Farley, the Cartesian revolution has distinct implications for the loss of Beauty. In Descartes Farley locates the beginnings of the association of Beauty with desire, relegating aesthetics to the realm of emotion. Farley situates the new problematic of Beauty emerging in mid-eighteenth-century England and France as the location of beauty as a human sensibility (vs. an external property). Here is the foundation of Beauty's downfall. "We must also acknowledge that the eighteenth century's location of beauty among human sensibilities has another long-term outcome: it sowed the seeds of Beauty's eventual demise in Western aesthetics."[15] While celebrating Kant's efforts to prevent Beauty from being reduced to pure subjectivity, Farley notes that in Kant's metaphysics the character of the ethical is separated from Beauty.

Offering a different take on the demise of Beauty, some theologians link this to Christian issues with the body. Frank Burch Brown, like many others, associates the theological neglect of the aesthetics to Christian ambivalence regarding the body. This is linked to the Christian dualism of the body and the soul, where the body and physical desires are often portrayed as the downfall of humanity. Due to its embodied nature, and its association with attraction and desire, Beauty is suspect.[16] Unlike Truth and Goodness, Carol Harrison notes, Beauty is problematic in the Christian tradition:

But beauty is more ambiguous: beauty allures the fallen, who want to possess it. A beautiful landscape or a beautiful piece of music may speak unambiguously of the divine source of beauty; but a beautiful painting, a beautiful woman . . . may provoke not just wonder but the desire to possess. . . . Moreover, they can easily be the occasion for actually turning man away from ultimate Beauty and can even be the occasion of his sin. Again, why is this? Is it because, of the three transcendentals, beauty is the most *embodied*, the most *incarnate*, the one which is virtually inseparable from matter?[17]

Linked to this is a denial of the body.[18] The body, and consequently the arts, can be interpreted as idolatrous and as distractions from one's life of faith. For the theologians examined below, however, the intersection of aesthetics and ethics is viewed as central to the theological task. Through their work, the ambiguous nature of Beauty is clarified, showing aesthetics, once again, to be fundamental to theology.

Latino/a Theology

As defined by Alejandro García-Rivera, "Theological aesthetics recognizes in the experience of the truly beautiful a religious dimension."[19] In other words, theological aesthetics contends that Beauty is a result of divine initiative. Because of its divine origin, for the human Beauty is always something that is received. Beauty exists in relationship. Beauty emerges from the divine and is then received and responded to by the human. García-Rivera situates this reception within the human heart. The task of theological aesthetics is to explore this reception and response, grounded in the divine as the source of Beauty. "Theological aesthetics attempts to make clear once again the connection between Beauty and the beautiful, between Beauty's divine origins and its appropriation by the human heart."[20] García-Rivera notes that in addressing both the objective and subjective dimensions of Beauty and its reception, theological aesthetics attempts to address modern suspicions surrounding the experience of beauty. By maintaining the origins of Beauty to be divine, García-Rivera argues for the objective reality of Beauty. However, that beauty is subjectively received and interpreted by the human.

In his theological aesthetics, García-Rivera places various strands of thought in conversation: von Balthasar's theological aesthetics, Latino/a theology, North American pragmatism, and semiotics. Building on the unity of the transcendentals as found in Hans Urs von Balthasar's theology, García-Rivera understands the True, the Good, and the Beautiful in terms of communities. This construction allows for a relational understanding of the transcendentals that addresses the reality of difference. Charles Sanders Peirce and Josiah Royce provide the philosophical framework for this task. García-Rivera further develops his aesthetics through his examination of the semiotics of Jan Mukarovsky, who understands Being as foregrounding. The aesthetic principle that emerges from this interweaving of voices is the lifting of the lowly, a subversive aesthetic norm with ethical implications.

The intersection of aesthetics and ethics plays a more central role in the theology of Roberto S. Goizueta. Arguing for the centrality of aesthetics in Latino/a theology, Goizueta contends that the role of aesthetics is integral and organic to the form and content of the Latino/a theological task, especially with its emphasis on popular religion. "If Tridentine Western theology stressed the fact that God is known in the form of the True (Doctrine), and liberation theology that God is known in the form of the Good (Justice), U.S. Hispanic theology stresses the fact that God is known in the form of the Beautiful."[21] Integral to his understanding of theological aesthetics is the relationship between form and content. Goizueta links their separation to the demise of aesthetics:

> One of the most devastating consequences of Western rationalism on Christian theology has been the divorce between theological form and content . . . the depreciation of preconceptual knowledge, now universally suspect because of its diffuse and hence "countless" character. In turn, the traditional forms of communicating such knowledge—symbol, ritual, narrative, metaphor, poetry, music, the arts—are necessarily marginalized as unacademic and unscholarly, that is, as pure (aesthetic) form without (conceptual) content.[22]

The separation of form and content has affected both the sources and norms of theology. This divorce leads to the privileging of the abstract over the concrete, and of theoretical knowledge over "common sense" knowledge.

Building on the work of early twentieth-century Latin American philosophy, Goizueta offers aesthetic experience as a way to interpret human action. The work of Mexican philosopher José Vasconcelos figures prominently, for he offers a philosophy grounded in aesthetic judgment. At the center of Vasconcelos's aesthetics is the "empathic fusion" that occurs in an aesthetic experience. In this aesthetic moment, the subject and the object of its gaze become one: "For Vasconcelos, human interpersonal action is fundamentally aesthetic action. Only through an aesthetic, empathic fusion with another can I truly relate to the other as a person."[23] This empathic fusion leads to an aesthetic unity where the uniqueness and particularity of the human being is not lost. Aesthetic fusion becomes the only manner in which we can know and love another person.

Goizueta sees popular religious practices in Latino/a communities as an example of the intrinsic value of the aesthetic:

> The symbols and rituals of popular religion are prime examples of the intrinsic value of beauty, and, hence, the intrinsic value of human life as beautiful, i.e., as an end in itself, for the goal of the community's participation in the stories, symbols, and rituals of popular religion is nothing other than that participation itself. . . . Popular Catholicism also represents the aesthetic character of human action in that popular Catholicism is perhaps the most important example of our U.S. Hispanic mestizaje. Popular Catholic symbols and rituals reflect an aesthetic, or "empathic fusion" of European, indigenous, and African elements.[24]

Popular religion also demonstrates the intersubjective nature of human action, where the human is only understood within community. Goizueta argues that unless scholars reject the separation of form and content, they will never truly understand the popular religious practices of Latino/a peoples. However, one cannot separate the reception of God's love from the socio-political embodiment of that love in social praxis. For Goizueta, the aesthetic is the foundation of the ethical. The aesthetic is mediated by and encountered in the ethical, and the aesthetic is also what gives meaning to the ethical.[25] Underlying Goizueta's assertions is the praxiological unity of the True, the Good, and Beauty. "And all three—imagination, reason, and ethics—have a single common and unifying ground: human praxis. More precisely, the affective, aesthetic, imagination, the rational intellect, and ethical-political commitment are all intrinsic dimensions of human praxis."[26] The praxiological unity of the three transcendentals guarantees that one cannot be emphasized at the expense of another. Beauty, Truth, and Goodness must always remain collaboratively in unison.

Latina theologians have not, as of yet, offered a comprehensive analysis of the role of aesthetics in their theologies.[27] Only scattered comments exist. Teresa Delgado is a Puerto Rican theologian who has explored aesthetic writing, specifically literature, as a theological resource. Delgado examines the contributions of four Puerto Rican women to Latina theology: Nicholasa Mohr, Judith Ortiz Cofer, Esmeralda Santiago, and Rosario Ferré. Delgado's article is grounded in the thesis that "I believe these Puerto Rican women writers are prophets for the Puerto Rican people, specifically, and for Latino/as in general. As such, their stories provide us with a *critical source* for the development of Latina feminist theology, in particular, and for U.S. Latino/a theology in general."[28] These authors, Delgado contends, present an understanding of what it means to be human through the use of narrative and story. Through the imagination, literature offers a vision of the future that is transformative of the status quo. Delgado's article is grounded on five presuppositions regarding the relationship between theology and literature. First, Puerto Rican literature embodies a tradition of subversion and freedom. Second, literature reveals something to us surrounding the contradictions of our humanity. Third, the response to these contradictions offers a vision for a transformed future. Fourth, theology must embody liberative action. Last, an authentic Puerto Rican theology must emerge from the connections between culture and ritual.[29] Delgado's selection of these four authors is based on the understanding and challenge they pose to contemporary Puerto Rican culture and religiosity.

Responding to the theme of aesthetics in Latino/a theology,

mujerista theologian Ada María Isasi-Díaz highlights two contributions Latinas make to the interconnectedness of Beauty and Justice. The first is the beauty of the struggle for Justice. Isasi-Díaz finds beauty in protesting and confronting injustice, for political action is a site for the encounter with Beauty. She locates the power of these rituals in their beauty, and their beauty is found in their vision of justice. Beauty becomes the language of the Good. "If today, then, action on behalf of justice is seen only as message, sermon, and prose, and not as vision, hymn, and poem, we are reaping the hegemonic effects of rationalization and analytic thought."[30] Her work, in many ways, echoes the sentiments of Goizueta. This theme ties into Isasi-Díaz's second point, the relationship between form and content and *mujerista* theology's understanding of praxis. Here she is responding directly to the work of Roberto Goizueta and his contention of the intersection of aesthetics, ethics, and intellect in human action. *Mujerista* theology affirms this claim as found in the narratives and daily lives of Latinas. Like Goizueta, Isasi-Díaz links the importance of aesthetics to the particular subject-matter of Latino/a theology.

Feminist Philosophy and Theology

The theme of aesthetics and historical research are integral to the task of feminist theology's methodology. As defined by Elizabeth A. Johnson, feminist theology is characterized by a threefold method. She writes, "[F]eminist theology engages in at least three interrelated tasks: it critically analyzes inherited oppressions, searches for alternative wisdom and suppressed history, and risks new interpretations of the tradition in conversation with women's lives."[31] In a similar vein, Anne E. Carr defines the method of feminist theology as occurring in three steps: critique of tradition, recovery of women in Church history, and theological reconstruction.[32] Both authors emphasize the critical lens of feminist theology and the historical dimension of feminist theological projects. Both Johnson and Carr address the idea of the "noninnocent" history of Christian theology and tradition, which must be examined in light of a feminist hermeneutics. As Elisabeth Schüssler Fiorenza writes, "Feminist scholarship unveils the patriarchal functions of the intellectual and scientific frameworks generated and perpetuated by male-centered scholarship that makes women invisible or peripheral in what we know about the world, human life, and cultural or religious history."[33] This first task in feminist theology is to be mindful of the function of power and marginalization in inherited and current theological discourses.

The second task of feminist theology is dominated by historical research. Through this work, the lost women's voices of Christian traditions are recovered through scriptural and historical scholarship. Part of this task is unearthing the role of silence that led to the marginalization of these women's voices. Schüssler Fiorenza highlights the importance of this step, for a feminist critical analysis must be accompanied by knowledge of women's intellectual contributions throughout history:

> Although women have questioned these explanations and internalizations throughout the centuries, we remain ignorant of our own intellectual traditions and foremothers. All "great" philosophers, scientists, theologians, poets, politicians, artists, and religious leaders seem to have been men who have for centuries been writing and talking to each other in order to define God, the world, human community and existence as "they saw it." However that does not mean that women have not been "great" thinkers and leaders. Yet their thoughts and works have not been transmitted and become classics of our culture and religion because patriarchy requires that in any conceptualization of the world men and their power have to be central.[34]

One should not, however, limit the subject matter of this task to the scholarship of women. Part of this second step includes unearthing the male voices that have been silenced, misinterpreted, or ignored. The third task of feminist theology creates new theological constructions in light of the prior two steps.

The work of Rebecca Chopp offers one avenue for opening up the implications of feminist scholarship for theology, especially in light of a recovery of Sor Juana. The work of French critical theorist Julia Kristeva informs her critique, for Chopp finds her method an extremely helpful tool in analyzing Christian theological discourse. The use of feminist theory as an analytical lens is an increasing practice in feminist theology.[35] Chopp's use of Kristeva, a "non-traditional" woman's voice in Christian theology, is yet another example of the broadening of conversation partners in feminist theology. A key thrust in Chopp's writing, as articulated in her groundbreaking book, *The Power to Speak*, is to liberate the oppositional construct of gender, moving towards a politics of difference which highlights plurality in discourses and significations, while challenging the present dichotomous social-symbolic order.[36] As a poststructuralist theologian, Chopp questions the normativity of Christian tradition based on its patriarchal contours.

> For Kristeva, the present symbolic order constitutes and is constituted through a binary opposition of gender relations. These relations, according to Kristeva, operate through cultural, linguistic, political, and psychic constructs of power and abjection, meaning and nonmeaning, order and chaos. In the West, these gender relations function through what she calls monotheism, the ordering principal of a symbolic, paternal community that requires men and women to have different relationships to the symbolic. This difference is the condition of relations between men and women.[37]

In Kristeva's writing the term monotheism denotes the ordering, at a societal, cultural, and linguistic level, of the symbolic order. Such ordering is given an ontological value, and consequently renders it unobjectionable. Kristeva's understanding of a monotheism that "secures the identity of the one through the devaluing and marginalizing of the other"[38] does not exhaust the use of the term as it is used in Christian theological discourse, but offers one dangerous interpretation that must be flagged. Kristeva's monotheism warns of the totalitarianism that can accompany assumed human ownership of the Absolute.

The symbolic order that functions in the monotheistic West is "scientific" and positivist, excluding rhythmic, poetic, or otherwise ambiguous discourse.[39] For Kristeva, women can only participate in the symbolic order through identification with the monotheistic Father. Any rupture of this participation leads to a *"discours marginal,"* a taboo break in the symbolic chain.[40] Women are therefore trapped in the monotheistic bind that regulates their access to politics and history, and keeps them marginal. How do women escape this bind? They must access that which is unspoken, the semiotic underlying the symbolic.[41] It is my contention that Kristeva, and consequently Chopp, would agree that Sor Juana's writing is such a discourse.

To offer a simple definition of Kristeva's notions of the semiotic and symbolic is perhaps to do injustice to their complexity. It may be best to turn to Kristeva's own words on the topic, in a concise answer given in a 1985 interview:

> But to be schematic, I would say for me signification is a process that I call *significance*, and to recognize the dynamics of this process, I distinguish two registers: the register of the symbolic and the register of the semiotic. By symbolic, I mean the tributary signification of language, all the effects of meaning that appear from the moment linguistic signs are articulated into grammar, not only chronologically but logically as well. In other words, the symbolic is both diachronic and synchronic; it concerns both the acquisition of language and the present syntactic structure. By semiotic, on the other hand, I mean the effects of meaning that are not reducible to language or that can operate outside language, even if language is necessary as an immediate context or as final referent.[42]

It is important to highlight that language, for Kristeva, is a process, not a system.[43] The symbolic represents the systematic, rational dimension of signification. The semiotic, on the other hand, represents the more corporeal or drive-related dimension of signification. The semiotic and symbolic, however, are not oppositional. As Jacqueline Rose notes, "The semiotic can never wholly displace the symbolic since it relies on that very order to give to it its albeit resistant shape."[44] The semiotic is therefore dependent and shaped by the symbolic.

Cleo McNelly Kearns, in her essay, "Kristeva and Feminist Theology," notes that "Kristeva's critique of theology rests on the assumption that, taken straight, and without the benefit of postmodern reading, it leans so heavily to the symbolic level that it violently represses the semiotic." Her solution to this is to carefully "negotiate" the line between semiotic and symbolic. "This negotiation allows us to relapse neither into the position of the patriarchal theologian nor into that of rebellious daughter."[45] This is a dangerous line, often ambiguous, and Sor Juana is an example of a life and a body of work that constantly negotiated it. Sor Juana is in fact an appropriate example of a Kristevan semiotic impulse in the symbolic canon of Western Christian theology, especially in the form of her writing. For Kristeva, poetry is an example of the semiotic, as is literature.[46]

Chopp emphasizes the significance of language in the discourse of Christian theology, especially as it relates to feminist political activity. She notes that historically women's words have been denied the right to speak of the Word (God), and consequently are not voices of authority. She understands her scholarship as an effort to overcome this marginalization. "As Word, God has traditionally been prevented from being represented by woman, while woman has been configured as taboo and placed on the margins of the Word. Yet there is a curious phenomenon occurring today in that women, from the margins of social, political, linguistic, and theological order, do speak of the Word, and speak to proclaim this Word to and for the world."[47] Chopp sees her work as striving for the transformation of Christian discourse that will lead to the proclamation of the Word in an emancipatory fashion. Part of this process is bringing forth voices that have been marginalized in the social-symbolic order. This will lead to the interruption and transformation of that order. Chopp's work, therefore, offers a methodological contribution to theology, in her emphasis on rupturing the current standards and norms of theological discourse. This will, in turn, lead to a transformation of the very content of theology, once these voices are given a space to articulate their contributions.

In a moving essay entitled "Poetry is Not a Luxury," Audre Lorde emphasizes the need for aesthetics and its relationship to ethics with a grace that more theoretical writing could never muster. "For women, then, poetry is not a luxury. It is a vital necessity of our existence. It forms the quality of the light within which we predicate our hopes and dreams toward survival and change, first made into language, then into idea, then into more tangible action. Poetry is the way we help give name to the nameless so it can be thought."[48] For Lorde, the aesthetic becomes the privileged means of expressing truth and an alternative to male European theoretical thinking. Poetry becomes the language of freedom for women, their only mode of survival. "Poetry coins the language to express and charter this revolutionary demand, the implementation of that freedom."[49] Poetry combines truth and beauty, and for Lorde provides the vision and the drive behind justice. Through poetry, women are free to have dreams of a better world and to draw a vision from them.

Elaine Scarry echoes these sentiments through her philosophical aesthetics with an emphasis on the interconnectedness of aesthetics and ethics. Scarry begins her book, *On Beauty and Being Just*, by examining three features of beauty: beauty as sacred, unprecedented, and lifesaving.[50] She then proceeds to argue for the alliance between Beauty, the True, and the Good. On Beauty and Truth she writes:

> I have tried to set forth the view here that beauty really is allied with truth. This is not to say that what is beautiful is also true. ... But the claim throughout these pages that beauty and truth are allied is not a claim that the two are identical. It is not that a poem or a painting or a palm tree or a person is "true," but rather that it ignites the desire for truth by giving us, with an eclectic brightness shared by almost no other uninvited, freely arriving perceptual event, the experience of conviction and the experience, as well, of error.[51]

Beauty makes Truth attractive; it invites one into a relationship with the True.

Turning to the relationship between Beauty and the Good, Scarry notes that contemporary discussions between aesthetics and ethics are marred by a critique of beauty at the expense of justice. The political critique of beauty is based on two arguments: the first says that beauty distracts from justice; the second says that the aesthetic gaze objectifies its object. The first assumes that the object would benefit from attention, the second that the object would suffer from it.[52] In contrast to these contentions, Scarry argues that beauty in fact aids in addressing justice issues.[53] Noticing an object's beauty, for example, often leads to handling it with care. The perception of beauty gives the perceiver the gift of life, while simultaneously giving that gift to the object in reciprocity. "Something that is perceived as beautiful is bound up with an urge to protect it, or act on its behalf, in a way that appears to be tied up with the perception of its lifelikeness."[54] Finally, she contends that beauty is distributional, leading to a "lateral disregard" that is extended to other objects. Scarry concludes by reaffirming the aesthetic as that which fuels and energizes the ethical.

For contemporary feminist theologian Margaret R. Miles, both beauty and moral responsibility require each other. "With Plato, I believe that perceptions of beauty fund a generosity of spirit that is essential to moral responsibility."[55] This is informed, in part, by the fact that Beauty is subject to the ambiguities that plague life. "Beauty is not innocent."[56] In stating this Miles highlights that Beauty has often been used to mask injustice and oppression. Not only is Beauty that which informs the Good; for Miles, religion is the space where aesthetics and ethics meet: "Religion occurs at the intersection of perceived beauty and moral responsibility. The two are not separate or antagonistic, for together they create orientation to a real world."[57] In other words, both ethics and aesthetics conjointly are at the foundations of religious life. The two must be held in unity.

An example of the emphasis on aesthetics in Miles's scholarship is found in her book, *Seeing and Believing: Religion and Values in the Movies.*[58] This study explores the religious and moral values found in contemporary films. The aesthetic impulse is found in the incorporation of film as a theological resource. Noting that such a study is often seen as trivial within the larger theological academy, Miles contends that in fact such scholarship is essential to the study of religion. "The study of religion is incomplete and impoverished when we study religious language to the exclusion of religious art. For religious images have informed the religious lives of our historical antecedents far more pervasively and profoundly than our slender attention to them in the academic study of religion would acknowledge."[59] Her scholarship on film not only engages a broader audience but also expands the sources of theological reflection in order to understand humanity's encounter with the divine and its expression in a more comprehensive manner.

Perhaps no other feminist theologian has argued for the aesthetic in theology as organic to the Christian message as effectively as Sallie McFague in her early writing on metaphor in theology. Highlighting the parabolic form as the primary manner of Jesus' teaching, McFague argues for a theology informed by parables, saying that one characteristic of the parabolic style is its use of secular language to portray religious themes: "A theology that takes its cues from parables finds that the genres most closely associated with it are the poem, the novel, and the autobiography, since these genres manifest the ways metaphor operates in language, belief, and life." Parabolic theology is "a kind of theology which attempts to stay close to the parables."[60] McFague notes Paul's letters, Augustine's *Confessions*, and Dietrich Bonhoeffer's *Letters and Papers from Prison* as key examples of this tradition in Christian theology. McFague contends that the poetic and the narrative are a means of "saving" theological discourse through an examination of the parable of the Prodigal Son, a poem by Gerard Manley Hopkins, and a story by Sam Keen:

> For many of us the language of the Christian tradition is no longer authoritative; no longer revelatory; no longer metaphorical; no longer meaningful. Much of it has become tired clichés, one-dimensional, univocal language. When this happens, it means that theological reflection is faced with an enormous task—the task of embodying anew. This will not happen, I believe, through systematic theology, for systematic theology is second-level language, language which orders, arranges, explicates, makes precise the first-order revelatory, metaphorical language. . . . It will be through the search for new metaphors—poems, stories, even lives— which will "image" to us.[61]

Situating the future of theology in the metaphorical, symbolic, and poetic, McFague favors aesthetics as the future of theological expressions. Aesthetics becomes the only appropriate language for theology.

Latin American Liberation Theology

Theological aesthetics is not new to Latin American liberation theology. However, with the heavy emphasis on ethics, Beauty has often been sidelined in the writing of Latin American theologians. The marginalization of Beauty, however, did not go unnoticed. Theologian María Teresa Porcile articulated the urgency of the need to recover Beauty in Latin American theology over fifteen years ago: "It is necessary and urgent to 'recover' the dimension of beauty in Theology. Theology has to be an expression of desire and attraction, of Eros. This dimension will be united to the poetic and the contemplative, and at the same time to prophecy and wisdom."[62] In linking the contemplative to the prophetic, Porcile emphasizes the relationship between aesthetics and ethics. The prophetic needs the aesthetic; social justice is futile without a vision behind it. Porcile is not alone in her assertions.

In María Pilar Aquino's theology, the role of the "primacy of desire" represents an aesthetic accent. Emphasizing the primacy of desire, Aquino holds, is a means of contesting the possibility of a detached, decontextualized, and purely abstract rationality. The primacy of desire highlights the role of emotion and desire in theological elaborations. This has implications for the very form of theological writing and sources. Aquino writes, "Therefore the language of poetry, play, and symbol becomes an appropriate way of expressing the understanding and wisdom of the faith, because it is the means of expressing the human person's deepest and most genuine aspirations and desire."[63] Sor Juana's writing, therefore, is a means of tapping into this primacy of desire that Aquino holds to be a central feature of Latina feminist theology. Again we find a privileging of the aesthetic as the most appropriate means of religious expression.

Aquino is not alone in her emphasis on desire in the theological task. María Clara Bingemer, whose work is foundational for Aquino, writes: "The cold circumspection of purely scientific inquiry must give way to a new sort of systematics springing from the impulse of desire that dwells at the deepest level of human existence. . . . Born of desire, theology exists as theology only if it is upheld and supported by desire."[64] Desire, for Bingemer, is in fact central to the theological task. In both Aquino and Bingemer there is an aesthetic turn in their theological writing, informing a broader change in the form of theological method. This aesthetic emphasis is understood as the only adequate means of expressing the human's deepest faith and sentiments. As Ivone Gebara notes, "In other words, to some extent this procedure means returning the poetic dimension of human life to theology, since the deepest meaning in the human being is expressed only through analogy; mystery is voiced only in poetry, and what is gratuitous is expressed only through symbols. Purely rational concepts do not take into account the meaning, desire, flavor, pleasure, pain, and mystery of existence."[65] Aesthetic form is the fullest expression of desire, emotion, and faith, which Aquino, Gebara, and Bingemer see as central both to the theological task and to an understanding of the human. Purely rational concepts are not adequate vehicles for expressing the fullness of the human.

Rubem A. Alves is the only Latin American liberation theologian who has placed aesthetics as central to his theology. In his aesthetics, Alves emphasizes the non-innocent nature of Beauty. "But there is no way out: if one wants the supreme joy of beauty, one must be prepared to cry. Sadness is not an intruder in beauty's domains."[66] Alves also laments the demise of aesthetics in theology. He sees this as directly related to the primacy of ethics in liberation theology. "And yet, how marginal beauty has been in our theological meditations! . . . Have we separated goodness from beauty? Is this the reason why our theological discourse has been dominated by the ethical motif—the divine imperative—as opposed to the aesthetical—the divine delight? . . . The ethical is not the end; it is only a means."[67] Alves sees the ethical as solely a means to the aesthetic. An ethics that ignores the aesthetic, in his eyes, leads to the objectification of peoples in the ethical process. In addition, Alves sees the ethical imperative of liberation theologies as an emphasis on works at the expense of grace. An ethics that is not grounded in beauty will result in a "heartburn" that leads to bitterness. Instead, Alves calls for political action based upon Beauty. "I am trying to suggest that human beings are moved by beauty. If we want to change the world, we need first of all to be able to make people dream about beauty. This has been totally forgotten by the Church."[68] The aesthetic is therefore that which grounds and informs the ethical. Given the earlier emphasis on Sor Juana's play *El Divino Narciso*, it is interesting to note that Alves uses the myth of Narcissus in his own theological aesthetics. For Alves, "Somehow God is like Narcissus: they both want to see their beauty."[69] In a similar vein to Sor Juana (and Aquinas), Alves sees the role of Beauty as pivotal in an understanding of the divine and creation. "The myths of creation are another version of Narcissus' myth. God created the universe as a mirror where his/her/its beauty could be seen. The beauty that we see in the world is the beauty which abides in our bodies."[70] Contrary to Sor Juana, however, Alves focuses his reflections on Narcissus in the realm of creation. For Sor Juana, the myth of Narcissus is a story of redemption.

Black Theology

The role of aesthetics in Black liberation and womanist theologies has not been studied extensively. While Black theologians clearly use aesthetic sources in their writing, the characterization of certain elements of Black theologies as theological aesthetics has not occurred. The use of aesthetic sources, however, is central to Black theology's method. This is usually situated within Black theology's emphasis on culture. In his excellent introduction to Black theology of liberation, Dwight Hopkins lists six sources for Black theology: the Bible, the African American Church, faith tradition of the struggle for liberation, culture, African American women's experience, and radical politics.[71] Hopkins says that the avenues for tapping into Black culture are art, literature, music, and folk tales. Aesthetic sources become a central means of accessing and expressing Black culture. The importance of a Black cultural foundation of Black liberation theology is central to the creation of a theology that can speak authentically of the Black experience in the United States.

An emphasis on culture, however, is not always a welcome project in liberation theologies. Early Black theology was marked by two trends: political and cultural. Political theologians emphasize social justice and praxis. For the cultural theologian, as elaborated by womanist theologian Diana Hayes, "One must, thus, look at the history, music, literature, art, etc. of Black people in order to develop the foundation upon which a true Black Theology can emerge. For without a past, a future cannot be dreamed of."[72] Cultural theologians emphasize the white supremacy of the sociology of knowledge underlying white theology, urging Black theologians to create new theological categories. As Audre Lorde writes, "The master's tools will not dismantle the master's house."[73] These political and cultural trends are not antithetical; in fact, they overlap. "Therefore, we can expect to find these two shades of difference united in the same path of a liberation journey."[74] The most recent generation of Black theologians blurs the lines between politics and culture. Hopkins's own work can be seen as an embodiment of the unity of the cultural and political dimensions of Black theology. His book, *Shoes That Fit Our Feet*, is divided into two sections: he begins with an exploration of Black folk religion (via a study of spirituals, slave narratives, literature, and folk culture); this is then followed by an examination of faith-based social movements.

A perusal of the writing of Black and womanist theologians over the past few decades reveals that music and literature are central aesthetic resources for their writing. James H. Cone, considered by many to be the father of academic Black theology, brought the importance of music to the forefront of Black theology in his 1972 publication, *The Spirituals and the Blues*. In this text Cone highlights the theological dimension of Black music:

> Black music is also theological. That is, it tells us about the divine Spirit that moves the people toward unity and self-determination. It is not possible to be Black and encounter the Spirit of Black emotion and not be moved. My purpose is to uncover the theological presuppositions of Black music as reflected in the spirituals and the blues, asking: What do they tell us about Black people's deepest aspirations and devotion? I will ask questions about God, Jesus Christ, life after death, and suffering; and I will investigate these questions in light of Black people's historical strivings for freedom.[75]

Cone's methodology operates with the presupposition that the spirituals are of theological value. As the method of the book demonstrates, the spirituals have a distinct theology that is linked to the cultural, social, and political context of slaves. The spirituals thus become a central resource for the study of slave religion. This emphasis on music as a theological voice does not end with the spirituals.[76] Cone also demonstrates that the blues offer an aesthetic resource for Black liberation theology.

The use of literature as a theological resource is central in the work of various womanist theologians. In her introduction to womanist theology Stephanie Mitchem highlights the importance of June Jordan's poetry, for example, to the development of a womanist consciousness. In one of the earliest texts of womanist theology, *Black Womanist Ethics*, Katie Cannon uses the literature and life of Zora Neale Hurston as a key interlocutor for womanist ethics. Cannon's work is ground-breaking at various levels. As Mitchem notes, "By valuing Black women's experiences, she challenged the basic assumptions of white, male, Christian ethics about individuals, personal and communal power, and acts of choice. Using Zora Neale Hurston's literature and life, Cannon points to the potential of Black literary traditions for social analysis."[77] In a later text, Cannon returns to the centrality of literature for womanist ethics: "It is my thesis that the Black women's literary tradition is the best available literary repository for understanding the ethical values Black women have created and cultivated in their participation in this society."[78] Literature becomes a central resource for accessing Black women's lives, culture, and world view.

The literature of Toni Morrison and Alice Walker are central voices in womanist theology. Noting that Delores S. Williams has used literature as a theological resource, Hopkins turns to Toni Morrison's writing as a source for a constructive Black theology. Morrison's literature is a key resource for understanding the spirituality of poor Black women. Hopkins argues, "Furthermore, to do theology from Black women's literature is precisely *theology*. Why? Because the God of justice and love presented and discovered in African American religious values, tradition, and contemporary witness is the same God who freely chooses to reveal an emancipatory spirit in Black women's stories."[79] In a similar vein, Cheryl Townsend Gilkes uses literature, specifically Alice Walker's *The Color Purple*, to explore the complexity of Black women's daily lives and realities. Walker herself speaks of the theological nature of her novel when she writes:

> Whatever else *The Color Purple* has been taken for during the swift ten years since its publication, it remains for me the theological work examining the journey from the religious back to the spiritual that I spent so much of my adult life, prior to writing it, seeking to avoid.... I would have thought a book that begins "Dear God" would immediately have been identified as a book about the desire to encounter, to hear from, the Ultimate Ancestor.[80]

Novels such as *The Color Purple* offer alternative theological resources that demonstrate that if one is going to attempt to recover the voices and experiences of a marginalized people, "traditional" avenues of research are not always appropriate.

While employing aesthetic sources in their theologies, womanist theologians are aware of the manner in which aesthetics can be oppressive. Beauty is ambiguous, for it can be used to marginalize and silence. For African-Americans, unrealistic beauty standards are linked to esteem issues within the Black community. As Gilkes thoughtfully points out, "As part of the racial oppression that African-American people experience, cultural humiliation based on beauty norms has serious implications for the self-esteem of African-American women and men. Such a concern may seem trivial in the face of drugs, violence, poverty, and social isolation, but many current social problems are often tied to low self-esteem or self-hatred."[81] This brokenness prevents the African-American community from creating a communal liberating vision. This is of special concern for African-American women. "Cultural humiliations assault Black women by undermining their capacities for self-love."[82] A theological aesthetics, however, which recognizes that Beauty is not equivalent to that which is culturally deemed beautiful will not fall into these oppressive pitfalls. Worldly beauty can never be equated with Beauty, aesthetics with aestheticism. In the writing of Hans Urs von Balthasar, one finds a repudiation of aestheticism as a central feature of his theology that is foundational to his aesthetics.

European and Euro-American Theologies

Roman Catholic theologian Hans Urs von Balthasar is one of the most significant and often overlooked figures in twentieth-century theology. His massive collection of theological texts covers a broad range of topics, from the classic theological loci of Christology and Ecclesiology to pastoral concerns such as women's ordination. This Swiss-born theologian, educated by and for some time a member of the Society of Jesus, is the author of the most substantial theological aesthetics of the twentieth century. Von Balthasar begins volume one of *The Glory of the Lord* by placing Beauty at the forefront of his theology, at the same time mourning its "demise" in modern discourse. "We here attempt to develop a Christian theology in the light of the third transcendental, that is to say: to complement the vision of the true and the good with that of the beautiful (*pulchrum*)."[83] This is an attempt, in von Balthasar's words, "to restore theology to a main artery which it has abandoned."[84] Beauty has lost its relevance. For von Balthasar, when Beauty suffers, so do the other two transcendentals, the True and the Good, for they lose their appeal; the ethical and aesthetic are in conjunction. The Good must be attractive; it must be Beautiful. As Edward Oakes notes:

> Here perhaps is the key that unlocks the whole point of the Aesthetics, for beauty is inherently attractive, meaning that it draws contemplators out of themselves and into a *direct* encounter with the phenomenon manifesting itself, and this beauty, the contemplator knows, testifies to itself in a way that the True and the Good cannot do. Although all three transcendentals, the Beautiful, the Good, and the True, in the traditional Platonic understanding, are all inherent aspects of the nature of Being, nonetheless, we may doubt, and often do, the inherent goodness and truth of the being of the world.[85]

Without Beauty, the True and the Good become obscured. Without Beauty, the Good ceases to be attractive, Truth stops being reasonable.[86]

Von Balthasar's discussion of theological aesthetics cannot be understood without treating his understanding of form. "Seeing the form" is a central concept in von Balthasar's aesthetics that is crucial to his Christology. The form is the active presence of the beautiful. It is something that affects the observer. Key to understanding von Balthasar's aesthetics is grasping this very complex notion of the form:

> The beautiful is above all a *form*, and the light does not fall on this form from above and from outside, rather it breaks forth from the form's interior. . . . Visible form not only "points" to an invisible, unfathomable mystery; form is the apparition of this mystery, and reveals it while, naturally, at the same time protecting and veiling it. . . . The content (*Gehalt*) does not lie behind the form (*Gestalt*), but within it.[87]

Various key themes emerge from this citation. First, there is an intrinsic relationship between form and content. The form emerges from the content, not vice versa. As noted by Peter Casarella, form and content are in organic relationship. "The manifestation of expressed content is neither just in itself nor merely in the external appearance. The disclosure of form lies in the organic whole constituted by the poles of exteriority and interiority. . . . The emergence of a concrete expression of the form codetermines the expressed content."[88] Second, this form radiates from the interior outward, not from the exterior inward. Here von Balthasar rejects a purely subjective understanding of Beauty, which reduces the objectivity of the form. Third, the form conceals as it reveals; the fullness of the form's expression is not available to humans. The mystery of the content is not "seen" in its fullness.

"Seeing" the form moves one to action. Beauty is engaging. As Edward Oakes observes, "Beauty by its very nature always elicits a response: one simply cannot experience a form or a phenomenon as beautiful without responding, without *assenting*."[89] One can see here the foundational connections von Balthasar draws between ethics and aesthetics. The experience of Beauty is an active event on both sides, objective and subjective, in its reaching out and in the human response to it. Von Balthasar often uses the language of the interrelationship between contemplation and action in order to describe the response elicited by Beauty's engagement.

To speak of Beauty in this day and age seems in many ways absurd. What is held as beautiful has been reduced to a subjective opinion. To refute this notion, von Balthasar begins by positing God as Beauty and Jesus Christ as the "super-form." This starting point, as highlighted by Edward Oakes, refutes any subjective interpretation of Beauty. "For a theological aesthetics there is, to be sure, an analogy between worldly beauty and divine beauty. But the criterion for beauty remains always with God and his revelation."[90] By positing the meaning of the form both in the interior and exterior of the form, von Balthasar repudiates a merely subjective interpretation of Beauty. For von Balthasar, God's Beauty is revealed in the *kenotic* self-emptying of Christ on the Cross. "We must not forget that even worldly aesthetics cannot exclude the element of the ugly, of the tragically fragmented, of the demonic, but must come to terms with these."[91] The "ugliness" of the cross paradoxically reveals God's glory through the path of humiliation.

Von Balthasar's academic formation was in literature, not theology, a fact that resonates throughout his writing. Von Balthasar is thus an interdisciplinary theologian who draws from a variety of fields in pursuing his theological task. Tied to von Balthasar's privileging of literature is his firm belief that culture must be a central category in theological elaboration. For von Balthasar, culture is essentially Christian. Von Balthasar holds literary, philosophical, and theological elaborations to converge under the Christian ethos, and thus are all equal subjects of study. For von Balthasar, the very nature of the human condition and human culture have been transformed by the incarnation, making theology aesthetic in its nature. Von Balthasar's intellectual background profoundly marks his theological method. As noted by Edward Oakes, "What makes a study of Balthasar's work with the German classics so important is the issue of interpretation: for it was from his study of the German classics that von Balthasar first received his training as a scholar and thus first came to his method of textual, and even theological, interpretation."[92] However, the significance of von Balthasar's use of literature goes well beyond his textual method; it offers an interdisciplinary theological contribution. For von Balthasar, literary sources are theological. He does not examine literature in order to find religious or theological themes therein. Instead, von Balthasar holds literature to be theological.[93] However, von Balthasar does not uncritically accept all literature as theology. For him there are certain literary figures who are also theologians. His aesthetics offers an example of his use of literature as theology. The use of literature as a theological resource and conversation partner is a hallmark of von Balthasar's theology. Emerging directly from his background in literary studies, von Balthasar's incorporation of literature gives theology an interdisciplinary dimension in its very foundation.

The link between theology and literature is emphasized in Philip A. Ballinger's recent study of the theological aesthetics of Gerard Manley Hopkins.[94] To understand Hopkins solely as a poet, Ballinger argues, is to miss the fullness of his writing. Instead, Hopkins is a theologian and philosopher whose poetry was a means of communicating the subtlety of his thought. His theology, Ballinger contends, carries a Christological emphasis that centers on Beauty. "His is a theological approach that emphasizes the perception of beauty in creation as revelation through an intensely Christological lens. . . . Revelation occurs, for Hopkins, in the perception of a thing's or experience's beauty—a perception which he ultimately held to be a kind of 'knowing' of the incarnate Word in matter."[95] Hopkins links aesthetic perception to the revelatory moment. Through his poetry faith and Beauty are reunited. The poetic form of Hopkins's theology is not inconsequential. As Ballinger notes, "For Hopkins, poetry is the use of language best suited for an approach to the transcendent. Even more, it seems that Hopkins tended toward a view of poetic language as 'sacramental' in function."[96] Thus, in Ballinger's retrieval of Hopkins's aesthetic theology, we find once again that the aesthetic is central to expressing the religious dimension of humanity.

Contrary to the writing of liberation theologians, for the most part contemporary European and Euro-American theologians who are writing in the field of theological aesthetics have not explicitly approached the relationship between aesthetics and ethics, especially from the perspective of marginalized peoples. While von Balthasar links aesthetics and ethics, this is not a strongly developed idea in his theology.[97] In the United States, Edward Farley goes so far as to downplay the aesthetic sensibilities of the oppressed. "Because an impoverished and marginalized life makes it very difficult for the slave, the poor or the disenfranchised to develop sensibilities, beauty as a culturally accessible value tends to become the possession of the citizen, the nobility, the gentry and the educated classes."[98] While not exactly denying the existence of aesthetic persuasions amongst the disenfranchised, Farley segregates the oppressed from the realm of beauty as cultural value. Earlier in his text Farley defines Beauty as that which is attractive. Theological aesthetics thus "uncovers the relation between what is intrinsically attractive and the life of faith."[99] Farley does not elaborate, however, on the implications of theological aesthetics for social justice.

A recent book by John W. De Gruchy offers a refreshing perspective on the interrelationship of aesthetics and ethics.[100] Underlying De Gruchy's work is the relationship between beauty and ugliness, which leads to the theological relationship between aesthetics and ethics. Beauty, De Gruchy argues, needs the Ugly. "Beauty may have the potential to redeem . . . but ugliness has the equally necessary capacity to subvert and deconstruct that which destroys life."[101] Just as the appeal of Beauty leads to attraction, ugliness's repellence can call one to contest and challenge it. For De Gruchy, Beauty is also fundamental for Truth, for without Beauty Truth loses its ability to persuade: "Truth without goodness and beauty degenerates into dogmatism, and lacks the power to attract and convince; goodness without truth is superficial, and without beauty—that is without graced form—it degenerates into moralizing. Alternatively, we could say that truth and goodness without beauty lack power to convince and therefore to save."[102] In a similar fashion to Goizueta, De Gruchy posits the aesthetic as the avenue for ethics and rationality. Beauty is the medium for the True and the Good.

Linked to the frequently cited interrelationship of Beauty and ugliness, and of special importance for Christian theology, is the cross. The "ugliness" of the cross paradoxically reveals God's glory through the path of humiliation. De Gruchy picks up on this theme in von Balthasar's theology, emphasizing that Beauty of the cross denounces the ugliness of human sin. This "alien beauty" is the source of human redemption. Only through assuming the ugliness of this world can Christ redeem humanity from it. As De Gruchy provocatively writes, "If it be so that Christ can only 'redeem what he has assumed' (Irenaeus), then it must be the case that only by assuming the ugliness of death on a cross erected on a rubbish dump outside the city, where 'there is no trace of beauty,' could Christ fully reveal the beauty of God and redeem the world."[103] Adopting a slightly different interpretation of the cross, Richard A. Viladesau finds the beauty of the cross in the action it represents. As an expression of love, the cross is beautiful.[104]

Aesthetics and Ethics

Having surveyed some contemporary voices in the theological arena, it is clear that aesthetics is poised for a return—though some would argue that this has already happened—as a central locus of theology. Theological aesthetics is not a monolithic school, however, but instead appears in many guises. Often it is accompanied by ethics; other times it is emphasized at the expense of ethics. Nonetheless, the implications of this return to Beauty are still unraveling, revealing an exciting moment in the history of theology. Beauty will not return in a manner identical to its previous incarnations; instead, aesthetics is shaped by the questions and concerns of modern/postmodern theology and culture. In this concluding section, I wish to highlight various features of the retrieval of Beauty in contemporary theology. The following chapter will explore these in light of my recovery of Sor Juana's theology.

To describe current writing in theological aesthetics as a return or retrieval is to imply that something has been lost. A central feature of many twentieth-century texts on aesthetics, beginning with von Balthasar's, is a lament for the loss of Beauty. This cry is accompanied by a reminiscence of an age long past, where Beauty was integral to theology. From the voices of European, Euro-American, Latino/a, and feminist theologians comes speculation surrounding the source of this loss: A fear of the body and embodiment? Wariness of Beauty's attraction? The reduction of Beauty to subjective opinion? All these answers are, in part, correct. They demonstrate the various fronts upon which Beauty was attacked. Implied in these are a sense that theology has somehow changed over the century, that in its attempt to become a scientific, academic discipline, theology has sacrificed its heart.

Interestingly, the writings of Black and womanist theologians do not include this grief over the loss of Beauty. Also, among those examined above, not one identifies their work as theological aesthetics. Instead, these scholars immerse themselves in historical research and contemporary interdisciplinary studies whose goal is the articulation of a theology that emerges from the Black community in the United States. The perhaps unintentional consequence of this research is the incorporation of aesthetic resources as central interlocutors for Black and womanist theologies. For Black theologians there is no lament for Beauty because, in their uncovering of historical Black sources, Beauty's historical presence is revealed. While European philosophers were picking away at the foundations of aesthetics, slaves were singing spirituals, finding their theological voice in music. Black and womanist theologians are unapologetic in their use of aesthetics. They do not spend chapters defending their use of spirituals, literature, and narratives. Instead, these sources are understood as organic to their theological task. A lesson can be learned here, especially for other liberation theologies. The assertion of Beauty's demise must be situated in its appropriate context, within academic European and Euro-American theologies. To deny the presence of theological aesthetics throughout the ages is to silence the marginalized voices of those who continued the tradition of seeing aesthetics as central to theological expression.

While certainly not the case for every thinker examined, the importance of the interrelationship between aesthetics and ethics is at the center of this recent impulse in theological aesthetics. Aesthetics cannot be emphasized in spite of, or in place of, ethics. Instead, the Good and Beauty, and the True for that matter, must remain organically united, existing in their interrelationship. Beauty is not a distraction from Justice, but the motivation behind it. Goizueta and De Gruchy are of special note in this area, for this is a central thrust in their writing. While Black and womanist theologians do not explicitly address the question of aesthetics and ethics, through the use of aesthetic sources in their liberation projects they affirm the unity of the two. In a similar vein, feminist theologians who recover forgotten women's voices from Christian history explore this interrelationship implicitly in their writing. Linked to this is the power of ugliness in aesthetics. As von Balthasar aptly points out, theological aesthetics must not be confused with aestheticism. God's beauty, in fact, is revealed in the suffering of the cross. Divine Beauty challenges human constructions of the beautiful.

The methodological implications of theological aesthetics are profound. Such an emphasis forces a comprehensive transformation of what is deemed theological discourse. The sources and methods of theology are expanded to include alternative expressions. Form and content are reunited. Beauty and glory return as central theological categories. Theology is no longer reduced to analytic, scientific discourse. However, the aesthetic in no way compromises theology's ability to make truth claims or speak meaningfully about this world. Instead, theological aesthetics redefines how one can speak authentically about the religious dimension of humanity. Sor Juana's theology, emerging at a time and place where this aesthetic expression was vital to the theological task, offers an essential resource in theological aesthetics, through both the form and content of her writing.

Notes

[1] Rubem A. Alves, "From Liberation Theologian to Poet: A Plea That the Church Move from Ethics to Aesthetics, from Doing to Beauty," *Church and State* 83 (1993):23.

[2] See Rosemary Radford Ruether, *Women and Redemption: A Theological History* (Minneapolis: Fortress Press, 1998).

[3] See Dwight N. Hopkins and George C.L. Cummings, eds., *Cut Loose Your Stammering Tongue: Black Theology in the Slave Narratives* (Maryknoll, NY: Orbis, 1991); Dwight Hopkins, *Down, Up, and Over: Slave Religion and Black Theology* (Minneapolis: Fortress Press, 2000). For a critique of Black theology's use of the slave narratives, see Victor Anderson, "Critical Reflections on the Problems of History and Narrative in a Recent African-American Research Program," in *A Dream Unfinished: Theological Reflections on America from the Margins*, ed. Eleazer S. Fernandez and Fernando F. Segovia (Maryknoll, NY: Orbis, 2001), 37-51.

184   THE ORGANIC UNITY OF BEAUTY AND JUSTICE

[4]See Manuel J. Mejido, "A Critique of the 'Aesthetic Turn' in U.S. Hispanic Theology: A Dialogue with Roberto Goizueta and the Positing of a New
Paradigm," *Journal of Hispanic Latino Theology* 8:3 (Feb. 2001): 18-48.

[5]Karl Rahner, "Theology and the Arts," *Thought* 57: 224 (March 1982):
27. Rahner makes the distinction between religious art and religious kitsch,
as well as art that is religious, though not explicitly so in content.

[6]Though this is a broad generalization, Beauty has historically been more
suspect in Protestant theologies, based on the iconoclasm of the Reformation.

[7]"The several books, essays and passages on beauty in twentieth-century
theology are too infrequent and too varied to permit a credible and clear
typology of approaches, though, with the inevitable exceptions that always
blur typological analyses, the texts do seem to fall roughly into Catholic and
Protestant approaches." Edward Farley, *Faith and Beauty: A Theological
Aesthetic* (Burlington, VT: Ashgate, 2001), 68.

[8]Amos N. Wilder, *Theology and Modern Literature* (Cambridge, MA:
Harvard University Press, 1958), 15.

[9]Wilder, *Theopoetic: Theology and Religious Imagination* (Minneapolis:
Fortress Press, 1976), 8.

[10]Rahner, "Theology and the Arts," 25.

[11]Roberto S. Goizueta, "U.S. Hispanic Popular Catholicism as Theopoetics"
in *Hispanic/Latino Theology: Challenge and Promise*, ed. Ada María Isasi-
Díaz and Fernando F. Segovia (Minneapolis: Fortress Press, 1996), 262.

[12]Hans Urs von Balthasar, *Seeing the Form*, vol. 1 of *The Glory of the Lord:
A Theological Aesthetics*, trans. of *Herrlichkeit: Eine Theologische Ästhetik*,
ed. Joseph Fessio, S.J., and John Riches, trans. Erasmo Leiva-Merikakis (San
Francisco: Ignatius Press, 1989), 494.

[13]Von Balthasar divides theological aesthetics into two eras: clerical, where
Beauty had an official place in the Church, and lay, where Beauty is found
outside of the Church. For von Balthasar, the chronological dividing line is
1300. After 1300, Christian spirituality became marginalized from theological discourse. The authors examined in *Lay Styles* are therefore found on the
margins of the institutional Church; their theologies were not that of the
mainstream. By naming these authors "lay" Balthasar is emphasizing this
marginalization. Two of the authors, Hopkins and St. John of the Cross, are
clerics, yet for von Balthasar they are "laymen" in light of the Church's
dominant discourse. John of the Cross, for example, is depicted as a response
to both the collapse of the Medieval world view and a response to the
Reformation. Hans Urs von Balthasar, *The Glory of the Lord: A Theological
Aesthetics*, vol. 2, *Studies in Theological Style: Clerical Styles*, trans. of
Herrlichkeit: Eine theologische Ästhetik, II: Fächer der Stile, I Klerical Style,
ed. John Riches, trans. Andrew Louth, Francis McDonagh and Brian McNeil,
C.R.V. (San Francisco: Ignatius Press, 1989), 105-171; and *The Glory of the
Lord: A Theological Aesthetics*, vol. 3, *Studies in Theological Style: Lay
Styles*, trans. of *Herrlichkeit: Eine theologische Ästhetik, II: Fächer der Stile,
I Laikale Style*, ed. John Riches, trans. Andrew Louth, John Saward, Martin

Simon, and Rowan Williams (San Francisco: Ignatius Press, 1986). As Edward Oakes explicates, von Balthasar's definition of a lay theologian is "someone who feels misunderstood and shunted aside from the central concerns of the Church *precisely because* of this concern for beauty." Edward T. Oakes, *Pattern of Redemption: The Theology of Hans Urs von Balthasar* (New York: Continuum, 1997), 180.

[14]John Navone, *Toward a Theology of Beauty* (Collegeville, MN: The Liturgical Press, 1996), 26.

[15]Farley, *Faith and Beauty*, 38.

[16]Frank Burch Brown, *Religious Aesthetics: A Theological Study of Making and Meaning* (Princeton: Princeton University Press, 1989), 3.

[17]Carol Harrison, *Beauty and Revelation in the Thought of Saint Augustine* (Oxford: Clarendon Press, 1992) 270-271.

[18]Highlighting the tense relationship between Christianity, the image, and the idol, John W. De Gruchy evokes Nietzsche's critique of Christianity as at times denying the body. Nietzsche writes, "Christianity was, from the beginning, essentially and fundamentally, life's nausea and disgust with life merely concealed behind, masked by, dressed up as, faith in 'another' or 'better' life. Hatred of 'the world,' condemnations of the passions, fear of beauty and sensuality, a beyond invented the better to slander this life, at bottom a craving for the nothing, for the end, for respite, for 'the Sabbath of Sabbaths.'" Friedrich Wilhelm Nietzsche, *The Birth of Tragedy* (New York: Vintage, 1967), 22-24, cited in John W. De Gruchy, *Christianity, Art and Transformation: Theological Aesthetics in the Struggle for Justice* (Cambridge, MA: Cambridge University Press, 2001), 15.

[19]Alejandro García-Rivera, *The Community of the Beautiful: A Theological Aesthetics* (Collegeville, MN: The Liturgical Press, 1999), 9.

[20]Ibid., 11.

[21]Goizueta, *Caminemos con Jesús: Toward a Hispanic/Latino Theology of Accompaniment* (Maryknoll, NY: Orbis, 1995), 106.

[22]Goizueta, "U.S. Hispanic Popular Catholicism," 261-288.

[23]Goizueta, *Caminemos con Jesús*, 92.

[24]Ibid., 102.

[25]Ibid., 128.

[26]Goizueta, "U.S. Hispanic Popular Catholicism," 264.

[27]María Pilar Aquino has written on the topic in her earlier work. However, since this was when she still identified her theology as Latin American, I have included those texts in the section on Latin American liberation theologies.

[28]Teresa Delgado, "Prophesy Freedom: Puerto Rican Women's Literature as a Source for Latina Feminist Theology," in *Religion and Justice: A Reader in Latina Feminist Theology*, ed. María Pilar Aquino, Daisy L. Machado, and Jeanette Rodríguez (Austin, TX: University of Texas Press, 2002), 24.

[29]Ibid., 26-28.

[30]Ada María Isasi-Díaz, "Doing Theology as Mission," *Apuntes* 18:4 (Winter 1998): 109.

[31]Elizabeth A. Johnson, *She Who Is: The Mystery of God in Feminist Theological Discourse* (New York: Crossroad, 1992), 29.

[32]Anne E. Carr, "The New Vision of Feminist Theology: Method," in *Freeing Theology: The Essentials of Theology in Feminist Perspective*, ed. Catherine Mowry LaCugna (San Francisco: HarperCollins, 1993), 9-11.

[33]Elisabeth Schüssler Fiorenza, "Breaking the Silence – Becoming Visible," in *The Power of Naming: A* Concilium *Reader in Feminist Liberation Theology* (Maryknoll, NY: Orbis, 1996), 168.

[34]Ibid., 171.

[35]See Serene Jones, *Feminist Theory and Christian Theology: Cartographies of Grace* (Minneapolis: Fortress Press, 2000); Rebecca Chopp and Sheila Greeve Davaney, eds. *Horizons in Feminist Theology: Identity, Tradition, and Norms* (Minneapolis: Fortress Press, 1997).

[36]"The phrase 'social-symbolic order' calls attention, in linguistic fashion, to how a dominant ordering operates in subjectivity, language, and politics. The social-symbolic order might also be called the present historical situation or contemporary existence. But the phrase 'the social-symbolic order' underscores the structural as well as the symbolic perspectives of language." Rebecca Chopp, *The Power to Speak: Feminism, Language, God* (New York: Crossroad, 1989), 14.

[37]Chopp, "From Patriarchy into Freedom: A Conversation Between American Feminist Theology and French Feminism," in *Transfigurations: Theology and the French Feminists*, ed. C.W. Maggie Kim, Susan M. St. Ville, Susan M. Simonaitis (Minneapolis: Fortress Press, 1993), 41.

[38]Ibid., 42.

[39]Ibid., 35-36.

[40]Ibid., 40-41.

[41]Julia Kristeva, *Des Chinoises* (Paris: Éditions des femmes, 1974), 43.

[42]Ina Lipkowitz and Andrea Loselle, interviewers, "A Conversation with Julia Kristeva," in *Julia Kristeva: Interviews*, ed. Ross Mitchell Guberman (New York: Columbia University Press, 1996), 21.

[43]Toril Moi, *Sexual/Textual Politics: Feminist Literary Theory* (New York: Routledge, 1985), 152.

[44]Jacqueline Rose, "Julia Kristeva – Take Two," in *Ethics, Politics, and Difference in Julia Kristeva's Writing*, ed. Kelly Oliver (New York: Routledge: 1993), 43.

[45]Cleo McNelly Kearns, "Kristeva and Feminist Theology," in *Transfigurations: Theology and the French Feminists*, 66-67.

[46]Kristeva, *Révolution du langage poétique* (Paris: Éditions du Seuil, 1974). "Literary language, especially as it has evolved in the West, not only offers a royal road to the particular sensibilities of women. It also points the way toward new, subversive, and sometimes prophetic religious and theological insights. Kristeva takes seriously the works of Western literature that

explore the nature and fate of the soul, and she looks for a postmodern critical, psychological, and religious discourse adequate to their range and depth." McNelly Kearns, "Kristeva and Feminist Theology," 51.

[47]Chopp, *Power to Speak*, 3.

[48]Audre Lorde, "Poetry Is Not a Luxury," in *Sister/Outsider: Essays and Speeches* (Freedom, CA: The Crossing Press, 1984), 37.

[49]Ibid., 39.

[50]Elaine Scarry, *On Beauty and Being Just* (Princeton, N.J.: Princeton University Press, 1999), 23-24.

[51]Ibid., 52.

[52]Ibid., 58-59.

[53]Ibid., 62.

[54]Ibid., 80.

[55]Margaret R. Miles, *Reading for Life: Beauty, Pluralism, and Responsibility* (New York: Continuum, 1997), 16.

[56]Ibid., 17.

[57]Ibid., 203.

[58]Miles, *Seeing and Believing: Religion and Values in the Movies* (Boston: Beacon Press, 1996).

[59]Ibid., x.

[60]Sally McFague, *Speaking in Parables: A Study in Metaphor and Theology* (Philadelphia: Fortress Press, 1975), 3.

[61]Ibid., 23.

[62]Maria Teresa Porcile, "El derecho de la belleza en América Latina," in *El rostro femenino de la teología*, ed. Elsa Tamez (Costa Rica: DEI, 1986), 105.

[63]María Pilar Aquino, *Our Cry for Life: Feminist Theology from Latin America* (Maryknoll, NY: Orbis, 1993), 111. As noted by Richard Viladesau, "Because they relate to a transcendent object, many of religion's expressions are appropriately nonverbal, and a 'negative' hermeneutic must be applied even to its verbal expressions. The latter are more related to the metaphorical speech of poetry, which addresses the existential human condition, than to the abstract concepts of science." Richard Viladesau, *Theological Aesthetics: God in Imagination, Beauty, and Art* (Oxford: Oxford University Press, 1999), 17.

[64]María Clara Bingemer, "Women in the Future of the Theology of Liberation," in *Feminist Theology from the Third World: A Reader*, ed. Ursula King (Maryknoll, NY: Orbis, 1994), 311.

[65]Ivone Gebara, "Women Doing Theology in Latin America," in *Feminist Theology from the Third World*, 56.

[66]Rubem A. Alves, *The Poet, The Warrior, The Prophet* (London: SCM Press; Philadelphia: Trinity Press International, 1990), 114.

[67]Ibid., 127.

[68]Rubem A. Alves, "From Liberation Theologian to Poet: A Plea That the Church Move from Ethics to Aesthetics, from Doing to Beauty," *Church and State* 83 (1993): 23.

[69]Alves, *The Poet, The Warrior, The Prophet*, 52.

[70]Ibid., 126.

[71]Dwight N. Hopkins, *Introducing Black Theology of Liberation* (Maryknoll, NY: Orbis, 1999), 42-46.

[72]Diana L. Hayes, *And Still We Rise: An Introduction to Black Liberation Theology* (New York: Paulist Press, 1996), 86.

[73]"Those of us who stand outside the circle of this society's definition of acceptable women; those of us who have been forged in the crucibles of difference – those of us who are poor, who are lesbians, who are Black, who are older – know that *survival is not an academic skill.* It is learning how to stand alone, unpopular and sometimes reviled, and how to make common cause with those others identified as outside the structures in order to define and seek a world in which we can all flourish. It is learning how to take our differences and make them strengths. *For the master's tools will never dismantle the master's house.* They may allow us to temporarily beat him at his own game, but they will never enable us to bring about genuine change." Audre Lorde, "The Master's Tools Will Never Dismantle the Master's House," in *Sister/Outsider*, 112.

[74]Dwight N. Hopkins, *Shoes That Fit Our Feet: Sources for a Constructive Black Theology* (Maryknoll, NY: Orbis, 1993), 5.

[75]James H. Cone, *The Spirituals and the Blues* (Maryknoll, NY: Orbis, 2000), 6.

[76]On music as a source for womanist theology, see Cheryl A. Kirk-Duggan, "African-American Spirituals: Confronting and Exorcising Evil through Song," in *A Troubling in My Soul: Womanist Perspectives on Evil and Suffering*, ed. Emile M. Townes (Maryknoll, NY: Orbis, 1993), 150-171; Cheryl A. Kirk-Duggan, "Justified, Sanctified, and Redeemed: Blessed Expectations in Black Women's Blues and Gospels," in *Embracing the Spirit: Womanist Perspectives on Hope, Salvation, and Transformation* (Maryknoll, NY: Orbis, 1997), 140-166; and Cheryl A. Kirk-Duggan, *Exorcising Evil: A Womanist Perspective on the Spirituals* (Maryknoll, NY: Orbis, 1997).

[77]Stephanie Y. Mitchem, *Introducing Womanist Theology* (Maryknoll, NY: Orbis, 2002), 69.

[78]Katie Geneva Cannon, *Katie's Canon: Womanism and the Soul of the Black Community* (New York: Continuum, 1996), 61.

[79]Hopkins, *Shoes That Fit Our Feet*, 83.

[80]Alice Walker, "Preface to the Tenth Anniversary Edition," *The Color Purple*, 10th anniversary ed. (New York: Harcourt Brace Jovanovich, 1992), xi.

[81]Cheryl Townsend Gilkes, "The 'Loves' and 'Troubles' of African-American Women's Bodies: The Womanist Challenge to Cultural Humiliation and Community Ambivalence," in *A Troubling in My Soul*, 232.

[82]Ibid.

[83]von Balthasar, *Seeing the Form*, 9.

[84]Ibid.

[85]Oakes, *Pattern of Redemption*, 143-145.

[86]"In a world without beauty . . . in a world which is perhaps not wholly without beauty, but which can no longer see it or reckon with it: in such a world the good also loses its attractiveness. . . . In a world that no longer has enough confidence in itself to affirm the beautiful, the proofs of the truth have lost their cogency." von Balthasar, *Seeing the Form*, 19.

[87]Ibid., 151.

[88]Peter J. Casarella, "The Painted Word," *Journal of Hispanic/Latino Theology* 6:2 (Nov. 98): 26-27.

[89]Oakes, *Pattern of Redemption*, 142.

[90]Ibid., 21.

[91]von Balthasar, *Seeing the Form*, 460.

[92]Oakes, *Pattern of Redemption*, 73.

[93]Alois M. Haas notes that von Balthasar would most likely not be accepted by literary scholars and theologians. "The reason is simply that von Balthasar lets the whole fullness of literary, philosophical, and theological mythical formulations converge toward an explicitly Christian mythic, while contemporary literary theology clearly tends toward a philosophical mediation between religion and literature." Alois M. Haas, "Hans Urs von Balthasar's 'Apocalypse of the German Soul': At the Intersection of German Literature, Philosophy, and Theology," in *Hans Urs von Balthasar: His Life and Work*, ed. David L. Schindler (San Francisco: Ignatius Press, 1991), 46.

[94]Philip A. Ballinger, *The Poem as Sacrament: The Theological Aesthetic of Gerard Manley Hopkins* (Louvain: Peters Press, 2000).

[95]Ibid., 2.

[96]Ibid., 3.

[97]For von Balthasar's critique of liberation theology, see Hans Urs von Balthasar, "Liberation Theology in the Light of Salvation History," in *Liberation Theology in Latin America*, ed. James V. Schall (San Francisco: Ignatius Press, 1982), 131-146. For a critique of von Balthasar's neglect of social justice see Thomas G. Dalzall, S.M., "Lack of Social Drama in Balthasar's Theological Dramatics," *Theological Studies* 60 (1999): 457-475.

[98]Farley, *Faith and Beauty*, 4.

[99]Ibid., viii.

[100]De Gruchy, *Christianity, Art and Transformation*.

[101]Ibid., 79-80.

[102]Ibid., 107.

[103]Ibid., 123.

[104]"The cross is not beautiful or good in itself: it is beautiful only insofar as it represents Christ's ultimate faithfulness and self-gift to God, even to the point of death, and insofar as this act is given eternal validity by God's overcoming of death itself. That is, the cross only has beauty as the expression of an act of love; and love is 'beautiful,' theologically speaking, precisely because it is finally not defeated, but victorious. . . . The cross, then, is not a beautiful thing; it is the symbol of a beautiful *act*." Viladesau, *Theological Aesthetics*, 197.

Conclusion

Sor Juana Inés de la Cruz

Latin American Church Mother

> *"I think it pisses God off if you walk by the color purple in a field somewhere and don't notice it."*[1]
> —Alice Walker

The ground is fertile for a revival of aesthetics in theology. Scholars from a variety of contexts are increasingly arguing that aesthetics is vital for the contemporary theological arena. In liberation theologies, theological aesthetics comes hand in hand with the centrality of the nonperson and attempts to recover marginalized histories within Christianity. This growing emphasis on aesthetics, however, can never come at the expense of the social justice that is essential to liberation theologies. In a similar vein, neither Beauty nor the Good can ever undermine the truth claims of theologies and their ability to speak meaningfully. Instead, Beauty and the Good expand the very way we understand Truth.

The theology of Sor Juana Inés de la Cruz offers an avenue for exploring the interrelationship between the True, Beauty, and the Good. The aesthetic form of her theology places Beauty at the center, though her concern for Justice and Truth also remains a fundamental component of her theology. In this concluding chapter, I explore several contributions Sor Juana's theology makes to contemporary conversations in theological aesthetics, with a particular focus on liberation theologies. Sor Juana's relevance cannot be limited to marginalized contexts. However, many of her interests and insights resonate with those raised by theologies from the underside of history. Before entering into her particular concerns, however, Sor Juana's broader impact on the discipline of theology must be established. Before Sor Juana's voice can gain access to the halls of the theological academy, the very nature of the discipline must be challenged and expanded.

Sor Juana: *Mujer Latinoamericana*

Josefina Ludmer has noted that in order to recover women's philosophical contributions, scholars must essentially transform their understanding of philosophy: "To the question of why there have been no women philosophers, one can answer that women have not engaged in philosophy from the space delimited by classical philosophy but rather from other zones; and if one reads or listens to their discourse as philosophical discourse, one can effect that transformation of thought. The same holds true for science and politics."[2] The transformation occurs at various levels. There is that of the reader, who must allow these marginalized voices to enter into the discourse of philosophy. Then there is the text or source itself, which, being marginalized, offers a new way of understanding the philosophical task. Finally, the very discipline of philosophy is transformed through the inclusion of this voice as a legitimate resource. This process depends on a porous definition of philosophy. As noted by Andrea Nye, however, this is organic to philosophy as a discipline: "Even when ratified by a version of intellectual history that covers up personal or political resources of philosophical wisdom or that privileges science as the only knowledge, philosophy's parameters remain unstable. The very insistence on what is 'real' or 'hardcore' philosophy against what is 'only' poetry, sociology, personal memoir, or politics itself renews the possibility of yet another philosophical reconstitution."[3] In other words, philosophy is constantly redefining and reinterpreting itself.

These remarks are in reference to the inclusion of women's voices into the "canon" of philosophical discourse. Turning specifically to the Latin American context, the work of philosopher

Ofelia Schutte offers a voice that addresses the absence of Latin American voices in philosophy. Schutte disputes the theory that the marginalization of Latin American philosophy is somehow due to a Eurocentric or Anglo-American bias, offering an alternative explanation:

> In my view, the error comes from a different source, namely, the fact that this rough model contains a limited conception of what counts as philosophy. Philosophy is defined exclusively or primarily either with the positing of universal truths or with the development of systematic theories of knowledge or value. . . . And yet, this analysis of philosophy as the end-product of the great system-builders may represent a misguided understanding of the great thinkers whom we call philosophers. For this reason an alternative understanding of what counts as philosophy is needed.[4]

Building on these remarks, Schutte provides an alternate definition of philosophy: "Coming to terms with the significance of human existence, together with all its theoretical, technological, political, ethical, and aesthetic implications—and not the building of systems as such—is the job of philosophy."[5] Like Ludmer, Schutte downplays the significance of the systematic nature of philosophy and instead attempts to address its actual subject matter in order to propose a broader understanding of philosophical resources and the philosophical task.

Turning specifically to the philosophy of Latin America, Schutte makes the distinction between philosophy *in* Latin America and philosophy *of* Latin America. The former merely refers to philosophical conversations and issues in Latin America, which she notes are dominated by European philosophy. Her concern is the latter: "In other words, I shall take the reference to Latin American philosophy as combining two important features: it is work rooted in Latin America historically and culturally; in addition, it is work which engages in reflecting upon the meaning of its historical and cultural origins."[6] In my view, Sor Juana's writing is a philosophy and theology *of* Latin America.

These two strains of thought, the feminist argument for the inclusion of alternative women's voices in philosophical discourse and the Latin American critique of a narrow definition of the philosophical task, are of special relevance to this project. While they do not specifically address the discipline of theology, their remarks resonate with the work of contemporary Latin American and feminist theologians. Sor Juana is subject to the twofold marginalization of being a woman and a Latin American. Too many theologians have not heard of Sor Juana and are unfamiliar with her work. Her gender and her geographic location play a major role in this.

Sor Juana's Contemporary Contribution

Pamela Kirk, one of few scholars who has examined Sor Juana's writing in light of contemporary theology, remarks that many themes in Sor Juana's writing echo concerns of contemporary theology: "Startling is the evidence of the concerns of today's theologies running like invisible threads through her work, forming patterns of connection between then and there and now and here. Among these are her concern for the process of evangelization and her sensitivity to the mingling of cultures, her exploration of Mary as a figure of power, and her incorporation of the voices of the poor into her religious celebrations."[7] In this concluding section I emphasize Sor Juana's contributions to contemporary theology. My remarks will focus on three areas in particular: her aesthetic theological method, her theological anthropology, and her inclusion of alternative sources for theology and philosophy.

Much has been said surrounding the methodological contribution of theological aesthetics. I do not wish to repeat earlier statements, but instead focus on the significance of Sor Juana's theology in light of contemporary theology. Through her introduction of the aesthetic within the theological task, Sor Juana makes the symbolic a privileged form of theological expression. She goes as far as stating that the aesthetic is *the most appropriate form* of theological expression. Pamela Kirk highlights the connections that can be made between Sor Juana's writing and Latin American and Latino/a theologies precisely on this topic. She indicates, for example, an explicit link between Sor Juana's

writing and María Pilar Aquino's: "Yet even the literary form of
her theological production corresponds to what María Pilar
Aquino, building on María Clara Bingemer, has described as the
'primacy of desire' over the purely rational in the theology of
Latin American women."[8] Sor Juana argues for the aesthetic as a
form of theological expression. In this her ideas resonate with
those of the Latino/a, Black, feminist, and Latin American theologians cited in the previous chapter. Accompanying the aesthetic
form of her theology is the interdisciplinary understanding of
theology that saturates Sor Juana's corpus. Theology is not merely
limited to what contemporary scholars today deem "theological" texts. Instead, literature, poetry, and drama become central
forms of theological expression. As noted by Herman-Emiel
Mertens, "[T]he theological use of literary fragments should not
be limited to only pretty ornaments of the theological texts. There
is more at stake than mere illustrations. When profane literature
discloses the deep levels of the Christian existence it can be inte-
grated into the theological reflection itself."[9] Literature becomes
a theological voice that contributes in an equally substantial way
to traditional forms of theological expression.

Ressourcement is another methodological gesture that Sor
Juana's aesthetics revives in contemporary theology. Scholarship
on Sor Juana is the *ressourcement* of a significant woman in the
Christian corpus. To use Schüssler Fiorenza's language, it is the
retrieval of an intellectual foremother. As a *Latin American Church
Mother*, Sor Juana's theology provides a Third World contribution within the project of *ressourcement*. Latin American liberation theology takes the contemporary nonperson as its primary
theological interlocutor. Sor Juana scholarship represents a historical resource that has been marginalized from theological discourse, while Sor Juana's theology provides a historical foundation for future projects.[10] As noted earlier, one particular dimension
of *ressourcement* in liberation theologies is the aesthetic emphasis. Sor Juana's theology offers yet another aesthetic, historical
resource.

A second area of Sor Juana's contribution is found in her theological anthropology. Sor Juana offers an egalitarian relational
anthropology that describes the human as constituted by his or
her relationships with others and with God, and defines the *imago*

Dei in terms of Beauty. Humanity is dynamic and responsive in Sor Juana's theology. Humanity must respond to God's grace and is a dramatic participant in salvation history. Anything that goes against this vision of humanity is deemed as corrupting the *imago Dei* in us. Thus, Echo and her cohorts are the exact opposite of humanity's intended state. Sor Juana devotes a significant amount of energy in her writing attempting to undermine those human constructions that contradict her vision of the human, with the construction of gender as the centerpiece.

To the modern reader, perhaps the most surprising dimension of Sor Juana's thought is her awareness of the manner in which gender is constructed to marginalize women. Sor Juana not only sees the construction of gender identity, she is conscious of its political function. Gender is used to oppress women. Combating this stereotype, Sor Juana philosophically deconstructs this social category. Through the characters in her plays and poetry Sor Juana creates a space for the stories and voices of marginalized women. We find Echo, who overcomes her state of repetition and becomes a narrative voice in *Divino Narciso*. Also in *Narciso* Sor Juana refutes the patriarchal anthropology of her era and emphasizes the feminine as a locus of redemption. The pantheon of transgressive women in *Primero sueño* accompanies Sor Juana in her challenge to male intellectual superiority. Resonating with historical retrieval in contemporary feminist theology, Sor Juana evokes litanies of women to support her theological position.

Mary is a key figure in Sor Juana's anthropology. Not merely a passive object of devotion, in Sor Juana's theology Mary is a theologian, Mother of the Word and advocate for the marginalized. It is no accident that many of Sor Juana's texts that defend and validate the humanity of Indigenous and African peoples are found in her Marian poetry. Sor Juana's defense of Africans and the Indigenous includes her use of non-Christian sources in her theology and her emphasis on the validity of the humanity and religious practices of non-Christians. This leads to the third area of Sor Juana's contribution: her expansion of the traditional sources for theology and philosophy. Accompanying her incorporation of African and Indigenous sources is her use of song and dance as part of her theological expression. Linked to this is her emphasis on *lo cotidiano* as a vital intellectual resource. Sor

Juana tapped into the popular imagination. She offered a public theology that reached the court elite and the popular masses. The public performances of her poems and plays allowed her voice to reach a broad and mixed audience. The public nature of her work, coupled with her self-proclaimed intellectual authority and her subject matter, set her apart from the other women religious writing in her era. As Pamela Kirk notes, "Sor Juana writes with the authority that comes from her intellectual and literary talents. Neither does she need to appeal to the mystical experience of the reader as a basis for understanding what she writes. Because she draws on both intellectual and devotional traditions, her religious writing is open to the educated reason of the elite, as well as the imaginative intuitive understanding of the uneducated populace."[11] In an era where the contributions of certain theologies are becoming increasingly isolated and irrelevant, the interdisciplinary project of recovering Sor Juana's voice seeks to rectify the seclusion of theology while simultaneously recovering a marginalized woman's voice.

This study claims to be a Latin American *ressourcement*, one that engages a historical voice as a living theological contribution to contemporary theology. Further study of Sor Juana's theology is needed in the contemporary arena, as is an examination of other women religious writing in colonial Mexico. One cannot, as Stephanie Merrim warns, fall into the Tenth Muse trap. "The tendency to succumb to the Tenth Muse trap—that is, to view Sor Juana in isolation, as an isolated ex-centric phenomenon—persists."[12] A Latin American *ressourcement* encourages further exploration of the other "lost" voices of Latin American theology, both men and women. This exploration does not need to be limited to textual sources. With their emphases on popular religion and popular devotions, for example, Latino/a theologians challenge the very understanding of the sources of theology and consequently the nature of the project of *ressourcement*. Even though my work on Sor Juana expands theological forms to include literature, it still remains a textual approach. However, an emphasis on aesthetics encourages a broadening of theological sources to include non-textual sources.

Why is Sor Juana such a significant source for contemporary theology? Gloria Inés Loya writes, "She is a source/*fuente* for theology because through her work she examined and expressed her religious concerns and theological understandings."[13] I would push the point a bit farther. Sor Juana is a source for contemporary theology because she is an intellectual foremother to Christian theologians; she offers a challenge to contemporary understandings of the theological task; and she sought to address the broader concerns of Christian theology and philosophy while remaining grounded in the concerns and issues of her context and era. Sor Juana Inés de la Cruz is a vibrant figure who offers an entry point into these and many other theological arenas. I find it only fitting to incorporate her words in my concluding comments. In a poem written for the dedication of a church to Saint Bernard she writes:

> A Church, Bernard and Mary,
> and good circumstances these are
> to bring the three together
> if only a Preacher I were;
> But no, no, no, no:
> I'm no tailor to cut such fine cloth.
> Yet supposing I were,
> what things might I tell you
> seeking a connection
> and going from text to text?
> But no, no, no, no:
> I'm no tailor to cut such fine cloth.[14]

If she were a preacher, Sor Juana notes, she would say these things. But no, she says, she is not one to cut such cloth. Many would argue that she is not cut from the cloth of a theologian. I disagree. Sor Juana in fact cut such fine cloth.

Notes

[1]Alice Walker, *The Color Purple*, 10th anniversary ed. (New York: Harcourt Brace Jovanovich, 1992), 191.

[2]Josefina Ludmer, "Tricks of the Weak," in *Feminist Perspectives on Sor Juana Inés de la Cruz*, ed. Stephanie Merrim (Detroit: Wayne State University Press, 1991), 93.

[3]Andrea Nye, " 'It's Not Philosophy'," *Hypatia* 13:2 (Spring 1998): 108.

[4]Ofelia Schutte, "Toward an Understanding of Latin American Philosophy," *Philosophy Today* 31:1/4 (Spring 1987): 22.

[5]Ibid.

[6]Ibid., 24.

[7]Kirk, *Sor Juana Inés de la Cruz: Religion Art, and Feminism* (New York: Continuum, 1998), 12.

[8]Pamela Kirk, "Sor Juana Inés de la Cruz: Precursor of Latin American Feminism," *Journal of Hispanic/Latino Theology* 5:3 (1998): 17.

[9]Herman-Emiel Mertens, "His Very Name Is Beauty: Experience and Christian Faith," *Louvain Studies* 20:2-3 (Summer-Fall 1995): 329.

[10]As noted by William Portier, the theological renewal of post-Vatican II Roman Catholic theology has been grounded in historical *ressourcement.* William Portier, "Introduction," in *American Catholic Traditions: Resources for Renewal,* ed. Sandra Yocum and William Portier (Maryknoll, NY: Orbis, 1997), xi.

[11]Kirk, *Sor Juana Inés de la Cruz,* 65.

[12]Stephanie Merrim, *Early Modern Women's Writing and Sor Juana Inés de la Cruz* (Nashville: Vanderbilt University Press, 1999), xiii.

[13]Gloria Inés Loya, "Considering the Source/*Fuentes* for a Hispanic Feminist Theology," *Theology Today* 54:4 (Jan. 1998): 496.

[14]OC 2:202.342 (EC).

Bibliography

Allen, Sister Prudence, R.S.M. *The Concept of Woman: The Aristotelian Revolution, 750 B.C.-A.D. 1250.* Grand Rapids: William B. Eerdmans Publishing Co., 1985.

Alves, Rubem A. "From Liberation Theologian to Poet: A Plea That the Church Move from Ethics to Aesthetics, from Doing to Beauty." *Church and State* 83 (1993): 20-24.

————. *The Poet, The Warrior, The Prophet.* London: SCM Press; Philadelphia: Trinity Press International, 1990.

Aquino, María Pilar. "The Collective 'Dis-covery' of Our Own Power: Latina American Feminist Theology." In *Hispanic/Latino Theology: Challenge and Promise*, ed. Ada María Isasi-Díaz and Fernando Segovia, 240-258. Minneapolis: Fortress Press, 1996.

————. *Our Cry for Life: Feminist Theology from Latin America.* Maryknoll, NY: Orbis, 1993.

————. "Theological Method in U.S. Latino/a Theology: Toward an Intercultural Theology for the Third Millennium." In *From the Heart of Our People: Latino/a Explorations in Catholic Systematic Theology*, ed. Orlando Espín and Miguel Díaz, 6-48. Maryknoll, NY: Orbis, 1999.

Arango L., Manuel Antonio. *Contribución al estudio de la obra dramática de Sor Juana Inés de la Cruz.* New York: Peter Lang, 2000.

Arenal, Electa. "The Convent as Catalyst for Autonomy: Two Hispanic Nuns of the Seventeenth Century." In *Women in Hispanic Literature: Icons and Fallen Idols*, ed. Beth Miller, 147-183. Berkeley, CA: University of California Press, 1983.

————. "Where Woman Is Creator of the Worl(l)d. Or, Sor Juana's Discourses on Method." In *Feminist Perspectives on Sor Juana Inés de la Cruz*, ed. Stephanie Merrim, 124-143. Detroit: Wayne State University Press, 1991.

Arenal, Electa and Amanda Powell. "Preface." In *The Answer/La respuesta*, ed. Electa Arenal and Amanda Powell, vii-x. New York: The Feminist Press at CUNY, 1994.

Arenal, Electa and Stacey Schlau. *Untold Sisters: Hispanic Nuns in Their Own Words*. Albuquerque, NM: University of New Mexico Press, 1989.

Arroyo, Anita. *Razón y pasión de Sor Juana*. Mexico: Editorial Porrúa, 1980.

Atamoros, Noemí. *Sor Juana Inés de la Cruz*. Toluca, Estado de México: Instituto Mexiquense de Cultura,1995.

Ballinger, Philip A. *The Poem as Sacrament: The Theological Aesthetic of Gerard Manley Hopkins*. Louvain: Peeters Press, 2000.

Beaupied, Aída. *Narciso hermético: Sor Juana Inés de la Cruz y José Lezama Lima*. Liverpool: Liverpool University Press, 1997.

Begbie, Jeremy S. *Voicing Creation's Praise*. Edinburgh: T & T Clark, 1991.

Beggs, Donald. "Sor Juana's Feminism: From Aristotle to Irigaray." In *Hypatia's Daughters: Fifteen Hundred Years of Women Philosophers*, ed. Linda Lopez McAlister, 108-127. Bloomington, IN: Indiana University Press, 1996.

Bénassy-Berling, Marie-Cécile. "Actualidad del sorjuanismo (1994-1999)." *Colonial Latin American Review* 9:2 (December 2000): 277-292.

———. *Humanisme et religion chez Sor Juana Inés de la Cruz: La femme et la culture au XVIIe siècle*. Paris: Éditions Hispaniques, 1992.

———. "La modernidad de Sor Juana Inés de la Cruz como católica." In *"Por amor de las letras" Juana Inés de la Cruz: Le donne e il sacro. Atti del convegno di Venezia 26-27 Gennaio 1996*, ed. Susanna Regazzoni, 107-112. Rome: Bulzoni Editore, 1996.

———. "Sobre el hermetismo de Sor Juana Inés de la Cruz." In *La creatividad feminino en el mundo barroco hispánico: María de Zayas – Isabel Rebeca Correa–Sor Juana Inés de la Cruz*, ed. Monike Bosse et al., 629-639. Kassel: Edition Reichenberger, 1999.

Bernstein, J.M. *The Fate of Art: Aesthetic Alienation from Kant to Derrida and Adorno*. University Park, PA: The Pennsylvania State University Press, 1992.

Beuchot, Mauricio. "Los autos de Sor Juana: Tres lugares teológicos." In *Sor Juana y su mundo: Una mirada actual*, ed. Sara Poot Herrera, 355-392. Mexico: Universidad del Claustro de Sor Juana, 1995.

———. *Estudios de historia y de filosofía en el México colonial*. Mexico: UNAM, 1991.

———. *The History of Philosophy in Colonial Mexico*. Translated by Elizabeth Millán. Washington, DC: The Catholic University of America Press, 1998.

———. *Sor Juana: Una filosofía barroca*. Mexico: UNAM, 1999.

———. "El universo filosófico de Sor Juana." In *Memoria del Coloquio Internacional Sor Juana Inés de la Cruz y el Pensamiento Novohispano*, 29-40. Mexico: Instituto Mexiquense de Cultura, 1995.

Bingemer, María Clara. "Women in the Future of the Theology of Liberation." In *Feminist Theology from the Third World: A Reader*, ed. Ursula King, 308-318. Maryknoll, NY: Orbis, 1994.

Børreson, Kari Elisabeth. *Subordination and Equivalence: The Nature and Role of Woman in Augustine and Thomas Aquinas*. Washington, DC: University Press of America, 1981. Reprint, Kampen: Kok Pharos Publishing House, 1995.

Brown, Frank Burch. *Religious Aesthetics*. Princeton, NJ: Princeton University Press, 1989.

Cannon, Katie Geneva. *Katie's Canon: Womanism and the Soul of the Black Community*. New York: Continuum, 1996.

Carr, Anne E. "The New Vision of Feminist Theology: Method." In *Freeing Theology: The Essentials of Theology in Feminist Perspective*, ed. Catherine Mowry LaCugna, 5-29. San Francisco: HarperCollins, 1993.

Casarella, Peter J. "The Painted Word." *Journal of Hispanic/Latino Theology* 6:2 (November 1998): 18-42.

Cevallos-Candaui, Francisco Javier, et al., eds. *Coded Encounters: Writing, Gender, and Ethnicity in Colonial Latin America*. Amherst, MA: The University of Massachusetts Press, 1994.

Chopp, Rebecca. *The Power to Speak: Feminism, Language, God*. New York: Crossroad, 1989.

Chopp, Rebecca and Sheila Greeve Davaney, eds. *Horizons in Feminist Theology: Identity, Tradition, and Norms.* Minneapolis: Fortress Press, 1997.

Cone, James H. *Black Theology and Black Power.* New York: Seabury Press, 1969; Maryknoll, NY: Orbis Books, 1998.

————. *The Spirituals and the Blues.* Maryknoll, NY: Orbis, 2000.

Congar, Yves. *I Believe in the Holy Spirit.* Vol. 2. Translated by David Smith. New York: Seabury Press, 1983.

Couch, Beatriz Melano. "Sor Juana Inés de la Cruz: The First Woman Theologian in the Americas." In *The Church and Women in the Third World,* ed. John C.B. Webster and Ellen Low Webster, 51-57. Philadelphia: The Westminster Press, 1985.

Cruz-Martinez, George. "Sor Juana Inés de la Cruz: Mother of Latin American Feminist Theology." *Apuntes* 12:2 (Summer 1992): 30-32.

De Gruchy, John W. *Christianity, Art and Transformation: Theological Aesthetics in the Struggle for Justice.* Cambridge, MA: Cambridge University Press, 2001.

Delgado, Teresa. "Prophesy Freedom: Puerto Rican Women's Literature as a Source for Latina Feminist Theology." In *Religion and Justice: A Reader in Latina Feminist Theology,* ed. María Pilar Aquino, Daisy L. Machado, and Jeanette Rodríguez, 23-52. Austin, TX: University of Texas Press, 2002.

Dietz, Donald T. "Liturgical and Allegorical Drama: The Uniqueness of Calderón's Auto Sacramental." In *Calderón de la Barca at the Tercentenary: Comparative Views,* ed. Wendell M. Aycock and Sydney P. Cravens, 71-88. Lubbock, TX: Texas Tech Press, 1982.

————. "Theology and the Stage: The God Figure in Calderón's *Autos sacramentales.*" *Bulletin of the Comediantes* 34:1 (Summer 1982): 97-105.

Dupré, Louis. "The Glory of the Lord: Hans Urs von Balthasar's Theological Aesthetic." In *Hans Urs von Balthasar: His Life and Work,* ed. David L. Schindler, 133-148. San Francisco: Ignatius Press, 1991.

————. *Passage to Modernity: An Essay in the Hermeneutics of Nature and Culture.* New Haven, CT: Yale University Press, 1993.

Elizondo, Virgilio. *Guadalupe: Mother of the New Creation.* Maryknoll, NY: Orbis, 1997.

Espín, Orlando O. *The Faith of the People: Theological Reflections on Popular Catholicism*. Maryknoll, NY: Orbis, 1997.

Farley, Edward. *Faith and Beauty: A Theological Aesthetic*. Burlington, VT: Ashgate, 2001.

Fornet-Betancourt, Raúl, ed. *Filosofía, teología, literatura: Aportes cubanos en los últimos 50 años*. Aachen: Concordia Reihe Monographien, Band 25, 1999.

Franco, Jean. *Plotting Women: Gender and Representation in Mexico*. New York: Columbia University Press, 1989.

García Alvarez, Jesús. *El pensamiento filosófico de Sor Juana Inés de la Cruz*. León, Gto.: Centro de Estudios Filosóficos Tomás de Aquino, 1997.

García-Rivera, Alejandro. *The Community of the Beautiful: A Theological Aesthetics*. Collegeville, MN: The Liturgical Press, 1999.

————. *St. Martín de Porres: "The Little Stories" and the Semiotics of Culture*. Maryknoll, NY: Orbis, 1995.

Gaspar de Alba, Alicia. "The Politics of Location of the Tenth Muse of America: An Interview with Sor Juana Inés de la Cruz." In *Living Chicana Theory*, ed. Carla Trujillo, 136-165. Berkeley, CA: Third World Woman Press, 1998.

————. *Sor Juana's Second Dream*. Albuquerque, NM: The University of New Mexico Press, 1999.

Gebara, Ivone. "Women Doing Theology in Latin America." In *Feminist Theology from the Third World: A Reader*, ed. Ursula King, 47-59. Maryknoll, NY: Orbis, 1994.

Gilkes, Cheryl Townsend. "The 'Loves' and 'Troubles' of African-American Women's Bodies: The Womanist Challenge to Cultural Humiliation and Community Ambivalence." In *A Troubling in My Soul: Womanist Perspectives on Evil and Suffering*, ed. Emilie M. Townes, 232-249. Maryknoll, NY: Orbis, 2001.

Glantz, Margo. *Sor Juana Inés de La Cruz: ¿Hagiografía o autobiografía?* Mexico: UNAM, 1995.

————. *Sor Juana Inés: La comparación y la hipérbole*. Mexico: CONACULTA, 2000.

Goizueta, Roberto S. *Caminemos con Jesús: Toward a Hispanic/Latino Theology of Accompaniment*. Maryknoll, NY: Orbis, 1995.

——. "Fiesta: Life in the Subjunctive." In *From the Heart of Our People: Latino/a Explorations in Catholic Systematic Theology*, ed. Orlando Espín and Miguel Díaz, 84-99. Maryknoll, NY: Orbis, 1999.

——. "A *Ressourcement* from the Margins: U.S. Latino Popular Catholicism as Lived Religion." In *Theology and Lived Christianity*, ed. David M. Hammond, 3-37. Mystic, CT: Twenty-Third Publications, 2000.

——. "U.S. Hispanic Popular Catholicism as Theopoetics." In *Hispanic/Latino Theology: Challenge and Promise*, ed. Ada María Isasi-Díaz and Fernando Segovia, 261-288. Minneapolis: Fortress Press, 1996.

Gonzalez, Michelle A. *A Latin American Ressourcement: The Theological Contribution of Sor Juana Inés de la Cruz in light of the Methodology of Hans Urs von Balthasar*. Ph.D. Diss., Graduate Theological Union, 2001.

——. "*Nuestra Humanidad*: Toward a Latina Theological Anthropology." *Journal of Hispanic/Latino Theology* 8:3 (Feb. 2001): 49-72.

——. "Seeing Beauty within Torment: Sor Juana Inés de la Cruz and the Baroque in New Spain." In *Religion and Justice: A Reader in Latina Feminist Theology*, ed. María Pilar Aquino, Daisy L. Machado, and Jeanette Rodríguez, 3-22. Austin, TX: University of Texas Press, 2002.

González Boixo, José Carlos. "Feminismo e intelectualidad en Sor Juana." In *Sor Juana Inés de la Cruz*, ed. Luis Sáinz de Medrano, 33-46. Rome: Bulzoni Editore, 1997.

Greider, Brett. *Crossing Deep Rivers: The Liberation Theology of Gustavo Gutiérrez in Light of the Narrative Poetics of José María Arguedas*. Ph.D. diss., Graduate Theological Union, Berkeley, CA, 1988.

Grossi, Verónica. "La loa para el auto sacramental *El Divino Narciso* de Sor Juana Inés de la Cruz frente al canon del auto oficial." *Monographic Review* 13 (1997): 122-138.

——. "Political Meta-Allegory in *El Divino Narciso* by Sor Juana Inés de la Cruz." *Intertexts* 1:1 (Spring 1997): 92-103.

Gutiérrez, Gustavo. *Las Casas: In Search of the Poor of Jesus Christ*. Maryknoll, NY: Orbis, 1993.

———. *A Theology of Liberation*, 15ᵗʰ anniversary ed. Maryknoll, NY: Orbis, 1988.

Haas, Alois M. "Hans Urs von Balthasar's 'Apocalypse of the German Soul': At the Intersection of German Literature, Philosophy, and Theology." In *Hans Urs von Balthasar: His Life and Work*, ed. David L. Schindler, 45-57. San Francisco: Ignatius Press, 1991.

Harrison, Carol. *Beauty and Revelation in the Thought of Saint Augustine*. Oxford: Clarendon Press, 1992.

Hayes, Diana L. *And Still We Rise: An Introduction to Black Liberation Theology*. New York: Paulist Press, 1996.

Hopkins, Dwight N. *Down, Up, and Over: Slave Religion and Black Theology*. Minneapolis: Fortress Press, 2000.

———. *Introducing Black Theology of Liberation*. Maryknoll, NY: Orbis, 1999.

———. *Shoes That Fit Our Feet: Sources for a Constructive Black Theology*. Maryknoll, NY: Orbis, 1993.

Hopkins, Dwight N. and George C.L. Cummings, eds. *Cut Loose Your Stammering Tongue: Black Theology in the Slave Narratives*. Maryknoll, NY: Orbis, 1991.

Johnson, Elizabeth A. *She Who Is: The Mystery of God in Feminist Theological Discourse*. New York: Crossroad, 1992.

Jones, Serene. *Feminist Theory and Christian Theology: Cartographies of Grace*. Minneapolis: Fortress Press, 2000.

Juan de la Cruz, San. "Cántico espiritual." In *Obras completas*, 5ᵗʰ ed., ed. Eulogio Pachi, 47-54. Burgos: Editorial Monte Carmelo, 1997.

Juana Inés de la Cruz, Sor. *The Answer/La respuesta: Including a Selection of Poems*, ed. Electa Arenal and Amanda Powell. New York: The Feminist Press at the City University of New York, 1994.

———. *The Divine Narcissus – El Divino Narciso*. Translated and annotated by Patricia A. Peters and Renée Domeier. Albuquerque, NM: University of New Mexico Press, 1998.

———. *Famas y obras póstumas del fénix de México, dezima musa, poetisa americana, Sor Juana Inés de la Cruz*. Mexico: Frente de Afirmación Hispanista, A.C., 1989.

————. *Obras completas*. Alfonso Méndez-Plancarte and Alberto G. Salceda, eds. Third edition. Vols. I-IV: *Lírica personal*; *Villancicos y letras sacras*; *Autos y loas*; *Comedias, sainetes y prosa*. Mexico: Fondo de Cultura Económica; Instituto Mexiquense de Cultura, 1995.

————. *Poems, Protest, and a Dream: Selected Writings*. Translated by Margaret Sayers Peden. New York: Penguin Books, 1997.

————. *A Sor Juana Anthology*. Translated by Alan S. Trueblood. Cambridge, MA: Harvard University Press, 1988.

Kirk, Pamela. "Christ as Divine Narcissus: A Theological Analysis of 'El Divino Narciso' by Sor Juana Inés de la Cruz." *Word and World* XII:2 (Spring 1992): 146-153.

————. "Sor Juana Inés de la Cruz: Precursor of Latin American Feminism." *Journal of Hispanic/Latino Theology* 5:3 (1998): 16-38.

————. *Sor Juana Inés de la Cruz: Religion, Art, and Feminism*. New York: Continuum, 1998.

Kirk-Duggan, Cheryl A. "African-American Spirituals: Confronting and Exorcising Evil through Song." In *A Troubling in My Soul: Womanist Perspectives on Evil and Suffering*, ed. Emile M. Townes, 150-171. Maryknoll, NY: Orbis, 1993.

————. *Exorcising Evil: A Womanist Perspective on the Spirituals*. Maryknoll, NY: Orbis, 1997.

————. "Justified, Sanctified, and Redeemed: Blessed Expectations in Black Women's Blues and Gospels." In *Embracing the Spirit: Womanist Perspectives on Hope, Salvation, and Transformation*, 140-166. Maryknoll, NY: Orbis, 1997.

Lavrin, Asunción. "Espiritualidad en el claustro novohispano." *Colonial Latin American Review* 4:2 (1995): 155-179.

————. "Sor Juana Inés de la Cruz: Obediencia y autoridad en su entorno religioso." *Revista Iberoamericana* 61 (July-Dec. 1995): 606-622.

————. "Unlike Sor Juana? The Model Nun in the Religious Literature of Colonial Mexico." In *Feminist Perspectives on Sor Juana Inés de la Cruz*, ed. Stephanie Merrim, 61-85. Detroit: Wayne State University Press, 1991.

Leonard, Irving A. *Baroque Times in Old Mexico: Seventeenth-Century Persons, Places, and Practices*. Ann Arbor, MI: University of Michigan Press, 1959.

López López, Alejandro. "Sor Juana Inés de la Cruz y la loa del *Divino Narciso*." In *Memoria del Coloquio Internacional: Sor Juana Inés de la Cruz Y El Pensamiento Novohispano 1995*, 221-230. Mexico: Instituto Mexiquense de Cultura, 1995.

Lorde, Audre. "Poetry Is Not a Luxury." In *Sister/Outsider: Essays and Speeches*, 36-39. Freedom, CA: The Crossing Press, 1984.

Loya, Gloria Inés. "Considering the Source/*Fuentes* for a Hispanic Feminist Theology." *Theology Today* 54:4 (Jan. 1998): 491-498.

Ludmer, Josefina. "Tricks of the Weak." In *Feminist Perspectives on Sor Juana Inés de la Cruz*, ed. Stephanie Merrim, 86-93. Detroit: Wayne State University Press, 1991.

Martinez-San Miguel, Yolanda. *Saberes Americanos: Subalternidad y epistemología en los escritos de Sor Juana*. Pittsburgh: University of Pittsburgh Press, 1999.

McFague, Sally. *Speaking in Parables: A Study in Metaphor and Theology*. Philadelphia: Fortress Press, 1975.

Merrim, Stephanie. *Early Modern Women's Writing and Sor Juana Inés de la Cruz*. Nashville: Vanderbilt University Press, 1999.

———. "*Mores Geometricae*: The 'Womanscript' in the Theater of Sor Juana Inés de la Cruz." In *Feminist Perspectives on Sor Juana Inés de la Cruz*, ed. Stephanie Merrim, 94-123. Detroit: Wayne State University Press, 1991.

———. "*Narciso Desdoblado*: Narcissistic Stratagems in *El Divino Narciso* and the *Respuesta a Sor Filotea de la Cruz*." *Bulletin of Hispanic Studies* 64:2 (April 1987): 111-117.

———. "Toward a Feminist Reading of Sor Juana Inés de la Cruz: Past, Present, and Future Directions in Sor Juana Criticism." In *Feminist Perspectives on Sor Juana Inés de la Cruz*, ed. Stephanie Merrim, 11-37. Detroit: Wayne State University Press, 1991.

Miles, Margaret R. *Reading for Life: Beauty, Pluralism, and Responsibility*. New York: Continuum, 1997.

———. *Seeing and Believing: Religion and Values in the Movies*. Boston: Beacon Press, 1996.

Mitchem, Stephanie Y. *Introducing Womanist Theology*. Maryknoll, NY: Orbis, 2002.

Montross, Constance M. *Virtue or Vice? Sor Juana's Use of Thomistic Thought.* Washington, DC: University Press of America, 1991.

Muriel, Josefina. "La vida conventual femenino de la segunda mitad del siglo XVII y la primera del XVIII." In *Memoria del Coloquio Internacional: Sor Juana Inés de la Cruz Y El Pensamiento Novohispano 1995*, 221-230. Mexico: Instituto Mexiquense de Cultura,1995.

Myers, Kathleen A. "Sor Juana's *respuesta*: Rewriting the *vitae*." *Revista Canadiense de Estudios Hispánicos* XIV: 3 (Spring 1990): 459-471.

Myers, Kathleen A. and Amanda Powell. *A Wild Country Out in the Garden: The Spiritual Journals of a Colonial Mexican Nun.* Bloomington, IN: Indiana University Press, 1999.

Navone, John. *Toward a Theology of Beauty.* Collegeville, MN: The Liturgical Press, 1996.

Oakes, Edward T. *Pattern of Redemption: The Theology of Hans Urs von Balthasar.* New York: Continuum, 1997.

Parker, Alexander A. *Los autos sacramentales de Calderón de la Barca.* Barcelona: Editorial Ariel, 1983.

———. "The Calderonian Sources of *El Divino Narciso* by Sor Juana Inés de la Cruz." *Romanistisches-Jahrbuch* 19 (1969): 257-274.

———. "The New World in the *Autos Sacramentales* of Calderón." In *Aureum Saeculum Hispanum: Beiträge zu Texten des Siglo de Oro*, ed. Karl-Hermann Körner and Dietrich Briesemeister, 261-270. Wiesbaden: Franz Steiner, 1983.

Paz, Octavio. *The Labyrinth of Solitude: Life and Thought in Mexico.* Translated by Lysander Kemp. New York: Grove Press Inc., 1961.

———. *Sor Juana Inés de la Cruz: O, las trampas de la fe.* Mexico: Fondo de Cultura Económica, 1994.

———. *Sor Juana: Or, the Traps of Faith.* Translated by Margaret Sayers Peden. Cambridge, MA: Harvard University Press, 1988.

Pfandl, Ludwig. *Sor Juana Inés de la Cruz: La décima musa de México.* Mexico: UNAM, 1963.

Picón-Salas, Mariano. *A Cultural History of Spanish America: From Conquest to Independence.* Translated by Irving A. Leonard. Berkeley, CA: University of California Press, 1966.

Porcile, María Teresa. "El derecho de la belleza en América Latina." In *El rostro feminino de la teología*, ed. Elsa Tamez, 85-107. Costa Rica: DEI, 1986.

Rahner, Karl. "Theology and the Arts." *Thought* 57:224 (March 1982): 17-29.

Ricard, Robert. *The Spiritual Conquest of Mexico*. Berkeley, CA: University of California Press, 1966.

Rivera-Pagán, Luis N. "Theology and Literature in Latin America." *Journal of Hispanic/Latino Theology* 7:4 (May 2000): 7-25.

Rodríguez-Holguín, Jeanette. "La Tierra: Home, Identity, and Destiny." In *From the Heart of Our People: Latino/a Explorations in Catholic Systematic Theology*, ed. Orlando Espín and Miguel Díaz, 189-208. Maryknoll, NY: Orbis, 1999.

Ruether, Rosemary Radford. "The Future of Feminist Theology in the Academy." *Journal of the American Academy of Religion* 53:3 (Dec. 1985): 703-713.

————. *Women and Redemption: A Theological History*. Minneapolis: Fortress Press, 1998.

Sabat de Rivers, Georgina. "Blanco, negro, rojo: Semiosis racial en los villancicos de Sor Juana Inés de la Cruz." In *Critica semiológica de textos literarios hispanicos*. Vol. II de Las Actas del Congreso Internacional Sobre Semiotica y Hispanismo *Celebrando en Madrid los dias de 20 al 25 de Junio de 1983*, ed. Miguel Angel Gallaro, 247-255. Madrid: Consejo Superior Investiaciones Cientificas, 1986.

————. *En Busca de Sor Juana*. Mexico: UNAM, 1998.

————. "A Feminist Rereading of Sor Juana's *Dream*." In *Feminist Perspectives on Sor Juana Inés de la Cruz*, ed. Stephanie Merrim, 142-161. Detroit: Wayne State University Press, 1991.

Salazar, Norma. *Foolish Men!: Sor Juana Inés de la Cruz as Spiritual Protagonist, Educational Prism, and Symbol for Women*. DeKalb, IL: LEPS Press, 1994.

Salyer, Gregory. "Introduction." In *Literature and Theology at Century's End*, ed. Gregory Salyer and Robert Detweiler. Atlanta: Scholars Press, 1995.

Scarry, Elaine. *On Beauty and Being Just*. Princeton, NJ: Princeton University Press, 1999.

Schons, Dorothy. "Some Obscure Points in the Life of Sor Juana Inés de la Cruz." In *Feminist Perspectives on Sor Juana Inés de la Cruz*, ed. Stephanie Merrim, 38-60. Detroit: Wayne State University Press, 1991.

Schüssler Fiorenza, Elisabeth. "Breaking the Silence – Becoming Visible." In *The Power of Naming: A Concilium Reader in Feminist Liberation Theology*, ed. Elisabeth Schüssler Fiorenza, 161-174. Maryknoll, NY: Orbis, 1996.

Schutte, Ofelia. "Toward an Understanding of Latin American Philosophy." *Philosophy Today* 31:1/4 (Spring 1987): 21-34.

Scott, Nina M. "'La gran turda de las que merecieron nombres': Sor Juana's Foremothers in 'La respuesta a Sor Filotea.'" In *Coded Encounters: Writing, Gender, and Ethnicity in Colonial Latin America*, ed. Francisco Javier Cevallos-Candau et al., 206-223. Amherst, MA: University of Massachusetts Press, 1994.

———. "'Ser mujer ni estar ausente, / no es de amarte impedimento': las poemas de Sor Juana al la condesa de Paredes." In *Y diversa de mí misma en vuestras plumas ando: Homenaje internacional a Sor Juana Inés de la Cruz*, ed. Sara Poot Herrera, 159-170. Mexico: El Colegio de México, 1993.

Sherry, Patrick. *Spirit and Beauty: An Introduction to Theological Aesthetics*. Oxford: Clarendon Press, 1992.

Tamez, Elsa, ed. *Through Her Eyes: Women's Theology from Latin America*. Maryknoll, NY: Orbis, 1989.

Tavard, George. *Juana Inés de la Cruz and the Theology of Beauty: The First Mexican Theology*. Notre Dame, IN: University of Notre Dame Press, 1991.

Trabulse, Elías. *Los años finales de Sor Juana: Una interpretación (1688-1695)*. Mexico: CONDUMEX, 1995.

———. "*La Rosa de Alexandría*: ¿Una querella secreta de Sor Juana?" In *Y diversa de mí misma entre vuestras plumas ando: Homenaje internacional a Sor Juana Inés de la Cruz*," ed. Sara Poot Herrera, 209-214. Mexico: El Colegio de México, 1993.

Viladesau, Richard. *Theological Aesthetics: God in Imagination, Beauty, and Art*. Oxford: Oxford University Press, 1999.

———. *Theology and the Arts*. New York: Paulist Press, 2000.

von Balthasar, Hans Urs. "Liberation Theology in the Light of Salvation History." In *Liberation Theology in Latin America*, ed. James V. Schall, 131-146. San Francisco: Ignatius Press, 1982.

————. *The Glory of the Lord: A Theological Aesthetics*, vol. 1, *Seeing the Form*, trans. of *Herrlichkeit: Eine Theologische Ästhetik*, ed. Joseph Fessio, S.J., and John Riches. Translated by Erasmo Leiva-Merikakis. San Francisco: Ignatius Press, 1989.

————. *The Glory of the Lord: A Theological Aesthetics*, vol. 2, *Studies in Theological Style: Clerical Styles*, trans. of *Herrlichkeit: Eine theologische Ästhetik, II: Fächer der Stile, I Klerical Style*, ed. John Riches. Translated by Andrew Louth, Francis McDonagh and Brian McNeil, C.R.V. San Francisco: Ignatius Press, 1989.

Vuola, Elina. "Sor Juana Inés de la Cruz: Rationality, Gender, and Power." *Journal of Hispanic/Latino Theology* 9:1 (Aug. 2001): 27-45.

Wardropper, Bruce W. *Introducción al teatro religioso del siglo de oro (La evolución del auto sacramental: 1500-1628)*. Madrid: Revista de Occidente, 1953.

Weber, Alison. *Teresa of Avila and the Rhetoric of Femininity*. Princeton, NJ: Princeton University Press, 1990.

Wilder, Amos N. *Theology and Modern Literature*. Cambridge, MA: Harvard University Press, 1958.

————. *Theopoetic: Theology and Religious Imagination*. Minneapolis: Fortress Press, 1976.

Williams, Delores. "Black Women's Literature and the Task of Feminist Theology." In *Immaculate and Powerful: The Female in Sacred Image and Social Reality*, ed. C.W. Atkinson, C.H. Buchanan, and M.R. Miles. Boston: Beacon Press, 1985.

Yates, Frances Amelia. *Giordano Bruno and the Hermetic Tradition*. London: Routledge, 1964.

Zanelli, Carmela. "La loa de 'El Divino Narciso' de Sor Juana Inés de la Cruz y la doble recuperación de a cultura indígena Mexicana." In *La literatura novohispana: Revisión crítica y propuestas metodológicas*, ed. José Pascual Buxó and Arnulfo Herrera, 183-200. Mexico: UNAM, 1994.

Index

aesthetics, theological. See Beauty

allegory and theology, 44, 85, 135. *See also El Divino Narciso; loas*

Alves, Rubem A., 171–72

anthropology, theological, 75–77, 80–82, 85, 106–11, 132–35, 194–95

Aquino, María Pilar, 15, 170, 194

Arenal, Electa, 67, 93–94, 98

Arrango L., Manuel, 80

art as central to religion, 155–56, 168–69. *See also* Beauty

Asbaje, Pedro Manuel de (father), 28

Asbaje y Santillana, Juana Ramírez de. *See* Sor Juana Inés de la Cruz

Augustine of Hippo, Saint, 59, 60, 107

Aunsibay y Arena, Antonio de, 34

authority and obedience, 48–49, 102–6, 137, 163

auto sacramental form, 63–68, 74, 77–78, 87–88n33, 88–89n39. *See also El Divino Narciso*

Aztec culture, 39–40, 116–17, 119–20

Ballinger, Philip A., 179

Baroque era in New Spain, 36, 37–43, 84

Beauty: allegory and theology, 44, 85, 135; in European

theologies, 176–81; fall from theological favor, 155–58; God as, 60–63, 69, 70, 72, 75, 79, 156–57, 178, 195; and the Good, 154–55, 158–62, 168, 170–72, 176–77, 180–83; and liberation theology, xii–xiii, 7–19, 170–76, 180–81; *loas,* 114–20, 135, 141, 142–43; and philosophy, 142, 159–70; relational nature of, 59, 60, 62–63, 158–59, 160, 178–79; social functions of, 42, 84; and theological method, 162–70, 193–94. *See also El Divino Narciso;* literature and theology; poetry

Bénassy-Berling, Marie-Cécile, 79, 82, 108, 110, 119, 120

Beuchot, Mauricio, 44, 74–75, 83, 127, 142

Bingemer, María Clara, 170–71

Blacks, 10–13, 39, 119–20, 172–76, 182, 195–96

body vs. soul concept, 49, 132–33, 157–58

Calderón de la Barca, Pedro, 64–66, 88n36, 117

Calleja, Diego, 27

Cannon, Katie, 174

Carreto, Leonor, 29

La carta atenagórica (The Letter) (Sor Juana), 33, 36, 138

Casarella, Peter, 177